# #IsraeliJudaism
Portrait of a Cultural Revolution

The Jewish People Policy Institute

# #IsraeliJudaism
# Portrait of a Cultural Revolution

---

Shmuel Rosner and Camil Fuchs

Translated from Hebrew by Eylon Levy
Edited by Yael Naamani and Matthew Schultz
Research and statistical analysis: Noah Slepkov

The Jewish People Policy Institute

Originally published in Hebrew as *Yahadut Yisraelit: Dyokan Shel Mahapcha Tarbutit* by Shmuel Rosner and Camil Fuchs (Dvir, JPPI, 2018)

ISBN 978-965-7549-26-1

Copyright © The Jewish People Policy Institute (JPPI) (Established by the Jewish Agency for Israel) Ltd. (CC) Jerusalem 2019/5779

All rights reserved. No part of this publication may be translated, reproduced, stored in a retrieval system or transmitted, in any form or by any means, electronic, mechanical, photocopying, recording or otherwise, without express written permission from the publisher.

JPPI, Givat Ram Campus, P.O.B 39156, Jerusalem 9139101, Israel
Telephone: 972-2-5633356 | Fax: 972-2-5635040 | www.jppi.org.il

Project management and publicity: Stuart Schnee

# Contents

| | |
|---|---|
| *A Note on Terms Used in this Book* | ix |
| *Srulik* | xi |
| Introduction: Israeli Judaism | 1 |
| First of All: One Chart | 11 |
| 1. What Is Israeli Judaism? | 15 |
| 2. Who Are the Jewsraelis? | 33 |
| 3. Chilun or Hadatah? | 47 |
| 4. Where Are You for the Holidays? | 59 |
| 5. Jewish or Israeli? | 77 |
| 6. The State or the People? | 91 |
| 7. Who Loves Shabbat? | 105 |
| 8. Who Is Secular? | 119 |
| 9. Who Are the Haredim? | 133 |
| 10. Who Are the Religious Zionists? | 147 |
| 11. Where Are the Non-Orthodox? | 159 |
| 12. Are We One People? | 171 |
| Afterword: The Essential Debate | 189 |

| | |
|---|---:|
| Appendixes | 195 |
| 1. The Survey and the Statistical Analysis | 196 |
| 2. The Participants: Demography, Gender, Age, and Religiosity | 198 |
| 3. The Questionnaire | 200 |
| 4. Being and Feeling Jewish | 205 |
| 5. Religiosity and Secularism | 209 |
| 6. The Axis of Nationalism and the Axis of Traditionalism | 212 |
| 7. The Jewish Streams | 218 |
| 8. Belief in God | 221 |
| 9. Political Beliefs and Ethnicity | 223 |
| *The Jewish People Policy Institute* | 225 |
| *Bibliography* | 227 |
| *Endnotes* | 241 |
| *Acknowledgments* | 267 |

"Go out and observe what the people are doing."
—*Talmudic saying (Babylonian Talmud, Eruvin 14b)*

# *A Note on Terms Used in this Book*

The study conducted by the Jewish People Policy Institute (JPPI) uses seven main categories to distinguish the Jews of Israel by levels of religiosity:

1. Totally secular (*hiloni la'chalutin*);
2. Somewhat-traditional secular (*hiloni k'tzat masorti*);
3. Traditionalist (*masorti*—not to be confused with the Masorti Movement, i.e., Conservative Judaism);
4. Liberal-Religious (*dati liberali*, a term that normally refers to liberal Orthodox Jews but also includes some Conservative Jews);
5. National-Religious (*dati*, which translates straightforwardly as "religious," but here refers to Religious Zionists, most of whom are modern Orthodox Jews);
6. Dati-Torani (also known as national-Haredi—generally speaking, the more strictly religious nationalist Jews, who border on ultra-Orthodox);
7. Haredi (ultra-Orthodox, including Hasidic and Yeshivish Jews).

The term "religious" or "Religious Zionist" will be used as a catch-all term encompassing the entire Liberal-Religious, National-Religious, and Dati-Torani spectrum. This should in no way be construed as implying that practicing Reform and Conservative Jews are not religious.

We also use the terms "Reform," "Conservative," and "Orthodox." These terms describe Jews' denominational self-identification, not the intensity of their religious or traditional practice.

We further use the terms "Ashkenazi" and "Sephardic" / "Mizrahi" to describe Jews who originate in Europe and the Middle East or North Africa, respectively. We also use the term "Russian" in a broad sense for Israelis who immigrated from the former Soviet Union.

# *Srulik*

The cartoon character that appears on the cover of this book was created by the famous Israeli cartoonist Dosh (Kariel Gardosh, 1921–2000) as the symbol that represented the State of Israel in his cartoons from 1951 onwards. The Gardosh family graciously agreed to let us use this character for the book.

The character of Srulik does not have roots in Jewish sources or ancient traditions. He was drawn as a typical Israeli youth: a native-born young man representing a new, young culture. The Israeli public soon came to know and love Srulik—a folksy, smiley boy, a pioneer and warrior with a tembel hat, sandals, and untucked shirt—and he became a national symbol and cultural icon for years.

In Dosh's words: "Srulik was born out of the encounter between me and my people, in the course of the great historic event that I was privileged to be part of: the establishment of the State of Israel. I turned this cluster of two-dimensional lines into a key witness of history. The eternal youth who rejoiced and cried, fought and failed, got disappointed, fell over, and picked himself back up like a roly-poly toy or modern Pinocchio, amid the unrelenting storm of Israel's existence."

# Introduction
# Israeli Judaism

Zionism was a political movement, with political objectives. Zionism was a spiritual movement, with spiritual objectives. Zionism sought to rescue the *Jews* from a bitter fate—persecution, antisemitism, and assimilation. Zionism sought to rescue *Judaism* from a bitter fate—exhaustion, paralysis, insignificance, and irrelevance.

Like the Jewish Enlightenment, Hasidism, the Reform Movement, Orthodoxy, and Kabbalah, Zionism was the Jews' response to a changing reality. The Jews cannot decide the direction the world will take. They are a small people with limited influence. The world goes its own way, and the Jews must adapt. If they fail to adapt, they will disappear. And like all nations, the Jews have a will to survive. They do not wish to vanish.[1]

Zionism offered the Jews a path for existence in a changing world. Not necessarily the only path, but a path based on a logic that was difficult to dispute and allowed the Jews to overcome three challenges. Since nations in the modern world exist in nation-states—we will build a nation-state for the Jews. Since religion in the modern world no longer serves the Jews as a strong glue—we will gather them to a place where their Judaism no longer depends on the strict observance of halakha. Since the modern world makes it easy for Jews to assimilate and disappear—we will create a social framework with no tangible possibility of assimilation.

The State of Israel *is* this environment. It is a secular nation-state, fit for the modern world. It is a place which preserves the Judaism of Jews who do not feel subject to the dictates of halakha. It is a social greenhouse which prevents assimilation. The Zionist thinker Ahad Ha'am foresaw this, if not precisely, in his celebrated essay "The Jewish State and the Jewish Problem." The Jews' abandonment of religion, he wrote, endangered their continued existence—but by returning to their historic homeland, they would be able "to live a life developing in a natural way."[2]

*A natural way.* This was the key. The Jews were ingathered: at first, few in number; now, almost half of the Jewish people. And as soon as they were ingathered, they started arguing about the nature of this "natural way" and its desired course. The State of Israel was founded to serve the Jewish people, but the question of how is left open to interpretation—and therefore also squabbling —between Jews of different opinions.

This book was written, and the research at its base was conducted, in the State of Israel's 70th year of independence. Long enough to learn something about the direction Israel is heading; not long enough to know what destination it will reach. Amongst ourselves, the book's working title was *"The Jewish Start-Up,"* because at this point in time, Israel is exactly that: a start-up enterprise in the service of the Jewish people. Like any start-up, an innovative concept is at its center—the notion of a future for the Jewish people in a nation-state. As with many start-ups, the concept exists, but the product is still in development. It requires further investment and there are many stages of trial and error yet to go. There will still be successes and failures. But there is also great promise. There is a dream. And from time to time, there is excitement for anyone who can briefly raise their eyes and gaze beyond the worries of the day-to-day.

Seventy years is a long time for a start-up company, but not for an ancient nation.

# Israeli Judaism

There is no reason to be surprised that Israel's culture is experiencing growing pains. There is no reason to be upset that there are arguments, sometimes ferocious ones, over the direction and path the country should take. There is no reason to be impatient—this will take time. We can try to enjoy the journey.

This book will present findings and articulate arguments about the Jews of Israel and their society. Chief among them is the proposition that the buds of a new Jewish culture in Israel are already visible. We shall call it "Israeli Judaism." This was practically inevitable, of course. Israel was founded in order to bring forth a new Judaism—to produce a culture that would allow Jews to live meaningful Jewish lives in the modern age. And this is exactly what it does—sometimes through careful planning, sometimes through inertia, sometimes by consensus, and sometimes by painful arm-twisting. Israeli Judaism differs in many respects from *non*-Israeli Judaism. Israeli Judaism also differs in many respects from *pre*-Israeli Judaism.

**This is a public Judaism.** The state slows down on Shabbat. The national flag bears the colors of the *tallit*, or prayer shawl. The holy tongue serves as the official language of the state. An Israeli Judaism is emerging from the freedom of Israeli Jews to design their public sphere in a way that reflects and preserves their Jewish culture. As for *how* Judaism should be reflected in the public sphere, there is no consensus—only arguments. But even these arguments set Israeli Judaism apart, because for thousands of years, until 70 years ago, such arguments would have been impossible. Jews could not argue about how the electricity company of a Jewish state should act or how the army of a Jewish state should conduct itself. They could not ask how, or whether, the state should keep its citizens aware of the Counting of the Omer. They could not debate whether there was still a reason to mourn for the destruction of a Jerusalem that has since been built anew.

**This is a national Judaism.** Israeli Jews see their residence in Israel, their life in Israel, and their sacrifices for Israel as a deeply meaningful component of their Jewish culture. The commandment to settle the Land of Israel—the precise elements of which are, of course, subject to fierce political debate—is a core imperative binding Israelis together. In this sense, the Israeli version of Judaism is only possible now, and it is only possible in Israel. It represents an innovation, therefore, in the history of the Jewish people.

**This is a free Judaism.** The State of Israel is a secular, civil creation. It is not bound by the laws of the *Shulchan Aruch*, and most of its citizens do not consider themselves obligated to a strict observance of the religious commandments. In this sense, the Israeli version of Judaism is appropriate for what the Jews want today. It allows them to do away with the elements of a religious lifestyle—from donning *tefillin* to keeping kosher—without losing their affinity for their people and its culture. One would struggle to find a similar phenomenon, lasting for any period of time, in the Jewish people's near or distant past.

Consider how the three missions that have challenged the Zionist movement are coming to some sort of completion:

- There are Jews in Israel, and they still want to be Jewish. Only five in 100 Jews in Israel say the fact that they are Jewish is "not important at all" to them;
- There are Jews in Israel, and they can be Jewish in their own way without feeling that their Jewishness is no longer relevant in the modern world. Nine in ten Jews in Israel feel very Jewish.[3]
- There are Jews in Israel, and they are not assimilating. Nine in ten Jews in Israel are certain that their children will be Jewish and think their grandchildren will also be Jewish.[4]

\* \* \*

A few words about this book—about the original Hebrew version and about this English translation.

This book is an initiative of the Jewish People Policy Institute in Jerusalem (JPPI), whose mission is to "ensure the thriving of the Jewish People and Jewish civilization."[5] The book's operating assumption is that an Israeli Judaism is developing in Israel, with its own unique characteristics. The book's mission is to better understand the Jews of Israel through comprehensive research into what they *feel* as Jews, how they *think* about their Jewishness, and in particular what they *do* as Jews, since actions often speak louder than words.

The two authors of this book, Shmuel Rosner and Camil Fuchs, were brought together for the purposes of this study. Shmuel Rosner is a Senior Fellow at the Jewish People Policy Institute. Camil Fuchs is a professor of statistics at Tel Aviv University and a leading Israeli pollster. The former is a man of words. The latter, a man of numbers. Together we compiled a questionnaire for a detailed and comprehensive survey, which was conducted in two stages and then analyzed and interpreted (for the methodology of the study, the nature of the questionnaire, and the methods of analysis, see the appendix at the end of the book). Together we tried to draw conclusions and insights, which was not always easy. To our great fortune, we received assistance from the entire team at JPPI, without whose wisdom, experience, professional expertise, and forbearance we would have been unable to complete this mission. Their names appear at the end of the book, and we give them our thanks. You will also be able to find many references to their works scattered throughout the footnotes. Besides these sources, we also used hundreds of other studies, polls, and books by other researchers. We thank them as well.

One remark about the difference between the study and this book: The study is, by its nature, colored in shades of gray. Every statistic comes with qualifications, every claim has its exceptions, and every figure requires explanations. The book, by its nature, was written for a general readership, which wants to understand the research material but also wants it to be interesting. This book was written, therefore, with broad brushstrokes and sweeping, decisive statements. It involves a necessary compromise: maximal clarity at the expense of maximal precision, and a tendency to generalize at the expense of meticulous details. As authors, we feel comfortable doing this. As researchers, less so. In making this decision, we reasoned thus: the book would be as clear as possible—and the qualifications, clarifications, precisions, details, and graphs would go in the footnotes and appendix. If you want to know where we have exaggerated a little ("*all* Jews do this or that"), where we have given ourselves leeway when dealing with reasonable hypotheses rather than cast-iron facts ("*these* are the Jews who are this or that"), or where we have jumped to disputable conclusions (saying "the Israelis *do* this or that," when we are really talking about what they *say* they do, not what we have observed them doing), then please also read the appendix and the footnotes.

What will you find in this book? Most readers of the Hebrew edition are Jews who live in Israel. They find here, almost without exception, themselves. Most readers of this slightly revised English edition—we presume—do not live in Israel. So you will find here customs that you may or may not observe; thoughts that you share or that annoy you; descriptions of disputes that preoccupy Israel; and groups of Jews with whom you identify or of whom you disapprove. You will find the full gamut of Israel's Jewish society. Some of its elements are likely to be deeply familiar to you; others will likely surprise you. At the end of each chapter, we have added a small dataset to help you place yourself on the map of Israeli Judaism, for comparison's sake—to see who answers like you, and who answers otherwise; who acts like you, and who acts otherwise.

What will you not find in this book? This book was not written with an agenda, other than a wish to describe Israeli Judaism as we understand it from reading about it, studying it, researching it and analyzing it. We have no desire to grade any Jews on what they do or do not do. We have no desire to rank Jews, to say who is a better Jew, or to rebuke anyone for not being as "good" a Jew as anyone else. In general, we have no agreed position on who is a "good" or "bad" Jew, or what is a "better" or "worse" form of Judaism. This is not an ideological book. It neither condemns Haredim who do not stand silent during Memorial Day sirens nor praises secular Jews who eat on Yom Kippur. It neither calls for anyone to wear a kippah nor proposes to partition the Land of Israel. This is a book that presents and analyzes *findings*. And these findings show that Israeli Jews do all sorts of things. This means that Israeli Jews are destined to continue arguing amongst themselves about many issues, even as we witness the consolidation of an Israeli Jewish culture, with its own common characteristics.

We will present the facts. We will also present possible conclusions. But we will leave the ideology to our (mostly Jewish) readers. We assume that some will welcome the findings, and others will lament them. Some will see a surprising success; others, a looming catastrophe.

\* \* \*

Israeli Judaism should be viewed through two lenses. Through one lens, we shall observe Israeli Judaism in the State of Israel as a *solution*—of greater or lesser desirability, depending on one's perspective—to the crisis of Judaism in the 21$^{st}$ century. Through the second, we shall observe the State of Israel as a *challenge*, which renders Judaism's complicated modern predicament even more complicated.

For the last few hundred years, Jewish culture has been at a crossroads. The historian Hannah Arendt dated the problem to the 17$^{th}$ century Shabtai Zvi crisis; others have dated it to a century later, but the essence is the same. Judaism's new predicament, Arendt wrote, "brought to a close—probably forever—the period in which religion alone could provide the Jews with a firm framework within which to satisfy their political, spiritual, and everyday needs… [The Jews were] henceforth to judge secular events on a secular basis and make secular decisions in secular terms." This happened because the Jews lost "their faith in a divine beginning and ultimate culmination of history" and therefore "lost their guide through the wilderness."[6]

This crisis was not unique to the Jews. The modern, science-driven, secularized world posed a challenge to many different religions and nations. They, too, had developed their own ways of thinking and living over the centuries. They, too, were confronted with a need to adapt their behavior to the modern age. But the Jews, scattered around the world, with no place to call their own, with no agreed leadership, with no arrangements for collective decision-making, had a twofold problem. "What they needed," wrote Arendt, "was not only a guide to reality, but reality itself; not simply a key to history, but the experience itself of history."[7] How did they cope with this difficulty? Some took up the offer of Reform Judaism; some erected the walls of Orthodoxy; others pursued the "isms" that proliferated across general society, such as communism and socialism; others emigrated to new lands that promised equality; and others chose Zionism.

Fast-forward three hundred years: Almost half of the Jewish people live in the United States and grapple with the identity problems of modern Judaism in a non-Jewish environment. Religious observance does not sustain the vast majority of American Jews, who have little desire for it. Meanwhile, the Jewish culture that is supposed to provide an alternative to strict religious observance has not fully crystallized, and assimilation rates are high. At the end of this book, we dedicate a chapter to explaining, in a nutshell, how our findings on Israeli Judaism compare with studies concerning American Judaism—and what challenges arise as we examine the implications of such a comparison.

Almost half of the Jewish people live in Israel and deal with identity problems of a different sort: how to adapt a Jewish culture tailored for a stateless nation to the life of a nation in a state of its own. Israel was established, as is written in its Declaration of Independence, as the state of the Jewish people. Not the state of the Jewish religion.

## Israeli Judaism

The Jews who built the State of Israel knew, more or less, what the Jewish religion looks like—but not what a Jewish state looks like. This is precisely what Israelis continue to argue about today.

The groups engaged in this debate call themselves by different names: religious, secular, Haredi (or ultra-Orthodox), traditionalist. They band together as camps, political parties, or "tribes" and fight for influence, resources, and values. Their day-to-day sometimes looks petty and aggressive: Will railway tracks be installed on Shabbat or not? Will the content of civics lessons be changed or not? Will female soldiers be able to sing in military ceremonies or not? Will university graduation ceremonies end with the singing of the national anthem, *Hatikva*, or not? Will Israel be prepared to evacuate settlements in Judea and Samaria or not?

These arguments can indeed be petty and aggressive. But they matter. Railway construction on Shabbat is one component of a much bigger question: What should Shabbat look like in a Jewish state? The question of civics lessons also has significant implications: How should Judaism be expressed in a Jewish and democratic state? The matter of female soldiers at military ceremonies will inform where, and to what extent, Israel should accept restrictions based on religious norms in the public sphere. The singing of *Hatikva* touches on issues of how the Jewish majority in the Jewish state should treat the country's non-Jewish minority. The question of settlements is a question of how important it is for the State of Israel to encompass the whole Land of Israel.

The findings presented in this book will provide an answer, albeit a provisional one, for some of these big questions. They show how Israeli Jews interpret their Judaism, how much importance they attach to it, and how they give it expression. They also show what Israeli Jews have preserved from their old culture in this new framework, what they have chosen to omit, and what they have renewed. Israel is a one big field experiment for Jewish culture. And we have gone out to the field, to observe what the people are doing.

# First of all
# One Chart

Sample questions: **More nationality**
*Does being a good Jew mean serving in the IDF?*
*Do you fly the flag on Independence Day?*

Sample questions: **Less nationality**
*Do you abstain from standing silent during the Memorial Day siren?*
*Should Israel not be a Jewish state?*

Sample questions: **More tradition**
*Do you make kiddush on Friday nights?*
*Does being a good Jew mean observing customs and festivals?*

**Sample questions: Less tradition**
*Do you consider New Year's Day (rather than Rosh Hashanah)
the beginning of the new year?
Would you prefer a secular burial?*

Look at the chart. Squint and look again. This is the first and last chart that you will see until the end of this book, in the appendix. This is the only chart we have insisted on including, despite not wanting to produce a book of charts and graphs.

This chart summarizes a significant part of the story we will present to you. Look at it and try to place the Israelis you might know. As you can see, most Israeli Jews (55%) are located in the upper right-hand corner. This box contains those who are developing a new culture, wrought from the Jewish past and the Israeli present, from traditional rituals and national customs, from ancient books and modern laws. More than half of the Jews in Israel are what we call "Jewsraelis," whose identity is an intricate amalgam of nationality and tradition. The other Jews in Israel are declining in number and influence. We shall discuss them too.

Three short comments about this chart.

The first concerns the numbers: The chart is based on the answers that Jews in Israel gave to 32 questions in a large-scale survey that we conducted. The questions presented here are only a sample of those used to prepare the model. We validated our results by examining different types of statistical models; you may learn about this in greater detail in the appendix. Notwithstanding minor differences, the models all produced sufficiently similar results for us to say: This is what Jewish society in Israel looks like. The majority are "Jewsraelis," the other groups are in the minority.

The second comment concerns definitions: We have called most Jews in Israel "Jewsraelis" because of the cultural compound they embody. We have called another group "Israelis" because its members emphasize their nationality and (relatively speaking) forgo tradition. We have called another group "Jews" because its members tend to emphasize Jewish tradition and (relatively speaking) demur from national sentiments. We have called an even smaller group "Universalists" because, compared to others, they show little interest in either Jewish tradition or Israeli nationality. These definitions should not be construed as making a value judgment about what is better than what, or to deny anyone an element of their identity. We are not saying that members of the "Universalist" group are less Israeli than the "Israeli" group. We are not saying that those in the "Jewsraeli" category are less Jewish than the "Jewish" group. These definitions are intended for ease of classification and understanding alone, no more.

The third comment relates to your placement, as the reader, on this chart: If you want to know where you are on the tradition-nationality graph compared to Israeli society, we can offer you a simple means. The website of the Jewish People Policy Institute (www.JPPI.org.il) contains an English-language survey, which is an exact copy of the original Hebrew version used to produce the map of Israeli Judaism. Answer the questions and you will be able to place yourself on the chart. Naturally, if you are not Israeli, you should expect your result to differ from most Jewish Israelis. It can still be an interesting exercise as an individual, family, or group.

**To access the English survey, scan this code**

# Chapter 1
# What Is Israeli Judaism?

*How can a culture of exile be adapted to an era of political independence? How can the culture of a religiously observant community be adapted to the reality of a secularized world? This is what Israeli Judaism seeks to do.*

Tractate *Yevamot* ("Brother's Widow") of the Babylonian Talmud deals with some strange laws. According to the laws of levirate marriage, for instance, a childless widow is obligated to marry her late husband's brother unless she performs the *halitza*—a ceremony relieving her of this duty. These laws are generally recalled, if at all, on the festival of Shavuot during the reading of the story of Ruth the Moabite, who left her homeland and joined the Jewish people.[8]

We shall not go into these laws in depth. Our purpose is only to sample them for an interesting observation by the Jewish sages. At one moment of disagreement (on whether the ceremonial removal of the widow's shoe requires an actual shoe or whether a sandal counts), Rabbah bar Nahmani quotes Rav Kahana quoting Abba Arikha as saying: "If Elijah the Prophet should come and say: One may perform *halitza* using a soft leather shoe, the Rabbis would listen to him. But if he says: One may not perform *halitza* using a hard leather sandal, they would not listen to him, for the people already have established the practice of performing *halitza* using a sandal."[9] In plain English, since the people were already accustomed to performing *halitza* with a sandal, even if the prophet Elijah came and said otherwise, they would pay no heed. Popular custom has the final say.

This is not the only instance in the Talmud of the instruction to "go out and observe what the people are doing."[10] What blessing, for example, should one recite over a cup of water? When the sage Abaye was asked, he replied precisely thus: Go out and see what blessing the people recite, and that will be the law.

"Go out and observe what the people are doing." May we suggest that this rule also applies to our present reality and therefore compels a reevaluation of the scope of Jewish tradition and the obligations it entails, according to what the people observe? The obligation to recite a blessing before drinking a cup of water has not changed under halakha, but the custom of most Jews today seems to be *not* to recite a blessing. The Abaye of the days of the Talmud might not have been able to imagine it (or perhaps he might), but this is the situation. In our survey of Jews we did not explicitly ask about water—we asked about food. Nevertheless, we can probably extrapolate from the answers: Only one-third (33%) of Jews in Israel say they recite a blessing before eating—most of the religious and Haredi populations, and almost nobody from the other Jewish groups. It is hard to imagine that a higher percentage might recite a blessing over water.

This is the public. This is its custom.

Can this custom, of not reciting a blessing, be considered a new *law*, as far as halakha is concerned? Does it abrogate the obligation imposed by Jewish tradition to recite a blessing before eating? What about the traditional obligation to don *tefillin* every day—a duty that a similar proportion of Jewish men in Israel observe (one-third[11])? And what about the duty to read the Book of Esther on Purim (41% observe this)? And what about the blessing over the

## What Is Israeli Judaism?

four species during Sukkot (34% observe this)? And what about reciting Selichot in the month of Elul (12%)? Can all these obligations be called into question because the majority of the public neglect them? Should we revise the relevant laws after going out and seeing what the people are doing?

Many Jews in Israel tend, at least implicitly, to make such a reassessment. Many believe that to be a "good Jew," one does not need to "observe all the commandments of halakha." In the eyes of these Jews, religious observance—including blessing the *etrog*, donning *tefillin*, and singing "*Adon Haselichot*" in the lead-up to the High Holy Days—is not the main criterion that defines Jewishness. Obviously, others disagree. Those who still observe the commandments in their traditional form generally believe that religious observance, including the *etrog* and *tefillin*, is still the main, if not exclusive, criterion that defines who is a good Jew (70% of religious Jews believe so, as do 91% of Haredim). These Jews would probably argue that the rule "go out and observe what the people are doing" was appropriate for the situation back when the sages first devised it. It was appropriate for a reality in which most of the Jewish public wanted to preserve the rabbinic tradition. In the absence of such a public, and in the absence of a public interest in the sages' instructions, this rabbinic rule would no longer be valid.[12]

"Go out and observe what the people are doing" is the imperative behind this book, whose purpose is to answer the question of what Jews *do*. More precisely: what Jews in Israel do. And we must say at the outset: They feel very Jewish. They place great emphasis on their Jewishness. And as for what it means to *be* Jewish, their answers generally correspond with their own behavior.

In other words: What Jews *do* generally also defines their perceptions of what they ought to do. Jews who hope to reach an agreement to separate from the Palestinians will say *this* is the Jewish thing to do. Jews who want to rebuild the Jewish Temple will say *this* is the purpose of Judaism and must be promoted. The rhetoric of Israelis who want Israel to be either more socialist or more capitalist contains a similar appeal to Judaism, as does the rhetoric of those who want Israel to be either more pluralistic or more homogeneous. Consider two examples from the survey: There is a good chance that Jews who raise their children to serve in the IDF will say that raising one's children to serve in the IDF is what good Jews should do (68% of Jews in Israel believe this[13]). There is a good chance that Jews who lean to the right politically will say that settling the whole Land of Israel is what good Jews should do (as 54% of all Jews in Israel believe, including 82% of those who define themselves as "right-wing").

\* \* \*

The Zionist movement aspired to reshape Jewish life and the collective identity of the Jewish people. Each of the streams that fought over the nature and direction of Zionism presented its own unique conception of Jewish identity. With the establishment of the State of Israel, and in the subsequent decades, some of these conceptions were also translated into a social reality.

- This reality is influenced by the fact that the political-national framework has become "the overarching authoritative framework of Jewish life and collective identity."[14] A considerable number of Jews consider the modern State of Israel to be a replacement for the old Diaspora tradition.
- This reality is influenced by circumstances: for example, the need to devote major resources, both material and mental, to the war for survival. This need creates a whole new set of priorities, which also translates into a hierarchy of desired behaviors (and thus, enlistment in the IDF has become an exemplar of Jewishness).
- This reality is influenced by world trends, which cannot be avoided in the age of globalization. The Jews do not live on a

desert island. They are influenced by what goes on in the wider world. The dawn of the age of secularization posed a challenge to the authority of religion. The intensification of the age of globalization also poses a challenge to conceptions of tribal belonging.

What is Israeli Judaism? First we need to answer what *Judaism* is, and as we know, there is no single, accepted answer. Many see Judaism as a nationality; others, as a religion. Many see Judaism as a system of values; others, as a way of life. Many see Judaism as a covenant of affinity to God; others, as a covenant of affinity to a people, based on a shared history. Stephen Prothero, a professor of religion at Boston University, proposes this pithy definition: "Judaism begins and ends with a story." To be a Jew, he writes, "is to tell and retell a story and to wrestle with its key symbols: the character of God, the people of Israel, and the vexed relationship between the two."[15] One need not agree. This is one of many possible definitions. But one way or the other, we can begin to ask whether Israeli Judaism is still the Judaism "of a story" or whether perhaps it has morphed into a Judaism of action.

To begin such a discussion, we must first elucidate the term "Israeli Judaism." Does it simply refer to the Judaism practiced by Jews in Israel—a factual geographic descriptor—or does it describe a unique and distinct cultural creation, influenced by geography but with a meaning which transcends geography? To continue Prothero's description: Is the Jewish story told by the Jews of modern Israel different from the one told by Jews in the past and by Jews overseas?

This question can not only be asked about Israeli Judaism but also Judaism elsewhere. Is Australian Jewry substantially different from Israeli Jewry? What about 19th century German Jewry? What about 15th century Italian Jewry? And what about the Jewry of the Golden Age in Spain or of the Geonic period in Babylon? Jews have lived in different places and periods, and their culture has been influenced by their local surroundings and global trends. Sometimes Jewish culture was influenced only in secondary matters—dress, food, and trade—and at other times it was influenced more profoundly, to the point of substantive cultural change. One's social being, as Karl Marx wrote, shapes one's consciousness. And the Jews' changing social being undoubtedly shaped their customs and consciousness, even if they successfully guarded their cultural continuity for thousands of years—all while adding new chapters to the same story.

There is no shortage of examples. The descendants of the Spanish conversos (Jews who were forcibly converted to Christianity), who played a role in the establishment of Jewish communities in Western Europe in the late 16th century, may have "taken upon themselves halakhic discipline," but "their Jewish, religious, and social experience was different from that of the rest of the Jewish people," in the words of Yosef Kaplan. They "flourished outside of traditional Jewish society" and absorbed values that originated on the Iberian Peninsula, including Christian values, "which left a profound mark on their beliefs and opinions."[16] These conversos had a role to play in the Jews' transition from their mediaeval to modern state.

They were preceded by the Jews of Alexandria in the days of the Roman Empire, and of course by their most prominent thinker, Philo, who preferred not to see the Jewish exile as a punishment for their sins. Here too we can see how integration into Hellenistic society produced a change in consciousness: in this case, the erosion of the political-national aspects of their identity and an emphasis on its religious dimensions. "Philo," wrote Aryeh Kasher, "sought to apply to the Jewish people an idea of abstract nationality, devoid of any real, tangible attachment to a race, a particular land, or political administration, but based on a pure consciousness of religion and culture, law and justice, and ways of life."[17]

What was true then remains true now. Later in the book, we shall devote a chapter to the differences between the two main Jewish communities of the modern age: the Jews of Israel and the Jews of the United States. But we shall make one point here, to illustrate how one's surroundings shape one's consciousness. The Jews of the United States have developed an entire culture around the value they call "*tikkun olam*"—repairing the world.[18] Why this, and why in the United States? The modern use of *tikkun olam* began around the Second World War. Jewish leaders used it at the time to illustrate the harmony between American and Jewish values. There is a genuine belief among Jews that the destiny and mission of the Jewish People is to "heal the world." And this belief gained prominence in response to widespread American social trends. The modern use of *tikkun olam* was, among other things, a response to the counterculture of the 1960s and was used by Jews as they adapted to the new discourse of a younger generation. *Tikkun olam* was cited in opposition to the Vietnam War and in support for the African American civil rights struggle. Later, this also meant supporting the rights of other minorities, the LGBT community, and migrants. Many other causes were brought together under the broad umbrella of *tikkun olam*, which is concerned with wider society and not with the predicament of the Jewish tribe alone. *Tikkun olam* allows the Jews of America to merge their values with those of their surroundings. To strengthen their own sense, and that of their non-Jewish neighbors, that "Judaism and Americanism reinforce one another," in the words of the historian Jonathan Sarna.[19]

Israel is not the modern United States. It is not 20th century Europe. It is neither Spain in the Middle Ages nor Babylon in the period of the Geonim. It has its own characteristics, which influence the Jews who live there. In Israel, Jewishness is the common denominator shared by most of the population, so there is no need to adapt it to a non-Jewish environment. But there is a need to adapt Israel's Jewish culture to other features of its environment: to the modern world, to the dangers of the region, and to the challenges of Jewish sovereignty. Israeli Judaism must also adapt to the Jews of Israel.

\#IsraeliJudaism

\* \* \*

The new Israeli Judaism is taking shape as a reaction to the collapse of the old Israeli Judaism. Or rather, as a reaction to the accelerated decline of three groups in Israeli society:
The decline of halakhic Israeli identity.
The decline of traditionalist Israeli identity.
The decline of secular Israeli identity.

We shall describe these declines, the demand that they subsequently generate for a new Judaism, and the unregulated market of suppliers who are trying to meet this demand.

Halakhic Israeli identity has two main branches. The first is the Haredi branch, which used to see Zionism as a problem and the establishment of the State of Israel as a difficulty. We shall dedicate an entire chapter to the Haredi sector later, but for now we shall merely mention that it is experiencing an update. Zionism is shaking up the Haredi world. The state is prospering—and the Haredim are integrating into Israel's society. As such, they are required to make decisions that impact Israel's future, and are increasingly involved in, dependent on, and partners in its government. Many Haredim still do not call themselves Zionists, but around one-third do[20], and around half believe that being a good Jew means raising one's children to live in Israel (49%) and even to settle the whole Land of Israel (45%). Almost all Haredim believe that to be a good Jew, one must contribute to society (79%). Around one-fifth of them watch the torch-lighting ceremony on Independence Day, and a large majority bow their heads and stand still during the Yom Hazikaron (Memorial Day) siren. The Haredi sector used to aspire to self-segregation, but in many respects it is now connected to the secular, modern, Zionist State of Israel. It retains its vitality, and it is growing numerically, but it is no longer a substitute for Israeli identity. It is part of it.

The second branch of halakhic Israeli identity is Religious Zionism. This sector used to aspire to a Zionist Israel governed by the spirit of the Torah. This aspiration has never been close to becoming reality. Although Religious Zionists see themselves as an Israeli elite, with outstanding representation in centers of power and government as well as political and cultural influence, their branch is shaky. Modern Israeli culture is seeping into the consciousness of the religious public, influencing it, and dividing it. We shall devote a chapter to this group as well, but we should already note: It is managing to sustain itself thanks to high birth rates, which compensate for the mass move towards secularism. It is stable and can boast impressive successes, but it does not represent a conceptual path that most Israelis will want to take. And to the extent that it does, the path is more nationalist than religious: A large number of Israelis do not see a need for halakha when there already exists a state that guarantees the Jewish future.

The branch of traditionalist Israeliness is also unsteady. Traditionalist Judaism, as existed in the first decades of Israel's independence, is in retreat. First, numerically. Around one-third of Jews who grow up in "traditionalist" homes become "secular" (36%[21]) in adulthood. Similarly, around one-third of "somewhat-traditional secular" Jews (31%) grew up in homes they define as "traditionalist." Traditionalism is contracting. It is being eroded by the secular majority and the religious minority. Its image is also in decline, as the scholars Yaacov Yadgar and Charles Liebman have argued: "There are Ashkenazim [Jews of Eastern European origin] who observe tradition to the same extent as most traditionalist Jews, but they refuse to identify as traditionalist because this category is reserved, as far as they are concerned, for Mizrahim [Jews of Middle Eastern origin]... There are Mizrahi Jews who shake off their Mizrahi identity and therefore define themselves as secular."[22] Put simply, Israelis feel less comfortable identifying as traditionalist because they perceive this category to be antiquated and linked to ethnic identity.

Most importantly, traditionalist Israeliness is in intellectual retreat. The foundations that used to form the base of traditionalist identity are cracking and crumbling. And this is one of the most interesting paradoxes of Jewish society in Israel. On the one hand, as we shall argue later, Israeli Judaism is built on a compound of tradition and nationality, which is similar to what traditionalist Israeli identity used to offer. On the other hand, fewer Israelis now see or conceive of themselves as traditionalist, favoring a secular identity. A key reason lies in their identification of sources of authority. The old traditionalism did not dispute the authority of the rabbinic model of halakha: traditionalist Jews recognized this authority, even if they personally chose not to live by its instructions. But the Israelis who are migrating from traditionalism to secularism no longer want this authority. They are not necessarily pushing back against tradition—against its customs, rituals, and the life cycle it preserves (a large majority [75%] believe that being a good Jew means observing Jewish festivals, rituals, and customs)—but they do not want religious law. They do not want the authority of religious law. Only a minority (34%) consider the observance of commandments to be what makes a Jew a good Jew.

The third branch that has been eroded is that of secular Israeli identity. This is not a matter of demographic erosion or collapse—the number of Israelis defined as secular is actually rising (more on this later). It is a political and intellectual erosion. At the end of the 19th century, many young Jews were flung into a profound spiritual crisis—and for some, Zionism was "a type of redemption." Nationalism served them as a substitute for a religious expression of their Jewishness. The author Micha Josef Berdyczewski described the choice thus: "To be or not to be! To be the last Jews or the first Hebrews."[23]

But the assumption made by some of the early Zionist leaders, that a secular Hebrew culture could be sustained without connection to the Jewish tradition, was unrealistic. Many of Israel's early thinkers, such as Martin Buber, Gershom Scholem, and Hayim Nahman Bialik could see this difficulty and sought, each in his own way, to create a compound that would embody both the vitality of the secular pioneers and the depth of Jewish culture. But their efforts were unsuccessful. After the first generation of pioneers, who were disbelievers, came the second and third generations, who were simply disengaged. These generations were the object of the well-known saying that is attributed to the Zionist activist Ya'akov Hazan: "We wanted to raise a generation of heretics, and we've raised a generation of ignoramuses."

This generation saw its political power wane when it proved unable to withstand the effervescent religious-messianic vitality of the Gush Emunim settler movement and the triumphant traditionalism of the Likud headed by Menachem Begin. The state's founders, who for the first decades of independence were supported by an establishment that appeared immortal and unassailable, lost control—exactly as one of the heroes of Amos Oz's novels predicted: "The religious and messianic energies, the irrational energies that the founders of Zionism endeavored to harness to their secular, contemporary struggle, would burst forth and sweep away everything those founding fathers intended to achieve here."[24]

No less importantly than their political decline, this generation was also damaged by the erosion of its intellectual vitality. Every social and political movement needs intellectual sources of meaning and identity. But secular Israeliness, as the scholar Gideon Katz observed, failed over time to serve as a sufficiently strong and stable engine for the Jewish aspiration for national and cultural revival.[25] The secular Zionist leaders presented the religious tradition "as a system of outdated, distorted symbols," and thereby "plug[ged] a wedge between the members of their group and their ancient symbols." This led to their alienation from other Jewish groups and provoked a crisis among secular Israelis, who found themselves—and this description is especially harsh—in a state of "cultural detachment, an inability to make do with the civil religion of Israel, and of what remained of the Jewish tradition within Zionism." The "absence of a shared cultural basis" prompted "assimilation into [the] global culture" and led to a "meaningless life."[26]

In summary: All the Jewish cultures that united under the roof of Israeliness are being eroded. The situation, place, and time are forcing them to contend with new challenges. Halakhic Jews recognize that halakha struggles to provide answers for modern times in a modern state—not least of all because most Israelis have no interest in adopting a halakhic discourse. Traditionalist Jews are losing the next generation, which no longer accepts the rabbis as authorities. Secular Jews are searching for an intellectual fulcrum, one which can enable innovation in the political sphere. This, simply put, is the nature of the demand. Israel's Jewish culture is emerging in a buyer's market, which is causing a seller's market to flourish: a chaotic, unregulated market in which an array of political forces, philanthropists, and organizations spread out their wares. Some promote ideas; others push initiatives. They line them up on the shelf, and Israel's Jews are taking their pick—to buy this and forgo that, to covet this and drop that.

Consider the festival of Chanukah. This is one example, out of many, of how Israeli Judaism is taking shape.

In the halakhic tradition, Chanukah is not a particularly important holiday. It is much less important than Sukkot. But the halakhic tradition is only one factor (and not the most important one) in ranking Chanukah's importance in Israel's Jewish culture. One piece of proof: Many more Israelis light Chanukah candles (nearly everyone does this) than sit in a sukkah on the first night of Sukkot (58%). How did this happen?

There are candles for sale, as well as menorahs and matches, oil and wicks. There are opportunities for people to light them—for whoever wants, whenever they want, as much as they want. On the supply side, actors advance their own interests: The education system decides what to teach about Chanukah and how much (in contrast to Sukkot, for which there are few study days because it is so close to Rosh Hashanah and Yom Kippur). Chabad vans make noise through loudspeakers and invite the public to light candles on street corners. Traders have an economic interest in a lively holiday, and they hold sales in order to sell more candles and Chanukkiot. Entertainment producers exploit the holiday to send children and their parents to music shows. Bakers promise a plentiful supply of doughnuts.

The demand for each of the festival's elements, old and new, entails practical outcomes. How many candles will be manufactured each year, how many will be sold, and at what price? The demand will dictate the look of Israel's public space—will the streets be lit up for the festival, and will there be a holiday atmosphere? The demand has implications for Israelis' lifestyles—should one expect a family get-together on the holiday? Perhaps to light candles together? Should Israelis light candles every night (73% do) or on only some nights (24%)? Will children expect Chanukah gelt (as 63% give their children), tickets for concerts (to which 42% go), and another serving of latkes (which 91% eat)? The demand dictates the holiday's ranking: what is Chanukah's role in the Israeli-Jewish calendar? What is its role in a Jewish state, which has no need for a festival to compete with Christmas? What is its role in a country that emphasizes its national character—warrior Maccabees versus priestly Hasmoneans? What is its role in a country that freely emphasizes its separatist side—Judaism versus Hellenism?

Connect the dots and behold this cultural creation: an Israeli Jewish Chanukah.

Is it different from the Chanukah of yesteryear? Absolutely. This festival has a much more prominent place in the calendar, and it places an emphasis on national motifs. It is a festival of "no miracle occurred to us, we found no vial of oil," and of "we hewed stone until we bled"—in the words of the popular song by the Zionist poet Aharon Ze'ev.

Is it different from the Chanukah celebrated by Jews elsewhere? Absolutely. It is conceptually different, because it pits Jews against gentiles without squirming around the question of mixed marriages. It is practically different, because Jews in Israel live in an atmosphere of Chanukah, not of Christmas, to which Chanukah has been appended as a junior partner in the Diaspora.

Does it contain Israeli novelties? Absolutely. The sages who enshrined Chanukah never imagined the power of the "*Festigal*," a highly popular Chanukah music festival for children, and other Chanukah entertainment shows. And by the way, the songs are in Hebrew. The joy is in Hebrew.

Supply and demand exist not just in relation to festivals and holidays. They can also be seen in the many varied spheres that express Jewish identity. Or at least the spheres about which we can ask, as we do repeatedly here, whether they too are Israeli expressions of Jewish identity.

There is demand, for example, for Israeli literature in Hebrew. Generally speaking, this is literature written by Jews. And it generally deals with the lives of Jews and their fate. Roughly half of the Jews in Israel (53%) say they read at least two books of Hebrew literature a year. Now we ask: Does reading Yochi Brandes' latest novel about the early days of Hasidism, or her previous book about the lives of the Mishnaic sages, count as an expression of Jewish identity? One-fifth of Jews in Israel (20%) believe that the most important element in Judaism is culture. Would they also consider reading Maya Arad's latest novel, about the lives of Israeli immigrants in America (like most of her books), to be an expression of Jewish identity? We can begin to answer this question by presenting a fact: More than half of the Jews in Israel agree that living in Israel is an important aspect of Jewish identity (56%). Then we can think again about the significance of Arad's novels concerning the lives of Israeli Jews outside of Israel.

Another example: Around half of the Jews in Israel (48%) say they feel sad on the anniversary of the assassination of Prime Minister Yitzhak Rabin. Nearly one in ten (9%) attends a communal remembrance event and a similar number (8%) light a candle in Rabin's memory. Again we must ask: Are these expressions of Jewish identity? Before answering, we should consider a few matters. This was the murder of a Jewish prime minister of the Jewish state by a Jewish killer, at the time of a fierce debate about Jewish national existence. Before answering, we should also remember that Rabin's assassination prompted substantial change, at least for a while, in Jewish discourse in Israel. New movements were born, with the aim of encouraging dialogue between Jews. New institutions were founded, with the aim of strengthening Jewish identity.

We should also bear in mind that for large sections of the Jewish population in Israel, any distinction between "Judaism" and "Israeliness" is artificial. The Jewish religion of Diaspora times, as the poet Heinrich Heine observed, was a mobile religion, which could be quickly packed up and moved around: a bag of *tefillin*, a *havdalah* candle, and a Hebrew Bible. Everything was compact. Everything was portable. But the Judaism of Israel is different: Israel's Judaism is rooted in a particular place. It has the Western Wall, and rabbis' tombs, and it has the Holy Land, and a state, which many Jews consider sacred as well.[27] Given the option, most Israelis define the stream of Judaism to which they belong as "Israeli Judaism" (55%). In effect, there are many more "Jewsraelis" in Israel than there are "Orthodox" or "Reform," "Chabad" or "Litvak," "Conservative" or "non-denominational." Most of the Jews in Israel have a sense of belonging to Judaism. And the primary means of belonging—especially for those who are not religious or Haredi—is through a self-definition that expresses the two primary axes of their identity: tradition and nationality. This is what it means to belong to the "Jewsraeli" stream. This is what we discover when we examine the key trends in Israel's buyer's and seller's markets.

*  *  *

Much can be done in 70 years, as the densely packed coastal skyscrapers in the Greater Tel Aviv area prove. But the creation of a culture is a long and complex process. It is particularly complicated when an ancient culture runs into an amazing and bewildering reality, which has had no parallel for thousands of years, and the likes of which has never really existed. This is modern Jewish political independence.

How can a culture of exile be adapted to an era of political independence? How can the culture of a religiously observant community be adapted to the reality of a secularized world? How can a common culture be created between those whose conception of Judaism is primarily religious and those for whom it is primarily national? This process is still in its early stages, and there are plenty of difficulties, dilemmas and quarrels. But this culture is progressing, and it has its own rules and distinctive features.

This culture is a compound of Jewish tradition and nationality. This compound is natural in a place like Israel. It becomes possible in a Jewish public space, where it is easy to imbue every act—from paving a road to reading a book—with Jewish significance. It is a compound which pits different and even contradictory worldviews against one another, but whose adherents must nevertheless live together and work towards the same goal—the prosperity of the society and state that they share.

The rules are simple: whatever works for as many Jews as possible who live in Israel. That is, not subordination to the rabbis and halakha—because most Jews do not want halakha. Nor a Judaism that operates parallel to and at a distance from the Israeli experience—because the Zionist sense of nationhood is a core feature of life in Israel. Nor a Judaism that is afraid of renewal—because in Israel, Jewish continuity is a given. Nor a secularism detached from tradition—because for Israel's Jews, tradition is their common cultural and historical infrastructure, as well as the language in which their new culture is being born.

What are the distinctive features of this process? We shall describe some of them in the next chapter.

\* \* \*

| Being a good Jew means... | "to a very great extent" | "to a great extent" |
|---|---|---|
| Being a good person | 61% | 26% |
| Remembering the Holocaust | 54% | 33% |
| Serving in the IDF | 40% | 32% |
| Caring for other Jews, whoever they may be | 33% | 45% |
| Working to improve the situation of the whole world | 24% | 32% |
| Raising one's children to live in Israel | 23% | 37% |
| Observing all the commandments of halakha | 13% | 21% |

# Chapter 2
# Who Are the Jewsraelis?

*Are Israelis splintering into tribes? It depends what you're looking at. The majority culture of Jews in Israel is the combination of an ancient Jewish tradition and the rituals of a young Israeli nationalism.*

"Passover is coming," wrote David Omansky from Kibbutz Ginegar to Israel's national poet, Hayim Nahman Bialik, in 1930. "And we are faced with the question of how to approach the hosting and arrangement of the holiday without making it banal, and without sinking into all the same religious rituals." Three years later, another letter landed in Bialik's letterbox. In it, Mordechai Kushnir from Kibbutz Geva explained why the pioneers on his kibbutz set out to till their fields on Shabbat. "Shabbat had been Israel's source of strength and stability in previous generations," wrote Kushnir, "[but now] all sentiment for this feeling has died." The Jewish customs were becoming "strange and foreign" to the generation of pioneers.

Bialik sought to create a modern Jewish culture that could respond to the needs of its time and place. He wanted to establish a code of Jewish law for the new age, even though halakha, in his words, "wears a frown."[28] He used harsh language—we shall quote it shortly—whenever he encountered what looked to him like the renunciation of Jewish culture. Letters received by Bialik from across the land in its pre-state days have been saved in the archives. Pioneers from the groups and kibbutzim in the Jezreel Valley, who were debating "basic questions about the shape of Jewish familial and group life," wrote to the poet for help. From the moment he moved to the Land of Israel in 1924, Bialik became a kind of spiritual shepherd, to the point that "no cow in the [Jezreel] Valley was named without consulting" him.

Bialik replied—gently to Omansky, aggressively to Kushnir. "You can't make up the festivals in your own head," he wrote to the residents of Ginegar ahead of Passover, "[therefore] celebrate the festival of your ancestors, and add something of your own in accordance with your own abilities, tastes, and circumstances." As for the Sabbath-desecrators from Geva, Bialik had no words of advice, only scorn: "It would be better for all of you to spare the honor of your God and the honor of the Land of Israel, which you are desecrating." Shabbat was Bialik's deepest passion: the "cathedral" of Jewish culture, the "central pillar of the renewal of halakha." Bialik used to smoke on Shabbat within the confines of his own home but he zealously protected the public character of Shabbat. "The Land of Israel shall not be built without Shabbat. It will be destroyed, and all your work will be for naught," he wrote to Kushnir.[29]

Consider another important early debate, which took place two decades later. At its core was a similar question: How should Shabbat be observed in the modern era? But unlike the situation at Kibbutz Geva, the issue here was not one of how secular Israeli society should deal with Shabbat as it turned its back on old-style religious observance, but rather one of how religious Israelis should deal with Shabbat in the context of a modern Jewish state.[30]

The man who triggered the debate was a well-known polemicist, and confrontations were his staple. There existed a serious problem that "religious Jews avoided," wrote Professor Yeshayahu Leibowitz. The problem was that Jewish religious law, which was written at a time when there was no Jewish state, was unsuited to solving the problems of life in a sovereign state. Simply put: Religious Jews could not strive for the ideal of a country governed by halakha when they were unable to offer halakhic solutions for the challenges facing the country. How can a state supply electricity on Shabbat and still keep Shabbat? How can it provide security, maintain a navy, and encourage heavy industry? Leibowitz called this new reality a "religious crisis," which was causing Sabbath-observant Jews to make do with merely "demanding that religious Jews not be forced to work on Shabbat." That is, the situation that these observant Jews sought to achieve in Israel was not substantially different from the one they had tried to realize when they lived among the gentiles. The only difference was that now, instead of a *Shabbos goy* (a gentile who performs tasks that religious Jews are forbidden from doing on Shabbat), they had the Jewish state.

Opposing Leibowitz was Rabbi Moshe Zvi Neria, dean of the Kfar Haroeh Yeshiva. Neria, later known as "the father of the knitted kippah generation," left a lasting mark on the nation's politics and culture as a leader of the Religious Zionist movement.

In Neria's understanding, Leibowitz was describing an imaginary crisis. He argued that halakha could cope with any problem that might arise. The rabbis could "solve the questions of every generation, including the questions of the State of Israel." From a practical perspective, however, the rabbis could not do so as long as most citizens did not observe Shabbat. Nor would there be any point in doing so. Neria believed that under the existing circumstances of a secular majority, any attempt to reform religious law would be like trying to square a circle: In the absence of a government "based on the Torah," it was impossible to begin to solve the country's problems using halakha. Such an effort would only provoke fears among secular Israelis (of religious coercion) and doubts among religious Israelis (about what was permissible and prohibited in present circumstances). Neria, therefore, described Leibowitz's demand to adapt halakha to the new political reality with the harshest term in all of Orthodox discourse: "Reform." In Neria's understanding, Leibowitz sought to make a Reform Judaism–style change to the Jewish religion.

The same question that irked Bialik in the 1930s caused Leibowitz and Neria to argue in the 1950s. What should Israeli Jews do on Shabbat? What should non-observant Jews do, and what should observant Jews do? What should Jews do in their homes, and what should they do outside, in the public square of the Jewish state? The dilemmas were diverse but the reasons for them were similar and continue to this day. What Leibowitz once described as "historical Judaism," namely "a system of Torah and *mitzvot,* the formalization of which is the world of halakha,"[31] is no longer the Judaism that is practiced by most Jews. But a comprehensive and satisfactory alternative has yet to be found. Nowadays, Jews all over the world identify with their Judaism in "diverse and pluralistic forms," which cannot easily be said to contain "a common set of basic values." The Jewish world is experiencing "a shift in identification from religious to secular, from ethnic to cultural, from community-oriented to individualistic and universal."[32] That is, the Jews are in a period of adjustment to a new era. They are coming to terms with a new existential reality.[33]

This does not mean that the Jews do not know who they are. A vast majority of Jews in Israel feel Jewish, or at least they say they do. When asked to rank how Jewish they feel on a scale of one to ten, more than half say ten. The rest also rank their own sense of Jewishness very highly.[34] This is true for a clear majority of religious Israelis and secular Israelis, of Mizrahim and Ashkenazim, of city-dwellers and villagers, of left-wingers and right-wingers, of synagogue-goers and of those who shop on Shabbat, of those with many children and those with few, of those who have complete faith in God and those who are disbelievers, of those who observe the Fast of Gedaliah and those who ride bicycles on Yom Kippur, of those who light candles on Chanukah every night and of those who do not know when a new month starts in the Hebrew calendar. The Jews in Israel practice diverse behaviors, but their sentiments are less diverse: They almost all feel Jewish. It is important for nearly all of them (87%) to be Jewish.[35] It is also important for nearly all of them that their children be Jewish (86%).

Why is their Jewishness important to them? We can guess. Perhaps it is because of a sense of belonging, or their upbringing, or a worldview, or faith. Why do they feel Jewish? This we can try to answer with more precision. Jews in Israel feel Jewish for many reasons, including that their environment is Jewish, their calendar is Jewish, their customs are Jewish, and their language is Jewish. In fact, it would be rather strange if they did *not* feel Jewish. The majority listen mainly to Israeli, Hebrew-language songs (60%). The large majority have a Hebrew Bible at home (91%). Only a small minority (4%) say they don't celebrate Jewish holidays such as Yom Kippur and Passover. *How* they celebrate these holidays is a different question, which will be covered later in detail. For now, it is important to note that they do.

It is also important to see that there are many customs that almost all, or at least a large majority, of Jews in Israel observe: Passover Seder, the eve of Rosh Hashanah, the Yom Hazikaron siren, bar and bat mitzvahs, Chanukah candle-lighting, Friday night dinner, rest on Shabbat, and male circumcision. A large majority of Jews believe in God (78%), even if this belief is sometimes accompanied by doubt. A large majority believe that a good Jew should be a good person, that Jews should care for other Jews whoever they may be (76%), and that being Jewish means remembering the Holocaust (84%). Most of them eat apples with honey on Rosh Hashanah (94%), doughnuts and latkes on Chanukah (91%), afikoman on Passover (76%), barbecue on Independence Day (63%), and dairy products on Shavuot (82%). A majority do not eat at all on Yom Kippur (67%), or only drink (7%). And when they eat again, they eat kosher, at least at home (64%).

\* \* \*

In 2015, when President Reuven Rivlin delivered his famous "Four Tribes" speech at the annual Herzliya Conference, he took what had been a vague sense felt by all Israelis and articulated it in clear language: "Israeli society is undergoing a far-reaching transformation. This is not a trivial change, it is a transformation that will restructure our very identity as Israelis, and will have a profound impact on the way we understand ourselves and our national home."

Rivlin was not speaking only of Jews, but of Jews and Arabs. His argument, at its root, was simple: Israel is home to four main tribes, which share the public space. The existence of these tribes is evident from the fact that Israel has four educational branches: secular, Arab, religious, and Haredi. "Children born in the State of Israel are sent to one of four separate education systems," said President Rivlin, "to a system whose purpose is to educate the child and form their worldview according to a different ethos or culture, religious belief or even national identity. A child from Beth El [religious settlers], a child from Rahat [Bedouin Arabs], a child from Herzliya [secular Jews], and a child from Beitar Ilit [ultra-Orthodox Jews]— not only do they not meet each other, but they are educated toward a totally different outlook regarding the basic values and desired character of the State of Israel."

Some of the facts the president presented are hard to dispute. Other facts and conclusions, however, can and should be disputed. "What is common to all these population sectors?" the president asked. "Do we have a shared civil language, a shared ethos? Do we share a common denominator of values with the power to link all these sectors together in the Jewish and democratic State of Israel"?[36]

Rivlin proposed an agenda for an Israeli partnership based on four pillars: security and dignity; shared responsibility; equity and equality; and a shared Israeli character of "Israeliness"—the precise nature of which he did not define.

Some celebrated this proposal. Here was a president who was prepared to respect minorities, set aside the ideological steamroller of Israel's early days of independence, make room for every tribe, and proclaim the creation of a full Israeli civic partnership. Others had difficulties with this speech. Some saw the trappings of "post-Zionism" or simply called it a "problematic ideology." The president, wrote Avrum Tomer, "went too far in eulogizing Zionism… The vast majority of Jews in Israel define themselves as Zionists, including a growing majority of the 'Haredi' tribe—and this majority would have been even larger if the Zionist ethos had not meant changing their lifestyles and traditions." Tomer believed that "the Zionist ideal is great and wide. It has enough space to include a range of different modes of realization by tribes with different worldviews, but the preservation of the overall framework is an absolute necessity."[37]

He was not alone in this belief, but whether or not he was correct is a question of one's worldview, which this book tries to avoid. But that does not mean there is nothing to talk about: The segmentation of Israeli society into tribes—*that* is a question of facts and figures. Whether these tribes are coming together or drifting apart—*that* is a question of analysis. And as happens often enough whenever such questions crop up, the answers are not unambiguous.

Yes, Israel contains tribes. Not only the tribes Rivlin identified, divided by streams in the education system, but also tribes divided along other lines. The researcher Charles Liebman divides Jewish society in Israel into three groups: one with a religious culture (either Zionist or Haredi), one with a secular Jewish culture, and one with a Western consumerist culture.[38] Another breakdown—used by the Pew Research Center, among other institutions—uses the terms "Haredi" (ultra-Orthodox), "*dati*" (religious), "*masorti*" (traditional) and "*hiloni*" (secular).[39] Some simply divide Jewish society into "Zionist" and "non-Zionist" groups. Others prefer a political segmentation: right-wing, center, left-wing. One could also divide society along party lines. The researcher Shlomo Hasson argues that there exist four main groups of Jews in Israel: "Secular Judaism with a nationalist orientation; secular Judaism with a post-Zionist orientation; National-Religious Judaism; and Haredi Judaism."[40]

The division of Israeli society into tribes is neither rigid nor immutable. It changes with the times. A few decades ago, Israel had an Ashkenazi tribe and a Mizrahi tribe, which were clearly discernible. They have obviously not disappeared, but their significance has waned. Most Israelis say it is unimportant for them to live "in a place where most people are from a similar ethnic group." (Note, ethnicity in the Israeli context refers to place of origin—such as Polish Jews, Moroccan Jews, etc.). That said, most Israelis *do* want to live in an area amongst people with a similar education. An even greater majority say it is important for them that their surroundings be religiously homogeneous.[41]

Nowadays, it is more common to divide Israeli society along economic lines. The economist Dan Ben-David has said: "There are two states here. One state of universities and hi-tech, which is truly phenomenal—and everyone else, who do not enjoy the conditions for work in the modern economy."[42] He called them "states," but one could just as easily say "tribes" or "sectors." The meaning is the same. These are divisions whose existence entails a social challenge.

When talking about tribes, it is clear that there are social sectors that do not think highly of other groups. Jews have a relatively negative view of Arabs (especially Muslims). So do secular Israelis of Haredim, and Haredim of Reform Jews. No wonder Israel's public discourse sometimes spills into harsh, and even violent, language.[43] Israeli society, as one high school civics textbook explained, is a "multi-cleavage society." The book counted five fissures in total (the first being between Jews and Arabs), which "express the tension, polarization, and divisions between the different groups in Israeli society and harm the country's social cohesion."[44] Public figures, rabbis, social activists, and columnists routinely warn against the tensions that undermine this cohesion.

The ideological roots of some of these divisions can be seen by examining just one of the survey questions we posed regarding the primary justification for Israel's existence as a Jewish state. Only a small minority of Jews in Israel want the state to cease being a Jewish state and become a neutral "civil Israeli" state (9%). The rest want Israel to be a "Jewish state," but not all for the same reason. A minority believe that the primary justification for the existence of a Jewish state is practical: to provide a refuge for the Jewish people (19%). Most Jews have grander aspirations. They want one of two things: the realization of the "national and religious ideals of the Jewish people" or "a modern Jewish existence in a secular state with Jewish cultural attributes." Here, then, is a rough sketch of the essential disagreement among those who want a Jewish state: Most Israelis who lean towards the religious and Haredi pole want the "realization" of the "national and religious ideals of the Jewish people," while most of those who lean towards the secular pole prefer a "modern" state with Jewish "cultural attributes."[45]

Israel is divided by groups and subgroups, and there are tensions between them along ideological, cultural and political lines. The groups fight over the distribution of resources and for primacy in the country's leadership. None of this is new information. Nor is it necessarily dramatic. The general impression is that Israeli society is "polarized, fragmented, and on the verge of disintegration," writes Professor Alexander Yakobson. It is the image of a society with various tribes that "are gradually withdrawing into hostile, alienated ghettos." Is this picture accurate? Yakobson believes it is not: "The main trend is the opposite," he writes. "Israelis are one people more than [they] ever were in the past." Alongside divisions in Israeli society, there is no small amount of convergence.[46] The ethnic divide is shrinking, there is broad consensus in the political arena on many matters, and groups that were once closed are being gradually integrated into wider society. We shall address their role in later chapters.

More often than not, the question is not whether the glass is full or empty—whether Israel is being torn apart or unified—but whether the beholder wishes to emphasize the (relative) fullness or emptiness of the glass. Do observers, leaders, scholars, writers, and the Twitterati choose to focus on the geographic self-segregation of Haredi and secular Jews? Or do they choose to see how a broad Israeli-Jewish culture now encompasses both secular and Haredi Jews together? After all, it is correct to speak of separation and conflict—but it is also correct to speak of consensus and Israelification. There are indeed profound divisions and significant rifts, but there is also a tangible sense of mutual responsibility, ongoing assimilation, a shared processing of a common symbology, and an active and ongoing conversation.

\* \* \*

In the picture of Jewish society in Israel sketched in this book—a picture based on the study of many thousands of data points, hundreds of books and articles, conversations, deliberations and sometimes arguments—one tribe stands out, clearly bigger than the others and with the strongest gravitational pull. This is the group we call the "Jewsraelis." They can be discerned from an examination of two axes: a nationality axis, and a tradition axis.[47] In simple terms: These are the people who observe both Jewish and Israeli rituals and customs and who espouse beliefs that combine

## Who Are the Jewsraelis?

Judaism and Zionism. Consider one illustrative example: Most Jews in Israel believe that being Jewish means observing festivals, rituals, and customs (73%), and a majority believe that being a good Jew means raising one's children to serve in the IDF (72%). That is—*Jewishness* means both observing festivals (tradition) and serving in the IDF (nationality). Whoever is characterized by this sort of Jewishness we call "Jewsraeli."

The Jewsraelis are a majority of Jews in Israel, but not a large majority. Alongside them, we can identify three further groups.

The first group consists of those who rank high on tradition and low on nationality. They can be called "conservatives" or simply "Jews," as in the chart at the start of this book (in order to distinguish them from "Jewsraelis"). Three in four Haredim (72%) belong to this group. They can be called by many names. What matters is their characteristics. The members of this group, by way of generalization, of course, are the Jews who *do not* fly the flag on Independence Day but *do* fast on Yom Kippur. They are the Jews who say that being a good Jew means being religiously observant but not necessarily living in Israel. They are Jews for whom Judaism is a religion, like it used to be. As if no Jewish state existed, or as if the state bore no significance for their Jewish identity.

The second group consists of those who rank high on the nationality axis and low on the tradition axis. We called them Israelis in the chart (again, to differentiate them from the "Jewsraelis"). They can be found in the kibbutzim, and noticeably most of them are Ashkenazi (52%), almost all of them are secular, and a relatively high proportion are even atheists. Three in four (72%) identify as "totally secular." But they are Zionists. They are Israeli patriots. They do not fast on Yom Kippur and have no interest in the Torah or religious commandments, but they do attend official ceremonies on Yom Hazikaron, and they do say that a good Jew is one who serves in the IDF. This type characterized the pioneering society of pre-state Israel. Perhaps they are the spiritual successors of the author Micha Josef Berdyczewski, who called for a change "from abstract Jews to Hebrew Jews."[48] They are the Jews for whom Israeli nationality has replaced Jewish religiosity.

The third group consists of those who rank low on both the tradition and nationality axes (or conversely, high on both the secularism and universalism axes). We have called them "Universalists" because they show no particular interest in either Jewish tradition or Israeli nationalism. They neither sit in a sukkah on Sukkot nor light Shabbat candles; they do not think that a good Jew must serve in the IDF; and in fact, they do not really care what a good Jew should do, because they do not consider it particularly important for their children and grandchildren to be Jewish. This is a group whose members do not always feel at home in Israel. They are almost all "totally secular" (83%); most belong to the political left (51% of those who identify as "left" belong to this group); many are childless (47%), and they feel that Israel has a great deal of religious coercion. Often, they consider their Jewishness more a biographical fact (sure, they were born Jewish) than a matter of cultural or intellectual significance.[49]

Together these three groups—roughly equal to one another in size—constitute less than half of the Jews in Israel (45%). The one dominant group, which contains a majority of Israel's Jews (55%), is the "Jewsraelis."

\* \* \*

The Jewish identity crisis began as early as the 18th century but escalated when some Jews added a political goal to their identity— a nation-state for the Jewish people—which they had to design and furnish. This crisis was on full display at the first session of Israel's Provisional Government, where arguments raged over the wording of the Declaration of Independence.[50] "The secular content and shape of this declaration, which serves as the foundational charter of the State of Israel, gravely offended my sensibilities," protested Meir David Levenstein from the ultra-Orthodox

Agudat Yisrael Party. He was opposed by Mapam (United Workers Party) representative Zvi Lurie, who promised to fight the forces of "clericalism."

The need to find a mutually accepted wording for this declaration momentarily obscured the disagreements, but they never disappeared. Factions of Israeli Jews were divided over the nature of the state's Jewishness, whether the laws of the Torah ought to be reflected in the law of the land, what the story of the Jewish people was, and whether the word "Jewish" even referred to a nation or a religion. Israeli Jews remain divided over these issues to this day. Almost half of the Jews in Israel (43%) believe that Judaism is first and foremost a religion. Roughly one-quarter (26%) see it primarily as a nation. Another one-fifth opt to describe it as a culture (20%). Another tenth or so see it chiefly as a matter of ancestral origin (11%).

Definitions like these entail behaviors, beliefs, and expectations. They forge feelings of social and political belonging. The Jews in Israel have been navigating their common surroundings for over seven decades and have kept up a struggle over the country's character this entire time. It often looks to them like this battle has been growing fiercer and wilder, but this isn't necessarily correct. They often think they understand which way the winds are blowing. This is not necessarily correct either. They often believe that there is no common denominator between the factions and that the battle will end in a split. This is a possibility, but not necessarily a plausible one. When we look at the Jews of Israel as a whole, examining a large number of questions, behaviors, beliefs, opinions, and lifestyles, we can identify interesting patterns of convergence. Most Jews in Israel share a common denominator, a common tradition, and a common culture: A Jewsraeli culture: a compound of Jewish traditions from the past and Israeli innovations from the present.

* * *

#IsraeliJudaism

| What do you do? What do you believe? | Rate among Jews in Israel |
|---|---|
| DOES fly the flag on Independence Day, AND makes kiddush on Friday night, AND IT IS important to be Jewish | 38% |
| DOES fly the flag on Independence Day, AND makes kiddush on Friday night, BUT IT IS NOT important to be Jewish | 1% |
| DOES NOT fly the flag on Independence Day, AND DOES make kiddush on Friday night, AND IT IS important to be Jewish | 12% |
| DOES NOT fly the flag on Independence Day, AND DOES make kiddush on Friday night, AND IT IS NOT important to be Jewish | 1% |
| DOES fly the flag on Independence Day, AND DOES NOT make kiddush on Friday night, AND IT IS NOT important to be Jewish | 4% |
| DOES fly the flag on Independence Day, AND DOES NOT make kiddush on Friday night, AND IT IS important to be Jewish | 18% |
| DOES NOT fly the flag on Independence Day, AND DOES NOT make kiddush on Friday night, AND IT IS NOT important to be Jewish | 8% |
| DOES NOT fly the flag on Independence Day, AND DOES NOT make kiddush on Friday night, AND IT IS important to be Jewish | 12% |

# Chapter 3
# Chilun or Hadatah?

*Is Israel becoming more secular or more religious? The answer is "both." Israel does not straddle an axis between religious and secular extremes: The space it contains is more complex, and the changes it is experiencing are more interesting.*

This short chapter will offer two propositions. Both are correct. The first—there exists *Hadatah* in Israel. This is the Hebrew word that describes a process of religionization. Israelis use it a lot, mostly as a negative description of a process they disapprove of. The second—there exists *Chilun* in Israel. This is the Hebrew word that describes a process of secularization. Israelis use it less often, but they all know what it means.

We believe that the questions of *Chilun* and *Hadatah*—questions that are frequently debated—obscure a more nuanced reality. Furthermore, the questions of *Chilun* and *Hadatah* are more political and psychological than sociological. The bottom line is that both phenomena exist in the eyes of the beholder. It all depends what one chooses to behold.

Consider this story. In the summer of 1940, the British Mandatory Government introduced daylight savings time in pre-state Israel. That meant pushing back the hour Shabbat ended and delaying the opening time of businesses on Saturday night. The British, however, did not stop with one ordinance—changing the clocks—and further decreed "the closure of all cafés and places of leisure at midnight." This left a narrow window of time in which businesses could be open on Saturday night. Cinema owners were placed in an especially difficult situation. If they chose not to open box offices on Shabbat, they would be unable to screen two consecutive movies in the evening. There would only be time for one. "This would have hurt the livelihoods of hundreds of families," explains the historian Yaron Harel, "especially since Saturday night was the public's favorite time for going out."[51]

In Harel's telling, the war over cinema openings on Shabbat in Mandate-era Jerusalem was a fascinating episode. It began with protests and entreaties, continued with pleas for the British authorities to take action against cinemas that opened on Shabbat, and culminated with a direct appeal by the chief rabbis to top Jewish movie producers in Hollywood. "Our explicit demand from the movie businesses and their agents is this," wrote Rabbi Ben-Zion Uziel, "when selling or leasing films to anyone in the Land of Israel (even to non-Jews, because of the possibility of fraud and because all productions are also screened to a Hebrew audience), they must do so on the condition, and to the extent, that they not be screened on Shabbat. And they must endeavor to enforce this condition, as merchants do."

Much in this old episode remains relevant today. The Israeli public sphere is still regularly rattled by ambiguity about what being Jewish demands of Israelis. A lack of clarity about the authority of religious institutions, as well as a mixture of religious and political power at the state level, leads to ongoing clashes between the desires of the religious-rabbinic establishment and the will of the public.

The end of this historical episode also teaches us something about the present. "The film distributors' promises were never honored," concludes Harel. "Sabbath desecration went on to capture an ever-greater place in the new Israeli public sphere." Cinema owners in Mandate-era Jerusalem did not seek to promote "cultural or national ideology of any sorts." Their eyes were pinned only on "their own economic profits." The result: "Economic competition was one of the reasons for the spread of Sabbath desecration."[52]

In a world of supply and demand, this was, in fact, the most predictable outcome. The Jews wanted cinemas on Shabbat, so they got cinemas on Shabbat. They had cinemas in Mandatory Palestine, and they went on to have them in a sovereign Israel.

The public defeated its rabbis, as it would defeat them many times again. The people would whine, then triumph; complaining about the rabbis' excessive power before flexing their own. These battles were not always won easily, and not always immediately. But ultimately, they were always won. And whatever the public has not yet achieved, it probably will. This shows that Israel is undergoing a process of *Chilun*, secularization. We can see it in the data. For example, the proportion of Jews who observe "part of the Jewish tradition" has gone down to one-third (34%) compared to roughly 40% a decade or two ago. At the same time, the proportion of Jews who "do not observe even part" of the tradition is around one-quarter (26%)—an increase from previous decades.

Consider another example (which will be discussed in more detail in the chapter on Shabbat). In Israel, 58 shopping centers, 218 supermarkets and mini-markets, 189 furniture shops, and some 85 garden centers are open on Shabbat. Fifty cell phone labs are open on Shabbat, as are 187 hardware stores. Simply put: There is commercial activity on Shabbat in Israel. Israel's growing consumer culture, as Prof. Guy Ben-Porat writes, plays a significant role in the secularization of society. Changes in Israeli society, he argues, have challenged the status quo and Orthodox monopoly since the '80s. The result is a less traditional Shabbat in the public sphere.[53]

This is the magic term: "status quo."

In June 1947, Israel's first prime minister, David Ben-Gurion, sent a letter to the leaders of the ultra-Orthodox community, promising that the future Jewish state would observe Shabbat as its day of rest for Jews, that marriage and divorce would be under religious authority, that official kitchens would be kosher, and that the Orthodox education system would retain its independence. His goal was to obtain the support of the Haredi community for the establishment of the new state.

The idea that there is a status quo on matters of religion and state—one which is reluctantly agreed upon and largely untouchable—was born of this letter. We believe, however, that the concept of the status quo as an immutable fact of Israeli public life is a sham. An illusion. It has never existed. The status quo remains in place—until it is changed. And whenever someone has the power to change it, they do. In an episode of the hit comedy *Seinfeld*, Jerry delivers an entertaining monologue about motor companies' habit of manufacturing certain cars in editions they call "limited." "It's a 'limited' edition," he says with a smile. "What did they make, fifty million of those? Yes, it's 'limited' to the number we can sell."[54] The religious status quo in Israel is similarly limited—for as long as the public wants it. In other words: It is not limited at all.

There is no "status quo" in Israel, nor can there be. Maintaining a status quo would be impossible in a country that has grown in 70 years from 650,000 Jews to 6.5 million Jews (as of mid-2018). Moreover, it is not even clear that a status quo would be desirable. There is nothing wrong with debates, power struggles, and self-examination. There is nothing wrong with change.

Consider, for example, that as of fifty years ago, female IDF soldiers were barred from serving in combat units. That status quo has changed. Not everybody is pleased with the change. For certain sections of the public (most secular Israelis), this is considered a change for the better; for others (most religious Israelis), it is a change for the worse. One way or another, this change entails further changes: for example, when religious soldiers serve in combat units alongside female soldiers. And of course, these changes also have their own ramifications and detractors.

What kind of state does Israel want to be? What kind of Jewish state does Israel want to be? The idea of the "status quo" is not an adequate answer. Not in theory and even less so in practice. It satisfies no one and fails to address reality. The existing situation might be suitable for today, but it might not be for tomorrow. Circumstances change, and Israel must adapt. The invention of the cinema was one such change, which led to a subsequent shift in the status quo. If and when the Haredi share of the population grows, this will be another change necessitating its own evolution in the status quo.

*  *  *

What is "*Hadatah*"? What is "*Chilun*"? Public discourse, often characterized by demagoguery and political agendas, does more to obfuscate these terms than to elucidate them. Nevertheless, we will attempt a concise summation.

*Hadatah* is the penetration of traditional or religious practices and discourse into Israel's secular-civil society. When textbooks for secular students convey the hidden or overt message that families that make kiddush on Friday night are better than those that do not—that is *Hadatah*. When military ceremonies refer to God, directly or indirectly, as the true commander of the paratroopers—that is *Hadatah*. When groups of Religious Zionist families move into neighborhoods and pressure local community centers to allocate separate swimming pool hours for men and women—that is *Hadatah*.

*Chilun*, by contrast, is the process whereby the public sphere is cleared of traditional or religious practices or discourse. When convenience stores that once closed on Shabbat open for business—that is *Chilun*. When local authorities decline to impose fines on restaurants that open on Tisha B'Av—that is *Chilun*. When schools devote less time for Bible studies—that is *Chilun*. When the courts rule that the state must give equal rights to couples whose marriages the Rabbinate does not recognize—that is *Chilun*.

The processes of *Hadatah* and *Chilun* are taking place in two parallel spaces: the institutional space and the social space. These spaces overlap and intersect but do not always operate at the same pace. Institutions are governed by a game of politics, which determines who is in charge of what, and how and to what extent they can thereby influence Israeli culture. Society, in contrast, operates chaotically in accordance with the will of its members, as long as the institutions do not impede them (and if they do, the public can replace those institutions). A large part of the difficulty in determining whether Israel is going through a process of *Hadatah* or *Chilun* stems from the confusion that results from the existence of opposite trends in these two spaces.

This is to say that some forces in the Israeli establishment are promoting developments that could be interpreted as *Hadatah*, while Israeli society is moving towards *Chilun*. What trumps what? Ultimately, the public is stronger than the establishment because it decides who holds the steering wheel. So, in the long run, Israel will be roughly as traditionalist or secular as the public wants it to be. But in the short run, owing to the quirks of its system of parliamentary government, the establishment also has power—and it uses that power to promote goals that are not shared by the public at large, including, occasionally, religious goals. Such instances are the main reason that fears over *Hadatah* have intensified in recent years. Since there has never been, nor will there ever be, such a thing as the "status quo," this change is inevitable and the fear is understandable. At the same time, the main reason for talk of *Chilun* is also fear. Those who do not want *Chilun* see trends that are eroding old habits and releasing Israel from the constraints of religion and tradition.

What is at the heart of the fear of *Hadatah*? Primarily, it is a fear about demographics—"they" are growing in number, and "they" will soon hold the reins. Religious and Haredi groups will be able to impose their values on the rest of society. It is also a fear about culture—"they" have already found sophisticated ways to infiltrate Israel's cultural piping and use it to instill their values in other sections of society.

The fear about demographics is exaggerated, at least in the short run. "They" are not yet a majority, nor will they be any time soon. The Israeli Central Bureau of Statistics forecasts that close to one-quarter of the Israeli population will be Haredi in 2040.[55] That is a lot of Haredim, but still not a decisive majority. Twenty years is also a very long time: too long to rely on projections that are based on many problematic assumptions—for example, that birth rates will remain constant, that the different populations' growth trajectories will continue in the same direction, that there will be no mass immigration of Diaspora Jews, and that there will not be a trend towards secularism. Such projections frequently turn out to be incorrect. This much was proven by a Taub Center study, which found that another forecast—which predicted that half of all Jews in Israel would be Haredi by 2059—was not necessarily coming true.[56] The study found that there is a "net flow of students from more to less religious education frameworks," which "seems to indicate the direction of religious mobility in Israeli society: a slowdown in the growth of the Haredi and religious populations and a slight increase in the growth rate of the secular population."

The fear about demographics is, therefore, partly based on an illusion: if religious families have more offspring, their populations must be growing at a much faster rate than the secular population. Why is this an illusion? Because such an assessment ignores changes in fertility rates (a rise in secular birth rates, and a decline among the Haredim) as well as the existence of Israelis who are born in one group and switch to another. Several studies have shown where they come from and where they go. Just as some pupils begin with a Haredi education and end up in the mainstream system, many Israelis migrate from the religious end of society—especially the National-Religious population—to its secular end. In other words, the high birth rates of religious families quite often boost the demographic growth of the secular community.

\* \* \*

What we are witnessing is a demographic race between different groups in Israeli society. The race can be won by whichever group has more offspring or is more effective in drawing members from other groups. For now, the situation is quite clear: Religious and Haredi Israelis are having more children but losing more members. Secular Israelis are having fewer children but recruiting more members. One-quarter of those who say they grew up Haredi (23%) has not remained Haredi. Within the Liberal-Religious public, more than half (52%) have not remained religious. So, on the one hand, levels of religiosity are declining with each new generation and Israelis are becoming increasingly secular. On the other hand, the high birth rates in the religious and Haredi sectors are having a dramatic influence on overall numbers. The result from the last few decades, which also saw substantial immigration of mostly secular Jews from the former Soviet Union, is roughly an even break. According to the data collated by Professor Uzi Rebhun, in 1990, 43% of Israeli Jews were secular, and 15% were religious or Haredi (the rest were traditionalist, in the middle). By 2000, the secular share had risen to 48%, but the religious and Haredi share had also risen to 17%. In 2008, there were even more secular Israelis—51%, a figure that is similar to our own study (49%)—but also more religious and Haredi Israelis, roughly 19%.[57]

But whereas the demographic fears are somewhat overblown, the cultural fears are quite understandable and often even justified. Israel will not have a Haredi majority any time soon, but the Haredi share of the population is growing. More importantly, the Haredi presence in society is also becoming more tangible. At the same time, the National-Religious community—despite losing almost half of its progeny to other groups—is gaining political influence and growing more socially assertive. Its power is being translated into ideological demands and political action. It is having an influence on the public sphere and on institutions such as the education system, government, and security forces. It is impacting school textbooks, which are being written with more traditionalist overtones. This means more demands for separate swimming hours for men and women and the imposition of modest dress codes in areas where they were not previously accepted.

The reality is undeniably changing. IDF kitchens are a clear example. Find a paratrooper from the 1950s and '60s, and he will gladly tell you how paratroopers used to keep their kitchens. They were hardly kosher. The paratroopers of the 2000s are much stricter about keeping their kitchens kosher. Sometimes even excessively so: In 2015, the country was in an uproar for a few hours over the confinement of a soldier who ate a non-kosher sandwich from home at a shooting range. His confinement to the base was soon lifted. Ten years earlier, a soldier was court-martialed for ordering a pizza to a military base during Passover. In his case, the detention was not revoked.

Is this *Hadatah*? Indeed, it is. The IDF of the new millennium is not the IDF of the 1950s. Its soldiers are not the same, its sensitivities have changed, and its needs have evolved. The IDF needs soldiers who keep kosher, and the soldiers who keep kosher have become more vocal. They are not prepared to bite their tongues when the laws of kashrut are violated. The status quo was once "we'll call it kosher but turn a blind eye to violations." This is no longer the case, and this change comes at a cost. Soldiers who want non-kosher sandwiches or crave *chametz* during Passover cannot eat them while on duty.

Of course, this assertiveness is not confined to the kitchens. The Israeli army, argues the researcher Yagil Levy, is undergoing a process of "theocratization, which is changing its culture and manners of operation." Levy believes that the accelerated push to expand the IDF's Jewish conversion program is "part of the Judaization of the army."[58] He also presents incriminating statements of rabbis who influence the army and its soldiers, the system of religious pre-military academies that send graduates to elite units, and recurring incidents of the exclusion of female soldiers from military activities. None of his examples are fabricated or unworthy of examination. But alongside these developments, several other things are happening: Female soldiers are being admitted to units once closed to them; Haredi battalions are being formed, and face challenges posed by the increasingly coed nature of the military. Levy writes much about *Hadatah* in the IDF, but there are no few religious and Haredi Israelis who believe that the army is actually experiencing *Chilun*. Shuki Friedman, of the Israel Democracy Institute, summarizes the situation thus: "On the liberal secular side, the picture is clear and sharp. The army, they argue, is undergoing a process of acute religionization... On the religious side, the feeling is precisely the opposite: Their frustrations about the secularization of the army, especially recently, are deepening."[59]

Consider another example: In 2004, Kibbutz Beit Alfa decided to make its kitchen kosher. "The Kosher Kibbutz," a documentary by kibbutz member Hagit Liron, tracked this complicated process. Beit Alfa was an extremely secular kibbutz, to the point of provocation. Weddings under a traditional *chuppah* canopy were banned, and on Yom Kippur the members barbecued meat. When discussions about kashrut began, kibbutz members were alarmed. It would not end with keeping kosher, one warned: "Afterwards, there'll be *mezuzot* on the walls [a parchment scroll affixed to the doorposts of Jewish homes]... They'll tell us what's allowed and what's forbidden." And she was right. A decade later, there were *mezuzot* on the doors of the kibbutz. As one of the initiators of the change explained: "We've installed *mezuzot*, we've decided not to drive on Shabbat by the side of the guesthouses... We've allocated separate times for men and women in the swimming pool… People are making their peace with this, reality is stronger than any particular worldview."[60]

By reality, he meant supply and demand. Demand from travelers and holiday guests who wanted a more traditional setting forced the kibbutz to decide what was more important: overt secularism or paying customers. The decision was quite easy but did not pass without anger and frustration. *Haaretz* columnist Uri Misgav included the Beit Alfa case in his list of events that prove that Israel is suffering "an epidemic of religionization." He urged his readers to wage a "determined battle" to clarify the "balance of forces" and articulate "the rules of the game and the conditions for coexistence."[61] But his plea was superfluous because what he wants is exactly what is happening: A determined battle is making the balance of forces perfectly clear. Whoever wants to be hospitable to all travelers must offer kosher food. In fact, the case of the kibbutz is not dissimilar from what happened with cinemas in mandatory Jerusalem. In both cases, ideology did not win—economics did. Whatever the public wants, the public gets.

\* \* \*

Here is the bottom line: Israeli society is not becoming more religious or more secular. It is becoming both. All other impressions are subjective. Most of the Israeli public think—or at least they did a few years ago—that Israel is becoming more secular (47%) as opposed to more religious (26%).[62] This is a reasonable assessment but not the only possible one. Most of the National-Religious public thinks that Israel is actually becoming more religious, or, in the words of researchers: "The feeling of the National-Religious sample group is of a mild shift in religious direction."[63] And of course, one's impressions about changes in society also entail conclusions about changes in one's own personal situation. Nearly half of Jews believe that there exists religious coercion in Israel. Around one-fifth believe that there exists secular coercion. The distribution by social sector is preordained: Secular Israelis complain about the religious side; the religious, about the secular side.[64] There is some *Hadatah*, there is some *Chilun*, but most of all, there is a great deal of complaining.

\* \* \*

| In your assessment, how much religious coercion is there in Israel? | | | | | | | | | |
|---|---|---|---|---|---|---|---|---|---|
| 1: not at all | 2 | 3 | 4 | 5 | 6 | 7 | 8 | 9 | 10 |
| 11% | 5% | 6% | 7% | 11% | 8% | 16% | 13% | 7% | 14% |

| In your assessment, how much secular coercion is there in Israel? | | | | | | | | | |
|---|---|---|---|---|---|---|---|---|---|
| 1: not at all | 2 | 3 | 4 | 5 | 6 | 7 | 8 | 9 | 10 |
| 23% | 10% | 11% | 11% | 14% | 8% | 7% | 5% | 3% | 5% |

# Chapter 4

# Where Are You for the Holidays?

*The Jews of Israel are changing practices, customs, and holidays. They are doing so in four separate ways: abolishing traditions, changing traditions, renewing traditions, and inventing traditions.*

What do Jews do on Yom Kippur? This is a question whose answer depends on the place, time, circumstances, and beliefs of the specific Jews at hand. It is a question that had a clear answer on the 8th of Av in year 70 CE—the eve of the destruction of the Second Temple—but which required a totally new answer a few weeks later—in the month of Tishrei just after the destruction. The Yom Kippur of the Temple was all about the high priest, the sacrifices, and the sprinkling of blood on the altar: a day with a clear geographic focus and organized rituals. The Yom Kippur of the year after the destruction of the Temple was an important date in search of new content. The holiday was eventually adapted for its new circumstances. If there are no sacrifices, let's compose prayers. If there is no priest, let's use a cantor. If there is no Temple, let's go to synagogue.

Circumstances change, and traditions change with them. The Talmud recalls how "the prominent men of Jerusalem" used to stay up all night during Temple times and make enough noise to keep the high priest awake. After the destruction of the Temple, the custom of staying awake continued in remembrance of the Temple, until it stopped. Why did it stop? Rabbi Abba Shaul provides the answer: "They would sin." Rashi explains further: "The men and women would participate in games together to pass the time."[65] Simply put: At first, the people stayed awake to practice Temple worship. Then they stayed awake to remember the Temple. Then they stayed awake for no particular reason and busied themselves in ways that were inappropriate for such a holy day. This led to the custom being abolished.

So what do Jews do on Yom Kippur? In contemporary Israel, the option of making noise is back on the table. Of course, there's no risk that cheerful children on bicycles will wake the high priest from his slumber. Still, their noise *can* be heard until very late at night in certain neighborhoods.

This is how the practice of riding bicycles on Yom Kippur was born: At first, a large number of Jews gathered in a single place—the State of Israel. Over time it became clear that although most of them were not religiously observant, they did not feel comfortable driving on Yom Kippur. Perhaps this was because of their upbringing, or on account of some historical consciousness, or a residual fear of God, or for fear of provoking a pious neighbor. Whatever the reason, on Yom Kippur, the streets were empty. Photographs from the morning of the outbreak of the Yom Kippur War are forever etched on the Israeli consciousness. The streets are deserted except for men wrapped in *talliot* rushing to pick up their uniforms and leave for the military collection points. These pictures rarely show bicycles on the streets, but about a decade later media reports of bike injuries on Yom Kippur were already routine.

The opportunity presented by the carless streets was not lost on Israeli children, who took to their bicycles each year in even greater numbers. After a decade, the phenomenon was keenly felt; after two decades, it was not just inconsiderate but dangerous to drive a car on Yom Kippur. The streets were absolutely packed with children on bicycles.[66]

Obviously, this practice is not shared by all Jews in Israel. Many see it as a perversion of what Yom Kippur—in their eyes—is supposed to be: a day for prayer, fasting, and introspection. As early as the mid-1980s, rabbis started putting out a "call for children and youngsters not to roam the streets on bicycles, which is forbidden on the holy day." The "main reason" to ban bicycles, wrote Rabbi Eliezer Melamed, was "on the grounds of *ovedin d'khul*," the principle prohibiting activities on Shabbat that are reminiscent of workday activities. "This is not a pleasure of rest but a pleasure of exertion." As Rabbi Shmuel Holstein put it: "This day is suitable for prayer and introspection... it is not suitable for cycling around the streets for no reason, and of course it is improper to add another sin on the holy day itself."[67]

Around one-third of all Jews in Israel (31%) say that Yom Kippur is a day for the synagogue, where they spend "the whole or almost the whole day." Two thirds of Jews (67%) say they fast the whole day—which of course makes it difficult to ride a bicycle.[68] But there are plenty of adults who do not fast, and some who fast only "part of the day" (8%) or "don't eat but do drink" (7%). And among them, there are also those who ride a bicycle. All in all, one in ten Israeli adults rides a bicycle on Yom Kippur, since it is "an ideal day to ride a bicycle," as one recent poll discovered.[69] Among children, the number is obviously much higher. Close to half of adults with children say their offspring ride bicycles (43%).

Israelis who live in secular areas tend to think that everyone rides a bicycle on Yom Kippur. They have good reason to think so. Children in more than half of secular families *do* ride bicycles. Among self-identifying traditionalist Israelis, the practice is less widespread. Around one-third of them (32%) say their children ride bicycles (and some 6% say they themselves do). Obviously,

#IsraeliJudaism

there are far fewer cyclists in religious communities. Only a small percentage of adults who self-identify as religious cycle on Yom Kippur (some observers would probably take issue with these individuals calling themselves religious) and the figure is only slightly higher among children. One-tenth (10%) of all National-Religious children and one-quarter (25%) of the small group of Liberal-Religious Jews ride bicycles. Among Haredi Jews, nobody cycles on Yom Kippur—neither adults nor children.

Is riding a bicycle on Yom Kippur an expression of Israeli Judaism? Is it an Israeli Jewish custom? We shall attempt to answer these questions.

First, is it "Judaism"? In order to decide whether riding a bicycle is a Jewish custom, one must first define "Judaism," and if we enter this minefield, we are in for a long ride (perhaps we can do it by bike). But there are a few simple facts we can all agree on: This form of cycling is tied to and rooted in an important date in the Hebrew calendar, Yom Kippur. Only on the holiest day of the Jewish year do the streets clear up. Only on this day does it become possible to cycle everywhere. And over time, this practice has become an unmistakable feature of this day—in Israel. This leads us to the next question.

Is it "Israeli"? Here the answer is even more straightforward. Only in Israel do the streets clear up for bicycles on Yom Kippur. On Yom Kippur, Jews living in Los Angeles find the highway jammed with cars. Jews in Paris need to maneuver the same unruly traffic as any other day. Israel's special circumstances connect a holy day with a brand-new custom. These circumstances are the existence of a substantial Jewish majority, whose absence from the roads clears the way for cyclists.

Some are already using this new custom (Israel is still young) to try to paint a modern picture of Yom Kippur. "Yom Kippur in Israeli towns is a thing of wonder," write two environmental activists. "Once dusk falls, all vehicles stop moving and masses of people go out to the streets, into the public space. On foot and by bicycle, they fill the major traffic routes. The environmental change is comprehensive: The places of cars, buses, and trucks are taken by women, men, and children. The sound of engines ceases, an almost total silence falls on the town, and the air becomes clear and clean." The authors of this essay see in the day's nature "an expression of an authentic and creative Israeli Judaism." They see the disappearance of cars from the streets as a way for the secular majority to "sanctify" Yom Kippur. They call it a "social fast" and a "consumer fast."[70] The researcher Hizky Shoham agreed that what we see is the emergence of "secular content" for Yom Kippur: "Unlike other festivals for which renewed interpretations were offered, in this case the modern significance was created as a result of the unintended development of holiday practices that trickled down from the culture of children to that of adults, so it cannot be seen as expressing a cultural initiative, only a retrospective interpretation."[71] That is: First bicycles emerged—and only later did some Israelis decide to imbue the new custom with meaning.

This new and evolving Yom Kippur is an exciting challenge for anyone who wishes to understand the direction in which the Jews of Israel are taking their culture. One option is to understand this custom as proof that the power of Yom Kippur is waning as the Jews of Israel become less Jewish.

After all, how do we usually measure commitment to Jewish culture? We ask about synagogue attendance and traditional Yom Kippur observance. There are no accepted metrics that use Yom Kippur cycling as a measure for one's Jewishness.

But what if a decline in synagogue attendance rates, along with a simultaneous increase in cycling on Yom Kippur, did not signal a *weakening* commitment to Jewish culture but simply a *change* in Jewish culture? Perhaps Israelis are not forgoing Yom Kippur so much as adapting an ancient tradition to the modern age, in which synagogues and prayers have less power to influence the soul than silence in the streets, children on bicycles, and the breathtaking view of the Ayalon Highway completely empty of cars—the sight of "the nakedness of the Ayalon," in Dr. Ruth Calderon's formulation.[72]

In modern Israel, a question such as this has practical implications. This much was proven by the dispute over the operation of the Tel-O-Fun bike-share system in Tel Aviv on Yom Kippur. Some thought it was inappropriate to allow people to rent bicycles on the holy day—because it was commercial activity. Transportation Minister Israel Katz said that renting out bicycles would harm "the holiest day of the Jewish people."[73] Those who saw bicycles as a key feature of the holiday found it unreasonable to stop people from renting them. After a brief tug-of-war, a compromise was hammered out: anyone with a subscription could take out a bicycle at zero cost, but anyone without a subscription could not pay for a rental during the festival.[74] This settled the matter, though such a debate might yet resume in the future.

One opponent of operating Tel-O-Fun on Yom Kippur explained that the bicycles should remain locked not because Yom Kippur is a religious day, but rather because "it is an Israeli day. It is one of the state's symbols."[75] In other words, he was not seeking religious coercion for the sake of a minority, but rather the preservation of a national symbol that enjoys a wide consensus. Needless to say, he was right. Yom Kippur is undoubtedly a symbol, which a clear majority of Israeli citizens respect and observe in some way. Three in four adults fast on Yom Kippur, at least occasionally and for at least a portion of the day. Two in three of them go to synagogue on Yom Kippur—around half for most of the day, and the other half "only for Kol Nidrei or Neila," the day's opening and closing services (32%).

Still, there is a problem with the argument that the Tel-O-Fun system "harms" one of the "state's symbols." This argument is based on the assumption that what was true in the past must be true in the future—that for Yom Kippur to remain a meaningful symbol, it must be a day for praying and fasting, not for cycling. If this were the case, then Yom Kippur would have been obliterated after the destruction of the Temple. A day of sacrifices was forced to become a day of prayers. Is it impossible to conceive of another dramatic change: that a day of prayers might become a day of cycling?

Such an idea can be shocking, or even disturbing, for many Jews, but there's nothing new here. History has already seen changes in Jewish customs. Many of them aroused controversy, sometimes to the point of rifts and even bloodshed, but ultimately, the evolving customs of Jews defined Judaism as much as Judaism defined the evolving customs of Jews. Since the Jews have no institution with the binding power to decide for them how they must realize their Jewish identity, the decider is the general Jewish public, in an iterative, collective decision-making process whose results often become clear only after several generations. In other words: If most Jews in Israel start cycling on Yom Kippur, a scholar of Judaism in the 22$^{nd}$ century will need to scour the archives to find the roots of this custom and identify the developments that imbued it with meaning and depth. And it *will* become a Jewish custom. Or for accuracy's sake: an Israeli Jewish custom, because it cannot be observed anywhere else. Not in the same way. Not on empty highways.

In fact, this is one of the most serious obstacles as we attempt to interpret bicycle-riding as a new Jewish custom. Can something be identified as a Jewish custom, when no Jews outside of Israel practice it? In theory, the same question could be raised about the American-Jewish tradition of eating Chinese food and heading to the movies on Christmas.

Throughout Jewish history, many customs have been accepted and absorbed while others have not. The Passover Haggadah, for example, contains additions that have won acceptance, such as *"Ha Lachma Anya,"* and others that remain the subject of dispute, such as "pour out your wrath on the gentiles." Other Passover practices ultimately failed to survive the test of time, like the custom of Amsterdam's Jews to abstain from eating chicken on Passover.

And so we skip ahead from Yom Kippur to Passover, to ask what Israeli Judaism will make of this festival.

\* \* \*

The Passover Seder is one of the most popular rituals in Israel. A vast majority of Israeli Jews celebrate it. Moreover, most of them do not merely see it as a special family meal. They read "the whole Haggadah" (64%).[76] The sociologist Dr. Shlomo Fischer believes this is proof that "all in all, the Seder night of Israeli Judaism remains very traditional in its nature."[77] Predictably, the more traditional the celebrants, the more likely they are to read the whole Haggadah.[78]

The modern age has seen no shortage of attempts to change the Haggadah. One of the best-known attempts was the Kibbutz Haggadah, an enterprise that included the composition of hundreds of different Haggadahs (200 of which are mentioned in a comprehensive book on this phenomenon[79]). Why did the kibbutzim feel compelled to write their own Haggadahs? Because they "wanted a version that would express their life experience— the abandonment of the Exile and the return to their native landscape." The poet Abba Kovner called these Haggadahs "the most original creation of the [kibbutz] movement in the field of festivals and culture since its inception."[80] This was undoubtedly a daring, innovative, and diverse undertaking, which teaches much about what kibbutz members were thinking from the early days of Zionism onwards. It also illustrates their desire to retain a connection with Jewish tradition, despite the unease of those who were not religiously observant.

The kibbutz Haggadahs reflected a certain ambivalence about the holiday's more faith-based content. Was the hand of God involved in the Exodus? Did the splitting of the Red Sea really happen? Unlike bicycles on Yom Kippur, one cannot argue that the kibbutz Haggadahs were random or unplanned or representative of an escape from the holiday's core features. "Some people object to this Haggadah out of a principled objection to changes in tradition," wrote the columnist and educator Uri Heitner from Kibbutz Ortal, "[and] I respect these objectors. But some are presenting the Kibbutz Haggadah as a 'slapdash' Haggadah, a 'Haggadah lite.' This position is completely groundless. The Kibbutz Haggadah is a most serious and profound piece of work."[81]

Indeed, in most of the Kibbutz Haggadahs, the authors' intimate knowledge of the Jewish tradition is evident and their critical engagement with that tradition is clear. These Haggadahs—barring, or perhaps including, the purposefully humorous ones—have an unmistakably serious dimension. What is also evident is the authors' desire to update the text of the Haggadah to address issues on the public agenda. Sometimes that meant boosting its agricultural content—Passover is the spring festival, and its agricultural themes are apt for a kibbutz environment. Other times it meant highlighting the Haggadah's specifically topical subject matter, such as the emphasis on the struggle for liberty in the Haggadahs published around the Warsaw Ghetto Uprising. Many of the Haggadahs include a famous quotation from Berl Katznelson, an intellectual tower of Labor Zionism: "A renewing and creative generation does not throw the cultural heritage of ages into the dustbin. It examines and scrutinizes, accepts and rejects."[82]

The kibbutz movement's burst of creativity did not continue with the same force into the present. It reached its peak at some point between the '40s and the '60s, and then it was institutionalized and lost steam. Despite the popularity of the kibbutz as a destination for visitors to celebrate Passover in the special kibbutz atmosphere (and perhaps also more cheaply than at home), efforts to rewrite the Haggadah failed to break out of the kibbutzim and sweep the masses, although they certainly played a role in encouraging other Israelis to include modern Israeli works in their own Seder night repertoires. One-fifth of Jews in Israel, a non-negligible minority, say they add "modern readings or texts" to the Haggadah (19%).

It is interesting to examine the groups that feel free to play with the Haggadah and refresh its content. Around one-fifth of self-identified "totally secular" Jews do so (22%). But religious Jews do so in even greater numbers: 21% of Dati-Torani Jews do so, as do 24% of National-Religious Jews and even more Liberal-Religious Jews (38%). Those who tend not to revise or add to the Haggadah are the traditional groups (somewhat-traditional secularists and traditionalists) and the Haredim (6%). We can try to guess why: The totally secular have no impediment to making changes; while the religious are sufficiently confident in their ability to make changes. Traditionalist Jews do not feel comfortable enough with the text to play around with it; while Haredi Jews do not feel comfortable with the very idea of playing with the text.

In many Diaspora Jewish communities, it is conventional to add new texts and rituals to the Haggadah. For Seder night in 1969, which coincided with the one-year anniversary of the assassination of Martin Luther King Jr. in the United States, American civil rights activists composed the "Freedom Haggadah." It drew inspiration from the Israeli kibbutz Haggadahs and included verses by the Beat Generation poet Allen Ginsberg, readings connected to African American rights, and texts against the Vietnam War. Moses, who delivered the Hebrews from Egypt, was depicted as a leader fighting for the rights of workers suffering under the yoke of their cruel employer, Pharaoh. Haggadahs composed in the United States since then have included texts about feminism, gay rights, the Palestinian struggle, migrant workers, and a whole panoply of topical issues, varying by year, agenda, and their authors' ideological dispositions.[83] After Donald Trump was elected president, some liberal American Jews sat down for a Seder with Haggadahs depicting Trump as Pharaoh (including one explicitly called "The Trump Passover Haggadah"). Trump was not, however, the first U.S. president to have this dubious honor: Ten years before him, a San Francisco synagogue published a Haggadah supplement that opened with the words: "In 2007, the President of the United

States has become the Pharaoh of the contemporary world." That president was George W. Bush.[84]

In Israel, the inclination to politicize the Haggadah is not as strong, and neither is the urge to make substantial changes to the traditional text. Israeli families are fulfilling the vision of Theodor Herzl, whose novel *Altneuland* includes a fairly traditional Seder night in Tiberias at its core. There, the participants first relate the story of the Exodus from Egypt, and only later start discussing the contemporary exodus of the Jews from their countries and the building of their new homeland in the Land of Israel.

\* \* \*

The reading of the traditional Haggadah has generally been preserved, but what about other Passover practices? What about the eating of *kitniyot* (legumes)? This is a fascinating question, which requires us to investigate at least three distinct cultural processes.

First, intermarriage between Jews from different ethnic groups in Israel is increasingly blurring the once-clear distinction between Ashkenazim—whose custom prohibits the consumption of *kitniyot* during Passover—and Jews of other origins. Whereas in the 1950s, only roughly one-tenth of Jewish weddings in Israel were between members of different ethnic groups, today these account for around one-quarter of all weddings. Over time, fewer and fewer Israelis hold to a clear "ethnic" tradition. Three in four Israelis grew up in a home with an either "Ashkenazi" or "Sephardic-Mizrahi" atmosphere, but nowadays only half will describe their homes this way. A growing proportion of Israelis (40%) say their home is either "both" Ashkenazi and Sephardic or "neither."[85]

The second process is a general decline in strictness among traditionalist Jews. These Jews are interested in practicing the key parts of the tradition but not necessarily adhering to its minutiae. Over time, the secular and traditionalist sectors of Israeli society are becoming more traditional in certain senses but less punctilious about religious observance.

The third process is an ongoing internal debate, including among religiously observant Ashkenazi Jews, about whether it is necessary to continue with the custom of not eating *kitniyot*, since the main reason for it—fear that the legumes might be mixed with particles of flour—is no longer relevant. Among those who identify as "Ashkenazi" in Israel, around one-third do not eat *kitniyot* on Passover (31%). The number of Ashkenazi Jews who say they keep kosher during Passover, however, is almost double (56%). So, it is indisputably clear that many Ashkenazi Jews in Israel both eat *kitniyot* and identify as keeping kosher for Passover. Among Israelis who identify as "mixed"—that is, neither Ashkenazi nor Mizrahi (or Russian or Ethiopian, as they could choose in the survey)—the proportion of those who keep kosher for Passover is similar to the rate among Ashkenazim (58%), but the rate of those who abstain from *kitniyot* plummets to one in ten. Thus, it seems a trend has emerged, which will probably continue: The number of Jews who abstain from *kitniyot* during Passover is in freefall.

Can the erosion of an ancient tradition also be seen as an expression of Israeli Judaism? Israel is undoubtedly a melting pot, mixing Jews from different places and thereby changing their culture. They can now relinquish the prohibition on eating *kitniyot* thanks to the breakdown of barriers between different ethnic groups. Israel is also undoubtedly a new phenomenon with the power to influence the identity and outlook of the Jews who live there. On the one hand, Israel allows Jews to live tribal lives and easily strengthen old customs and traditions; on the other, it also makes it easier for them to break old habits, because there is no tangible threat to their collective identity as Jews. This ease is often expressed through their brazen displays of self-confidence in renewing traditions (eg., the Kibbutz Haggadah) or in abolishing traditions whose time has passed (eg., *kitniyot*).

In the specific case of the prohibition on *kitniyot*, Rabbi Michael Avraham writes: "We are chained to a strange custom that developed over the years and has become a monster devouring our

Passover."[86] His weariness with this custom is increasingly common among Israelis, including among the strictly observant. He also joins many others in thinking that this prohibition should be abolished. Several rabbis have indeed permitted the consumption of *kitniyot* during Passover on the grounds that Jews in Israel are neither Ashkenazi nor Sephardic but "Land of Israel Jews." In effect, they have decided that the new state of affairs in the State of Israel permits new local customs, including the abolition of "this odd practice."[87]

Will this prohibition be retired? We can offer a reasonable forecast on the basis of developments to date. The custom will be discontinued among a majority of the Jews of Israel, either because they will intermarry and cease to be "ethnic" in their practices, or for lack of interest in the minutiae of strict observance, or thanks to dispensations from their rabbis to relinquish the custom. The Haredim are the exception. As a group they are majority-Ashkenazi (some 60%).[88] Haredi Jews also keep to their ethnic groups: Ashkenazi and Sephardic Haredim rarely intermarry. Reports of discrimination by Ashkenazi Haredim against Sephardic Haredim occasionally make headlines, especially in the context of school admissions. The Haredim attach relatively greater importance to the separation between different groups. Around one-third say it is important for them "to live in a place where most people have a similar ethnic origin to me"—whereas roughly one-fifth of non-Haredi Jews say the same.[89] And, as we know, Haredi Jews are hesitant about abolishing religious stringencies, so no important rabbis have emerged to annul the prohibition on *kitniyot*.

In other words: A custom that was once general became a matter of tradition, then contracted to just the religious public, and may certainly become exclusively Haredi in a generation or two, no different from black brimmed hats and long sidelocks.

There are several dates in the Israeli calendar on which different groups can be distinguished by the customs they observe. Some customs are primarily National-Religious (singing *Hallel* during

Jerusalem Day prayers); others are primarily Haredi (not shaving during the Three Weeks, the period of mourning before Tisha B'Av); others are primarily secular or traditionalist (the religious and Haredi groups do not attend New Year's Eve parties—secular and traditionalist Israelis do).

Other customs divide Israeli society along different lines. On Tisha B'Av, National-Religious, Dati-Torani, and Haredi Jews go to pray at the Western Wall. Not all of them, of course, but very many. Why does this matter? Because this custom is an Israeli novelty as well, which only became possible after the Six-Day War, when the Western Wall became accessible to the general public. As we have already said, the facts of modern Israel are changing Jews' patterns of behavior, which is just as true of this custom as a similar one—the Priestly Blessing at the Western Wall in the intermediate days of Sukkot.

If you are secular or even traditionalist, you have probably never expressed an interest in this custom. You might have come across a photograph in the newspaper depicting it. You might have once been startled to see masses of people rushing to do something of which you have no experience. And indeed, these are *masses*. This much is reported by those who visit the Western Wall on the day of the mass benediction during Sukkot. This much is also clear from our survey: 5% of Jews in Israel say they attend the Priestly Blessing at the Western Wall during Sukkot. That translates to some 300,000 people. It is unlikely that such a large crowd would fit in the Western Wall Plaza, so we can assume that many attend but not every year. Or that they would want to go but cannot always make it. Either way, this is an Israeli Jewish custom, because one must be *in Israel* to observe it—but it is not a custom of *all* Israeli Jews. Noticeably, only two groups participate: the Dati-Torani group (15%) and the Haredi group (18%). Among the various types of secular, traditionalist, and even religious Israelis, participation rates are either much smaller than among these groups or negligible.

## Where Are You for the Holidays?

The Western Wall Plaza is also crowded during the fast that commemorates the destruction of the Temples. Israel fought, liberated (or occupied, depending on your politics), cleared, renovated, and expanded the area, and it now maintains it and facilitates access. What was, throughout much of Jewish history, difficult or even impossible, is absolutely possible today, and that possibility is enticing. Every Tisha B'Av, tens and possibly hundreds of thousands of grieving worshippers descend on the Western Wall Plaza. (Reports vary depending on the newspapers' sectoral affiliations—online you will find everything from "thousands" to "tens of thousands" to "hundreds of thousands" in reports from the same year.) According to our research, the figure is one in twenty Jews (4%). But on Tisha B'Av, the range of participants is much wider than at the Priestly Blessing during Sukkot and spans the entire spectrum of the observant sector, from Liberal-Religious (9%) to National-Religious (8%), Dati-Torani (9%) and Haredi (10%).

\* \* \*

There are significant differences between the many examples presented in this chapter. They include innovations (e.g., bicycles on Yom Kippur), additions (e.g., new texts in the Passover Haggadah, or mass gatherings at the Western Wall), and total or gradual abolitions (e.g., that of the prohibition on *kitniyot* during Passover). But these examples have one thing in common, which must be noted: They all involve changes in the *practice* of Jewish festivals. The Jews of Israel have not given up on the general framework of their festivals. Very many observe Yom Kippur, and almost everyone observes Passover. And these festivals still retain strong elements of tradition: walking to synagogue, fasting, Seder night, keeping kosher, reading the Haggadah, sitting in the sukkah, and so forth. For most of the key dates in the Jewish calendar, it is clear that the changes Israelis are making point not to a *revolt*— a rejection of tradition in order to erase it—but to an *update* of the tradition—an adaptation to new circumstances. This is the reality for the majority of Israelis who are not religiously observant but still feel Jewish and want to express their Jewishness. This is the reality of Jewish sovereignty, which allows Jews to be flexible without fearing they will lose control of their identity. It is a reality of coexistence between different communities, which requires them to be considerate of one another. Everyone sees everyone else, everyone learns from everyone else, and everyone imitates everyone else—sometimes out of choice, and other times subconsciously.

This process is clear not only from the waning of "ethnic" traditions, as with *kitniyot* during Passover, but also from the spread of such traditions. Ashkenazi Jews are losing the battle over *kitniyot*, perhaps for their own good, but another group—which is being absorbed into the Israeli mainstream—is winning the battle over another custom: Mimouna. This festival, which is celebrated by Jews from Morocco and elsewhere in North Africa, stopped being a merely "ethnic" custom long ago. It is a national holiday. In 2016, then-environment minister Avi Gabbay decided to exempt Mimouna (like Independence Day) from the general ban on making noise after 11 p.m. The celebrations and late-night ululations received an official stamp of approval.

Mimouna, celebrated at the end of Passover, is a tradition that was imported by a minority: a "marginal, sectoral" festival that received the "status of a national holiday, partly religious, partly civil," as Rachel Sharabi wrote in her book on the subject.[90] Moroccan immigrants celebrated it at home until someone had the idea of taking it public in the mid-1960s. Initially, a few hundred came, then thousands, then tens and hundreds of thousands, and with them the politicians, who understood the electoral power represented by the revelers. Mimouna caught on so quickly that some people are already complaining that the switch "from the erasure of a culture to its appropriation" was too speedy. That is, at first Israel pushed Moroccan immigrants and their culture to the margins, but the smell of *mufletot*—the traditional Mimouna pancakes—persuaded them to appropriate this culture.[91]

## Where Are You for the Holidays?

Around half a million Moroccan immigrants, whether first- or second-generation, live in Israel today.[92] This corresponds with our finding that one-tenth of Jews in Israel (9%) say they "host Mimouna at home." Around half of the hosts also "wear traditional dress" on Mimouna (4%). These numbers point to a traditional "ethnic" holiday. Mimouna, however, requires not only hosts but also guests. In Morocco, the Jews used to invite their Muslim neighbors. In modern Israel, they invite their Jewish compatriots from other communities, who are not fortunate enough to have such a beautiful festival of their own.

Almost four in ten Israelis are hosted for Mimouna (38%). More than one-quarter of Ashkenazi Jews say they are hosted for Mimouna (27%). A similar proportion of Jews from the former Soviet Union say the same (28%). The proportion is even higher among Mizrahi Jews (48%) and Israelis from mixed families (43%). Thus, from a simple calculation of hosts and guests, we discover that almost half of Israel's Jewish population celebrates Mimouna. Is it an "ethnic" holiday? Prime Minister Benjamin Netanyahu told his Mimouna hosts in 2017 that what had begun as a solely Moroccan tradition "has turned into a holiday for all the ethnic groups."[93] He did not have exact numbers in front of him, but politicians have a good sense of what is popular and no longer sectoral. Netanyahu was right: Members of all ethnic groups celebrate Mimouna.

Here we can begin to wrap up. Jewish society in Israel is revising its traditions, customs, and holidays. It is doing so in four different ways: abolishing traditions, changing traditions, renewing traditions, and inventing traditions. The prohibition on *kitniyot* falls under abolitions, even if only partially and inconclusively. Bicycles fall under the second category—Yom Kippur still exists, including abstinence from driving, but its character is changing. Under renewals come the Jews who visit the Western Wall on Tisha B'Av, or practices like the offering of the first fruits on Shavuot in Israel's agricultural settlements.

And what about the last category—the invention of new traditions? That is a no less complicated matter. It is the subject of the next chapter.

\* \* \*

| Groups/ Practices | Do your children ride bicycles on Yom Kippur? | Do you read the whole Passover Haggadah, including the sections after the meal? | Are you hosted for Mimouna? | Do you visit the Western Wall on Tisha B'Av? |
|---|---|---|---|---|
| All Jews | 34% | 64% | 38% | 4% |
| Totally secular | 52% | 22% | 28% | 0% |
| Somewhat-traditional secular | 47% | 58% | 45% | 0% |
| Traditionalist | 32% | 79% | 47% | 3% |
| Liberal-Religious | 25% | 88% | 50% | 9% |
| National-Religious | 10% | 96% | 43% | 8% |
| Dati-Torani | 7% | 99% | 38% | 9% |
| Haredi | 1% | 99% | 24% | 10% |

# Chapter 5
# Jewish or Israeli?

> *New holidays and customs are being added to the Israeli calendar: days of national remembrance, mourning, and celebration. Are they Israeli holidays? Are they Jewish?*

No question is more vexatious and familiar for Israelis than the question: "What are you first, Jewish or Israeli?" The late Israeli humorist and politician Uri Orbach once wrote, "That's more or less like asking me: 'What are you more, a man with glasses or a man with a mustache?'"[94] Nevertheless, this question is familiar to any Israeli who has been a member of a youth movement, engaged in a dialogue about Israeli and/or Jewish identity, been through an IDF course, or traveled abroad as a *shaliach* (emissary of a Jewish organization). In short—it is familiar to almost every Jew in Israel. Like the question of whether you love your mother or your father more (which is almost never asked), or whether Israel should be a Jewish or a democratic state (which is asked all the time), the question of "Israeli" versus "Jewish" forces Israelis to choose when it is not clear that a choice exists. Moreover, it is not always clear that the meaning of this choice is understood the same way by the questioner and the respondent.

The question appears in different forms in various studies and surveys, but the results are almost always the same. More Israelis identify primarily as Jewish than as Israeli. When presented with the formulations "Jewish first" or "Israeli first," 46% responded that they are Jewish first and 35% that they are Israeli first.[95] When presented with the wording "Which of these terms best defines your identity?" their answers did not change much: 51% said "Jewish" and 41% said "Israeli." Other formulations, such as whether they would like to have been born Jewish or Israeli if given a choice, also reveal a preference for "Jewishness" over "Israeliness."[96]

But what, exactly, does the choice of "Jewishness" signify? Perhaps a partial answer is that it signifies one's level of religiosity: Israelis who are more religious tend to choose Jewishness (as did three in four National-Religious and traditionalist Jews); while those who are less religious tend to choose Israeliness (as did some two-thirds of all secular respondents). This is not entirely surprising: 43% of Jews in Israel—including a clear majority of traditionalist and religious Jews—say that the "main element of Judaism" is "religion."[97] So when Jews in Israel answer whether they are Jewish first or Israeli first, many are really answering a different question: "How religious are you?"[98]

But the meaning of "Jewishness" is more complex than such questions imply. This can be confusing for pollsters, but even respondents struggle to give consistent answers. For example, when Israeli Jews are asked whether "being Jewish" or "being a good Jew" means being religiously observant, most say no. Suddenly, it no longer sounds reasonable to them to define Judaism in terms of religious practice. Only around one-third (who are predominantly religious and Haredi) believe that being a good Jew means being religiously observant.

So what makes a Jew a Jew? And what makes a good Jew a good Jew? One option: They live in Israel. Most Jews in Israel (56%) believe that living in Israel is essential for being a good Jew.

Can you spot the dog chasing its own tail? We just explained that most Israeli Jews consider themselves Jewish first. Now it is clear that most of them also think that being a good Jew means living in Israel: i.e., being Israeli. In order to be *Jewish* first, one must first be *Israeli*. And vice versa.

Our purposes in pointing out this paradox are not to make fun of Jews or Israelis, but to clarify an important point: Over time, Jewishness and Israeliness are being fused into a new compound. Some elements belong exclusively to the religiously observant; others are strongest among those who are not observant. But there is much that is common to everyone, or nearly everyone. These are the buds of a new culture—of Israeli Judaism. A culture that bears both fresh thinking and fresh features. A culture in which being a "good Jew" means both "observing festivals, rituals, and customs" and "serving in the IDF." Only the totally secular believe that one can be a good Jew without observing rituals and customs (77%), and only the Haredim believe that service in the IDF is not an expression of being a good Jew (83%). For Jews in all the other identity categories, there is no great dilemma. Israeli Judaism means *both* traditional customs *and* military service.

* * *

Israeli Judaism did not emerge out of thin air. Founded upon ancient strata, it has added elements that emerged from the new reality of national independence. Consider, for example, the history of Yom Hazikaron—Israel's Memorial Day for fallen soldiers—a date on which this Israeli-Jewish amalgam is clearly recognizable. It is a unique day, which generates great emotional power, and the decision to hold it back-to-back with Yom Haatzmaut, Independence Day, amplifies the resonance of both days.

As in other countries, Israel's Memorial Day is a civil—Israeli—day of remembrance. It is also a Jewish day of remembrance, whose Jewish nature is evident from its symbols. "May the People of Israel remember its sons and daughters," Israelis say on Yom Hazikaron as they recite the Yizkor memorial prayer. But who is "the People of Israel"? Is it the Israeli nation, mourning the victims of the wars that guaranteed its security—just as the French, Belgians, or Americans mourn the victims of their own wars on their respective memorial days—or is it the ancient Jewish nation, which is also called "the People of Israel"? Continue reading the text of Yizkor and other such questions will arise. What is "*t'kumat Yisrael*"? Does it mean the "birth" of a modern state, or the "rebirth" of an ancient nation?

The example of Yom Hazikaron reveals how new days and practices, rooted in national revival, are being added to the Jewish calendar in Israel. The State of Israel is playing an active role in making this happen. Still, we must ask: Does Israel's Memorial Day for fallen soldiers and terror victims actually constitute a Jewish day? Moreover, if it does, we must also ask if it's proper for the civil bureaucracy of a modern state to establish new Jewish customs and impose them on an ancient culture that has always been governed by a colorful anarchy rather than a guiding, authoritative government.

Israel's original Independence Day started as a peculiar event called Yom Hamedina— State Day—which was set for the 20th of Tammuz, the anniversary of Theodor Herzl's death. It was celebrated in 1948, the year Israel was established, only a few months after independence was declared. The next year, it was supplemented by a new day: Yom Hakomemiyut—Independence Day, but with a different Hebrew word for "independence." The date was the 5th of Iyar, the anniversary of the declaration of independence. The earlier date, the 20th of Tammuz, became Army Day, but it soon became clear that this division in the state calendar was illogical. David Ben-Gurion abolished Army Day and insisted on "Yom Hakomemiyut" but ultimately conceded and accepted the new name—"Yom Haatzmaut."[99] The final decision to append it to Yom Hazikaron was decided by a committee, which only started deliberating in 1951, after the War of Independence was over, in light of complaints from bereaved parents about the typically haphazard memorial services for their loved ones. The committee explored four possible dates for Yom Hazikaron: Lag Ba'Omer, a day of Jewish heroism; the 11th of Adar, the date of the famous 1920 Battle of Tel Hai in northern Israel; the 20th of Tammuz, which had become available with the cancellation of State Day; and the 4th of Iyar, the eve of Independence Day.[100] Ultimately, the last option was chosen, mainly because families of fallen soldiers were already in the habit of visiting the cemeteries on this day.

The program for Yom Hazikaron was designed to include civil elements—a siren, military formations, and flags lowered to half-mast—but also many components that are discernibly Jewish. The official state ceremony, for example, takes place at the Western Wall Plaza. Prayers are recited. Memorial candles are lit. The day lasts—by law—from sunset on the evening of the 4th of Iyar until stars appear the next evening in accordance with the conventional structure of days in the Jewish calendar.

Accordingly, most of the debates about the observance of Yom Hazikaron also relate to its Jewish content.

The Yizkor prayer customarily used by the IDF was composed by Labor Zionist leader Berl Katznelson, who "adopted the form of religious prayers but changed their logic to a national meaning," in the words of his biographer, Anita Shapira.[101]

In Katznelson's prayer, it is *"Am Yisrael,"* the people of Israel, who remember and mourn their fallen on Yom Hazikaron, though an updated edition, which begins "May God remember," was written at the initiative of IDF Chief Rabbi Shlomo Goren, who saw Katznelson's version, which erased God, as a "malicious distortion."

In 2011, after a bitter public debate, a committee appointed by then-IDF Chief of Staff Benny Gantz was tasked with deciding which of these two versions should be used at remembrance ceremonies.[102] The committee moved to abolish Goren's God-based version and restore Katznelson's. General Yishai Bar, who headed the committee, explained the decision with an interesting combination of religious sensitivity and secular civics: "Yom Hazikaron is a sacred day, in both the religious and secular senses—a unifying day. We reasoned that it would be appropriate to facilitate in the cemeteries, alongside the unity of hearts, also a uniformity of texts. It became clear to us that some of the secular bereaved families do not feel comfortable with the religious sections in the ceremony. Elements of the *Tziduk Hadin* ('Justification of Divine Judgment') prayer are difficult for them. They find it difficult to accept that the Lord is Full of Mercy."

A "sacred day," but not necessarily sacred in a religious sense. This is Jewish sanctity expressed by a modern state: not by God but by the people. This sanctity is indeed a unifying force, as General Bar stated. Almost all Jews in Israel (85%) say they feel sad on this day. Even more stand for the siren, whether in public or at home (94%).[103] This means that of all the day's customs—including visiting cemeteries, lighting memorial candles, reciting Yizkor or *El Malei Rachamim*, and attending official or alternative ceremonies—the secular custom (the siren) is the one most observed. Around half of Jews in Israel attend Yom Hazikaron ceremonies, either organized by the state, by schools, or elsewhere. Very few Jews in Israel (6%) say it is "a regular day" for them. The outliers are the Haredim, only a minority of whom (4%) attend Yom Hazikaron ceremonies.

Of course, Yom Hazikaron is not the only newly sanctified day in Israel's Jewish calendar. Independence Day straddles the same line between a national holiday and a Jewish one. Its particular customs are practiced by most of Israel's Jewish population, a large majority of whom (discounting the Haredim) fly the Israeli flag on Independence Day. They purchase more than one million flags every year.[104] Religious and traditionalist Jews do so somewhat more than others (73%), and secular Jews do so somewhat less.[105] Flag-waving might look like a secular practice, but the Israeli flag is intimately tied to Jewish culture. In committee deliberations, the representative of Hapoel Mizrahi, Zerach Warhaftig, enumerated the principles used to guide the design of the flag, including: "The rule will prevail that the more ancient, the more sacred."[106] The result was a national flag like any other, but its resonance for the Jewish people is unmistakable. With a Star of David at its center, the white flag's two azure strips conjure the image of the *tallitot* worn by Jews in prayer. "No other symbol is considered by Jews and gentiles to be as Jewish as the Star of David," stated David Ben-Gurion at a cabinet meeting in July 1948.[107]

According to our survey, watching the traditional torch-lighting ceremony on Independence Day is almost as popular a practice as flying the flag. Fifty-eight percent of Israelis say they do so (though television ratings point to a lower figure of around 35%). Why torches? There is no organized account of the decision to light torches on the eve of Independence Day, but on Israel's first Independence Day, members of youth movements lit torches in several settlements across the country—probably recalling the practice of lighting torches on mountaintops in the ancient days of Hebrew rule in the Land of Israel. On Independence Day in 1950, this had already become a formal ceremony. Twelve torches were lit, representing the tribes of Israel—a further display of how this ceremony superimposed the historic narrative of the Jewish people upon the civil existence of the State of Israel.

The data show that most Israelis who fly the flag also watch the torch-lighting ceremony, and half of those who both fly the flag and watch the ceremony also go out to celebrate in the streets. Some Independence Day practices have developed in a top-down fashion, such as watching the official ceremony or tuning into the International Bible Contest (which is also an expression of Independence Day's connection to the Jewish past). Other customs emerged bottom-up, such as exploring the great outdoors, flying the national flag, and overeating at barbecues.

Independence Day drew on Jewish tradition, and as a result, it is gradually becoming a Jewish tradition: a secular tradition for secular Jews, and a religious tradition for religious Jews.

\* \* \*

On the 8th of Nissan, 5709 (April 7th, 1949), Israel's two chief rabbis, Yitzhak HaLevi Herzog and Ben-Zion Meir Hai Uziel, wrote to the Chief Rabbinate Council:

> "The fundamental turning point in God's compassion for us, the declaration of our independence in the Land, which saved us and redeemed our souls, obligates us to uphold and keep this day of the fifth of Iyar, the day of the declaration of the State of Israel, for all generations, as a day of joy at the beginning of the redemption for all of Israel, and to exempt the day of this great miracle from all customs of mourning of the Omer period."[108]

It is worth dwelling on this event, whether or not you care for rabbinic rulings or consider the State of Israel to be the beginning of the Redemption. This story illustrates not just the influence of Jewish culture on the Jewish state, but also the dramatic influence of the Jewish state on Jewish culture. Two respected rabbis, whose authority was accepted by many, issued a statement decreeing a new festival in the Jewish calendar. Not a civic holiday, but a religious one. Similar to the wording about Purim in the Book of Esther, which enjoins the Jews to "keep… yearly… a day of feasting and gladness,"[109] the wording in the rabbis' letter also mandated "for all generations… a day of joy."

Independence Day takes place in the middle of the Counting of the Omer, a period of mourning. The chief rabbis decided to suspend the mourning for the sake of joy. Perhaps even to permit weddings, as on Lag Ba'Omer. It is interesting to imagine how this decision might have changed the nature of Independence Day, the eve of which could have been filled with weddings alongside national and personal celebrations. But this we can only imagine, because Herzog and Uziel's decision provoked a storm of strife. The chief rabbis ran into opposition from the Chief Rabbinate

Council. Consequently, they walked back their comparison of Independence Day to Lag Ba'Omer. The joy was still on. The weddings were off. At least for now.

The argument over the religious connotations of Independence Day concerned two further matters: Should the *Hallel* prayer be recited, and if so, should it be said with or without the blessing? Similarly, should the Prayer for the Welfare of the State of Israel be recited, and which version? One can detect in these arguments a certain religious pedantry, but one can also see the crisis of a religious culture encountering a new reality to which it was forced to adapt. Suddenly there was a Jewish state, a Jewish sovereign entity with an array of powers—and a decision had to be made about what to do with them. Must Judaism, as a culture, be indifferent to the existence of the Jewish state, or does the existence of the State of Israel call for an "Israeli Judaism" with adaptations for the new era?

The contours of this debate demarcate the line between Religious Zionists and religious but non-Zionist (and of course anti-Zionist) Haredim. Around two-thirds of Religious Zionist men (Liberal-Religious, National-Religious, and Dati-Torani) recite the *Hallel* prayer on Independence Day, compared to only a small fraction (6%) of Haredi men. Haredi society remains strongly characterized by its rejection of the state's religious significance. So, while religious and Haredi Jews generally agree (religious 70%, Haredi 90%) that "in order to be a good Jew, one must observe all the commandments of halakha," they are profoundly divided on questions relating to Israel. For example, a sizeable majority of Religious Zionist Jews believe that "being a good Jew means serving in the IDF" (74%), while far fewer Haredim (16%) believe the same.

But the debate over religious practice in an Israeli context is not just between religious and Haredi populations. The Religious Zionist public has its own internal arguments about the customs and prayers that follow from the fact of the state's existence.

#IsraeliJudaism

At the time of the Oslo Accords, several religious groups changed the wording of the Prayer for the Welfare of the State of Israel because they considered it improper to pray for "ministers and advisers" who were acting contrary to their wishes. Similarly, during the Gaza Disengagement, some wondered whether they should even celebrate Independence Day and recite *Hallel* for a state that was (in their minds) betraying its mission. One can see from each of these junctions how the Jewish state poses a challenge to traditional Judaism. It forces the Jews to react. To change, to resist, to update. It creates new conditions, which allow for the modernization of ancient festivals, such as Yom Kippur (see the previous chapter). It creates a new calendar, which can recharge its batteries with fresh Jewish content. It inserts Jewish customs into ceremonies that embrace all Israelis, including those who identify as totally secular. The young Israelis who lit candles after the assassination of Prime Minister Yitzhak Rabin, for instance, instinctively expressed their grief in the language of Jewish tradition. Their candles were memorial candles. Till today, some Israelis still light candles on the anniversary of the assassination (8%); occasionally, some even propose making it a fast day. No mass movement has emerged from this initiative, but the need to express grief remains. As we have already recalled, around half of Jews in Israel say they feel sad on the anniversary of Rabin's murder.

\* \* \*

From grief over Rabin to a more ancient sorrow. Tisha B'Av fell relatively late in 1997, towards the middle of August. About two weeks earlier, at the end of July, the Knesset Constitution Committee convened to discuss a bill to "prohibit the opening of entertainment venues on Tisha B'Av." They were obviously pressed for time. The chairman, MK Shaul Yahalom, a member of a Religious Zionist party, hoped to avoid a lengthy debate about values and quickly pass the bill. In fact, as he hinted to the committee members, there was nothing controversial about this legislation. "We copied from the Holocaust Martyrs' and Heroes' Remembrance Day Law," he said. Committee member Yael Dayan pressed him: "I want to understand. It's summer and a tourist wants to find somewhere to eat on the eve of Tisha B'Av and can't find anywhere, what happens then?" "Closed," Yahalom replied. Cafés, however, would be "open in Jaffa." This is to say that the proposed law would not be applied to areas with non-Jewish majorities.[110]

What was meant to be a technical discussion about the nuts and bolts of the legislation ended up stirring an indispensable debate about principles.

"What about completely secular communal settlements that don't want this law to be applied to them on this day?" pressed MK Hagai Marom.

"This is not a religious law or a secular law," replied Yahalom. "It's a national law. We are saying that Tisha B'Av is a day of national mourning."

Nevertheless, as MK Alex Lubotzky noted, this bill was being proposed and promoted specifically by the religious parties. "It's like this is another attempt at religious coercion." In Dayan's eyes, there was no doubt about this. She saw the proposed prohibition on Tisha B'Av as "a religious matter" and therefore considered the comparison to Yom Hashoah—Holocaust Remembrance Day—absurd.

The Knesset Interior Committee debated similar issues three years later, when the law needed to be amended. MK Yosef Paritzky from the secular Shinui Party argued that cafés were not "entertainment venues" and therefore there was no reason to close them.

"[If so,] you will need to explain why there is a prohibition on opening cafés on Yom Hazikaron and Yom Hashoah," replied United Torah Judaism MK Moshe Gafni.

Paritzky doubled down: "There is a difference between Tisha B'Av and Yom Hazikaron, if only because nobody has a personal memory of the destruction of the Temple."

Yahalom struggled to understand his point: "Does that mean we will need to abolish Yom Hashoah in a hundred years?" he asked, noting that by then nobody who has "personal memory" of the Holocaust will still be alive.

This argument irritated Paritzky: "Do you not understand the difference?" Obviously, the answer was a resounding no. The law passed. Tisha B'Av, like Yom Hashoah, was declared a day of national mourning, on which entertainment venues are prohibited from opening. But while the respective laws are similar, there is a vast difference between these two dates in the consciousness of Israelis: Four in five Jews in Israel say they "feel sad" on Yom Hashoah (78%). It is a day on which the totally secular (81%), the somewhat-traditional secular (82%), the Liberal-Religious (74%), and even two-thirds of the Haredim feel sad (Haredim express their grief over the Holocaust in the context of the Asara B'Tevet fast but do not deny the power of the state's Yom Hashoah). Yom Hashoah is a day on which the left (77%), the right (77%), and the political center (79%) all feel sad. Only one-tenth of Jews in Israel (9%) say that, for them, Yom Hashoah is a completely regular day.

The situation on the other national day of mourning, Tisha B'Av, is quite different. More than half of Jews in Israel (55%) feel that Tisha B'Av is a "completely regular day." This is true of almost all Jews who identify as totally secular (97%), a large majority of somewhat-traditional secular Jews (84%), and also half of the traditionalists (50%). The same goes for most of the political center (75%) and a large majority of the left (91%).

The law notwithstanding, Tisha B'Av is not really a national day of mourning, as anyone who goes tubing down the streams of the Galilee, bathes at the beach, or visits the zoo can see on this summer day. Restaurant owners also seem unfazed by the day's grief, opening their doors despite the prohibition, the law, and the fines.

Tisha B'Av has remained "Jewish" in the religious sense and has not been assimilated into the new Israeli culture. Perhaps because it is marked during the summer holidays, when the education system has no opportunity to instill its significance into the minds of pupils. Perhaps because it is hard to mourn for a temple that many prefer not be rebuilt. Perhaps because it is difficult to grieve for the destruction of Jerusalem when Jerusalem has been rebuilt and is bigger than ever. Around one-third of Jews in Israel fast for the whole day on Tisha B'Av; the overwhelming majority of those who fast are religious or Haredi. The state's legislative efforts have not achieved their national objectives. Attempts by renowned ideological leaders, such as Berl Katznelson, to preserve Tisha B'Av in the general Jewish consciousness have also failed.

The story about Katznelson is quite familiar to many Israelis. The Labor leader was shocked to discover that the HaMahanot HaOlim youth movement had taken its members to a summer camp on Tisha B'Av, "the very night when the Jewish people laments its destruction, its enslavement, and the bitterness of its exile." In an article for the *Davar* newspaper, he wondered: "What is the value and product of a liberation movement that lacks *rootedness* and indulges in *forgetfulness*?"[111]

This was certainly a piercing essay, but its influence on reality was limited. Members of the youth movement, joined by those who resented Katznelson's rebuke, argued that Tisha B'Av was a religious event. As secularists, they had no interest in it. Moshe Shner of Oranim College, who did not accept Katznelson's position, later articulated the fundamental dispute thus: "There is a profound, polar difference, touching the root of the matter, between the sanctification of Tisha B'Av as a day of mourning and the renewal of the Jewish present in the democratic State of Israel."[112] Tisha B'Av, he explained, is stuck in the past and alien to the present. Whether he was right or wrong, the nation is voting with its feet. Against Katznelson—and for Shner. Against a national day of mourning—and for a day of remembrance exclusively for the religious public.

\* \* \*

#IsraeliJudaism

The Jewish calendar is changing. For Jews who live in Israel it is becoming an Israeli Jewish calendar. The force of history adds new dates. The state institutions add new customs. But the real power remains in the hands of the only sovereign in Jewish tradition: the public, which sometimes embraces the new—and sometimes rejects the old.

\* \* \*

| A national sense of Jewishness | |
|---|---|
| I feel sad on Yom Hashoah | 78% |
| I travel a lot around the country | 70% |
| Being a good Jew means serving in the IDF (and/or raising one's children to serve in the IDF) | 68% |
| I watch the torch-lighting ceremony on Independence Day | 58% |
| Being a good Jew means living in Israel | 56% |
| The definition that describes me is "Israeli Jew" | 55% |
| In my eyes, the main feature of Judaism is "nation" | 26% |
| I fly the Israeli flag on Jerusalem Day | 24% |
| I go to a rally or light a memorial candle on the anniversary of Rabin's assassination | 14% |

# CHAPTER 6
# The State or the People?

*The Israeli state is deeply involved in the creation of an Israeli Judaism. The state has registered several successes in this design process—and quite a few failures.*

In 1997, the Yaakov Neeman Committee was appointed "to develop ideas and proposals regarding the issue of religious conversion in Israel." The stakes of their commission were high: nothing less than "the unity of the Jewish people" was at risk.

Twenty years later, the Moshe Nissim Committee was tasked with the same mission.[113]

In both cases, two detailed reports by men of undisputed wisdom and experience in politics and law were placed at the disposal of the state. The issue at hand was the utter lack of consensus regarding what constitutes a Jewish conversion. The two reports suggested a solution: the creation a uniform path for "accepting the Jewish faith and joining the Jewish people," as Nissim put it in his report.

The recommendations made by Neeman and Nissim provoked discussion, but in both cases, any possibility of practical implementation was torpedoed. That is what happens when one tries to solve political problems with the tools of faith, or religious problems with the tools of politics. Either way, it doesn't work.

The question of conversion is a weighty one, but not necessarily because of the danger of assimilation, as one might surmise from the Nissim Report.[114] It is significant because it points to a major difficulty faced by Israeli Judaism: the difficulty of adapting an ancient and chaotic tradition—which developed organically, without anybody in charge—to a modern, civic system with a proprietor (the state), decision-making institutions (the Knesset and the courts), and deliberations that must ultimately produce decisions (in legislation or court rulings).

\* \* \*

As we started explaining in the previous chapter, the State of Israel is deeply involved in the design of Israeli Judaism. It is involved in fixing dates in the calendar, legislating codes of conduct, and setting goals and expectations. The state has registered several successes in this process and no small number of failures. Take the example of Jerusalem Day. The state intended this day, the anniversary of the reunification of Jerusalem in 1967, to be a national day of celebration. This is not what they got. With time, the day became a religious holiday. More precisely, a National-Religious holiday. This was a direct reversal of what occurred with Tisha B'Av, when the state tried (and failed) to transform a religious occasion into a national one.

Statistics attest to the failure of Jerusalem Day. Almost three in four Jews in Israel say that Jerusalem Day is "a normal day" for them. This is the case with Israelis on the political right (60%) and even more so for those on the political left (96%). Non-religious Israelis do not see any special significance in this day. Neither do most Haredim (87%). Only Israelis who identify as both religious *and* Zionist consider Jerusalem Day to be special, though one could further specify that it is a holiday narrowly observed by those Religious Zionists who associate with the political right. After all, Jerusalem Day is heavily politicized. Fixed in the calendar after the Six-Day War, it is associated with

Israel's conquest of Judea and Samaria and the unresolved Israeli-Palestinian conflict.

On Jerusalem Day, it is predominantly Religious Zionists (Liberal-Religious, National-Religious, and Dati-Torani Jews) who celebrate. Over half of them fly the Israeli flag (54%), a large proportion recite the *Hallel* prayer (44%), and around one-third go "to a party, march, or ceremony." Only a very small minority (4%) of totally secular Israelis take part in a Jerusalem Day event. Only one-tenth of them fly the flag on Jerusalem Day; in comparison, around half of them do so on Independence Day.

In other words, Jerusalem Day is a policy failure, and a plainly identifiable one. This isn't the end of the world. Some festivals catch on, others don't. Jerusalem Day might not have taken off as a national holiday, but neither is it a flashpoint between Jews who celebrate it and Jews who don't (it is, however, a flashpoint between Jews and Arabs in Jerusalem). Alas, not all of the State of Israel's cultural design failures have gone over so easily. The state's attempts to shape Passover, for example, have had costs. Perhaps also benefits. It is not easy to conclusively measure these costs and benefits due to their subjective nature.

Passover does not seem like a festival that requires outside interference. Certainly not the support of the state. Many studies demonstrate that Seder night is one of the most popular Jewish rituals in (and out) of Israel. According to the Pew Research Center, 93% of Jews in Israel participated in Seder night "last Passover" (the rate among American Jews is 70%).[115] A Guttman-AVI CHAI survey found that 90% of Jews believe it is "very important" to attend a Passover Seder.[116] According to the Israeli Central Bureau of Statistics in 2009, nine in ten Jews who identify as secular or traditionalist take part in Seder night. Among religious and Haredi Jews there are no exceptions.[117] In our study, almost all respondents (97%) replied in the affirmative as to whether they "celebrate Seder night or are hosted for Seder night."

Seder night is thus one of the only Israeli Jewish practices that is observed in almost equal measure by the full gamut of religious, political, and social sectors of the Jewish population. Moreover, as a previous chapter detailed, most Jews in Israel not only sit down to eat on Seder night but also practice a meaningful ritual by reading the Passover Haggadah. There is only one other family meal as consistently observed by a similar majority of Jews: the festive dinner on the eve of Rosh Hashanah (97%).

So why would the state interfere with such a powerful festival? Why try to fix what is not broken?

Here is the story in brief: In the mid-1980s, the Knesset passed what was called the "Chametz Law," which restricts the sale of food that is not kosher-for-Passover during the seven days of the holiday. MK Avner-Hai Shaki from the National Religious Party thought there was simply no choice but to pass the legislation: "There is a growing wave of *chametz* sales in stores, kiosks, canteens, and restaurants during Passover, and these *chametz* products are being displayed in public, which deeply injures the feelings of the majority of the religious, national, and traditionalist public."[118] But why, asked secular Mapam Party MK Victor Shem-Tov, should that prejudice his right to buy whatever he wants? "Because the Torah forbids it," answered MK Rabbi Chaim Druckman.

This answer exposed one thread in a tangle of confusion. Rabbi Druckman was talking about a Torah prohibition, but the Chametz Law does not legislate prohibitions on behalf of the Torah—it does so on behalf of the state. After two thousand years of exile, the Jews are now able to impose Jewish culture using the state's powers of coercion. Since Israel was established several decades ago, the Jews have been conducting various experiments with this power. Some argue that these measures are counterintuitive—alienating Jews from their culture. Others see them as a necessary bulwark against cultural deterioration. For them, it is clear that if the state can make it illegal to drive through a red light, it can also prevent the public display of *chametz* during Passover.

# The State or the People?

One way or another, MK Shaki did not see the proposed ban as a matter of religious coercion. "I am appealing to members of the Knesset not just on religious grounds, but also on national, cultural, and spiritual grounds," he said, echoing the reasons given in the debate over the Tisha B'Av law. Shaki claimed that the bill was rooted in the principles expressed in the Declaration of Independence. He argued (it is unclear on what basis) that "the overwhelming majority of the Jewish people in the Diaspora" probably shared his positions. "The state's Jewishness finds expression in the outward manifestations of its cultural and spiritual life, and in its primary symbols, which bear the imprint of Jewish history—including Shabbat, Jewish holidays, kosher food, the Jewish family, and a Jewish education," he declared.

MK Mordechai Virshubski from the secular Shinui Party disagreed: "Once again in this day and age we bear witness to a law that is fated to be an amusing anecdote… and I call on everyone to vote against this absurdity, which will increase hatred and polarization among the Jewish people."

Over 30 years have passed since, and the debate has not ended. It is occasionally stirred by proposals to scrap the law, court rulings that undermine its efficacy (the most prominent, in 2008, set strict rules for defining the public "display" of *chametz*), and policies of specific government ministers who increase or forgo the enforcement of the law (Interior Minister Eli Yishai from Shas enforced the law; Interior Minister Avraham Poraz from Shinui did not).

Around two-thirds of Jews in Israel say they eat only kosher-for-Passover food on Passover (64%). Even more of them (68%) take care to eat only kosher-for-Passover food on the first day of the holiday. An additional one-tenth of Jews do not eat bread during Passover but are not strict about observing "all the rest" (9%). Supporters of the Chametz Law flaunt these numbers as proof that the fear of hurting public sensibilities falls on their side—a substantial majority of the Jewish public refrain from eating *chametz* and so probably prefer not to see it in public. The law's opponents have their own counter-arguments, saying that it is not the state's business to protect religious customs; that the law is impractical to enforce; that the law has become a joke; and further, that there is no reason for a national law when local authorities can handle the issue as they see fit.

It is difficult to find Israelis who do not have strong opinions about laws like the Chametz Law. It is equally difficult to have a clear and well-substantiated answer about whether the Chametz Law has produced benefits (and for whom) or caused damage (and for whom).

Its supporters claim they have bucked a dangerous trend. Without this law, they argue, Israel would have been full of *chametz*, and more people would have been tempted to give up on observing the customs of Passover. Its opponents say that the law makes people hate Judaism, and that Pesach observance does not need to be legislated when most Israeli Jews celebrate it.

Its supporters point to how the ban on commerce on Shabbat has eroded due to a dearth of sufficiently strict laws. Its opponents retort by pointing out Yom Kippur, which is observed by quiet agreement, without a need for legislation.

In all fairness, the validity of these arguments cannot be verified. If the public really wants to, a simple majority in the Knesset can repeal the law, but the issue isn't high on anyone's agenda. Whoever wants *chametz* can find it without difficulty; whoever does not can pretend it doesn't exist.

\* \* \*

*Outlawed Pigs*, by Israeli Supreme Court justice Daphne Barak-Erez, deals with the politics, religion, and culture of Israel's laws about pigs. Since the 1980s, the legitimacy of laws restricting the rearing of pigs and the sale of pork has been eroded, as has the strength of their enforcement. Barak-Erez lists four possible explanations: changing attitudes about pork; the fragmentation of Israeli society into diverse communities; the reinforcement of protections for individual freedoms; and general changes in the relationship between religion and state in Israel.[119]

These explanations are all clearly connected. The "national dimension of these [anti-pork] prohibitions was self-evident" in Israel's early days, Barak-Erez writes, but now there is a "new narrative that associates pig prohibitions exclusively with religion and religious views."[120] This change is rooted in various factors, including Israeli Jews' tendency nowadays to choose communities—whether religious or secular—that define them and their positions. According to Barak-Erez, the secular community defines itself in opposition to the religious community. "Rejecting the compelling nature of traditional prohibitions is part of the definition of their new identity."[121] From this group's perspective, the prohibition on pork has become a symbol with a contrary meaning from what it had in the past. It now stands for "their opposition to what they perceive as religious coercion."[122] More explicitly, there is a section of the public that wants to consume pork as a sign of its freedom from the threat of coercion. In this sense, the prohibition on eating pork is similar to many other customs, which have come to be seen as religious. The pattern is clear: once a custom is labeled religious, Israelis with no interest in religion will reject the argument that these are national symbols and oppose the custom. We have already listed similar cases: The opening of cafés on Tisha B'Av and the ban on displaying *chametz* during Passover. There is no meaningful difference between what lawmakers did in these cases and what they did with the anti-pork laws.

Nowadays, 34% of Jews in Israel eat kosher in all circumstances, both at home and outside.[123] There are also Jews who eat kosher at home but not outside (7%), and even some who eat kosher in Israel but not when they travel abroad (2%). About a quarter of Jews in Israel do not eat kosher and will even eat pork. An additional 9% do not keep kosher but abstain from eating pork.

As we have said, nobody can know for sure what would have happened without the anti-pork laws (these laws restrict pig farming and the selling of pork in certain areas). Perhaps abstinence from pork would have remained a national symbol, but even more widespread. Alternatively, perhaps pork would have quickly started being sold on every street corner. What is clear is that here too, the state tested its powers to shape Israeli culture and, as before, it enjoyed only partial success in attaining the objectives set by lawmakers. The legislation ended up boosting the impression of "religious coercion" among the ban's opponents, who see such restrictions as illegitimate.

The law was labeled "religious legislation." The term has stuck—a lasting testament to the law's failure. The moment the public conceives of a particular law as a piece of religious legislation, a majority will oppose it.[124]

Not only does the public oppose religious laws, it also regards any attempt to pass such legislation—sometimes justifiably, sometimes less so—as illegitimate "coercion." But what exactly is religious coercion? Justice Aharon Barak, in a ruling about traffic on a main road on Shabbat, proposed a formulation that could be adopted as a definition: "Considerations that take religious sensibilities into account are precluded if religious coercion is the final goal of such considerations. In contrast, religious sensibilities may be taken into account if they are intended to give expression to religious needs."[125] Most of the public believes there is "religious coercion" in Israel and feels uneasy with this situation. Secular Israelis obviously sense this coercion most keenly. Most even feel there is a "threat" to their secular identity in Israel.[126]

This too is a contribution of the state to Israeli-Jewish culture. On the one hand, the state can initiate, promote, and empower Jewish culture. On the other, it can erode Jewish culture by alienating the public. In fact, the key to assessing the state's policies on such matters is to understand the following: The public accepts with open arms whatever it understands to be a "national" need; it rejects as excessive coercion whatever it understands as a "religious" need. The law shutting cafés on the eve of Yom Hazikaron is therefore considered obvious—and accepted. But the law shutting cafés on the eve of Tisha B'Av is opposed—and increasingly ignored. When is something perceived as national and when is it religious? This too has quite a simple and generally accurate answer: Policies initiated by the religious parties and promoted by the Chief Rabbinate—or any rabbis—are labeled "religious." Policies understood as cross-societal initiatives—and not as the result of small-time political horse-trading—these are labeled "national."

\* \* \*

Back to conversion.

For many generations, there were only two ways to be considered Jewish: Jewish (matrilineal) descent or conversion, which involved a standard system of steps (circumcision for men, ritual immersion, and authorization from a Beit Din, or religious court).[127] Several internal developments within the Jewish people disrupted these paths, leading to a much more flexible understanding of what constitutes Jewishness. These developments and changes can be gathered under three headlines: fragmentation and secularization in the Jewish world; the integration of Jews into wider society; and the establishment of the State of Israel.

The integration of the Jews into Western societies has had unavoidable and tangible consequences. Since the Enlightenment, the boundaries and definitions that used to separate the Jews from the rest of society have been gradually disappearing. These boundaries used to be delineated and policed through strong social norms (both within the Jewish community and in non-Jewish society), which preserved the cohesiveness of the Jewish world; but they collapsed like the walls of Jericho. As a result, young Jews increasingly started marrying non-Jews, and the number of families with one Jewish and one non-Jewish parent rose dramatically.[128] Under the traditional halakhic criteria, many of their children are not Jewish. But many Jews dissent from the presumption that only someone with a Jewish mother is Jewish, as halakha traditionally requires, favoring a more flexible definition that gives weight to how people choose to identify. A Guttman-AVI CHAI poll has found that a large proportion of Jews in Israel (40%) see no difficulty in accepting as Jewish anyone "born to a Jewish father and non-Jewish mother," and around one-third of Jews in Israel (33%) are prepared to accept as Jewish anyone who "feels Jewish but their parents are not Jewish."[129] A poll for Bina has found that around one-quarter of Jews in Israel, including nearly half of secular Israelis (42%), are prepared to recognize as Jewish anyone who wants to be recognized as such.[130]

The weakening of the religious component of Judaism is clear from many studies. Nowadays most of the world's Jews do not fully observe a system of laws and customs that could mark them as a cohesive group. No less importantly, Jews no longer accept the authority of rabbis or a written code of halakha to decide rules of behavior for them. In effect, two parallel processes are taking place. On the one hand, fewer Jews believe that rabbis should be the ones to decide who is Jewish. On the other, the Jews who still prefer rabbinic authority refuse to accept the authority of rabbis who are not "theirs." The status of the Israeli Chief Rabbinate, which suffers dismal approval ratings, provides a clear illustration. Secular Israelis dislike it because they are not content for the rabbis to have authority. Many Religious Israelis dislike it because it does not reflect their particular worldview.[131]

The State of Israel complicated this picture even further. As an official sovereign entity, the state has a need to apply clear, defined criteria for belonging to the Jewish people. This is because in Israel, being Jewish bears practical and legal implications. It bears direct implications for Israeli citizens (what schools will they will attend? Will they need to serve in the army? Who will officiate their weddings?); for non-Israeli Jews (are they eligible to immigrate to Israel under the Law of Return?); and for the future of the state (will it be a country with a Jewish majority?).

## The State or the People?

This is why the State of Israel aspires for definitions, which are not necessarily accepted (and potentially *cannot* be accepted) by all Jews. There is an unavoidable collision here between two forces: the Jewish people on the one hand, as it moves towards a more flexible and hazy definition of Jewishness—and the Jewish state on the other, aiming for clear and rigid criteria.

Connect these trends to the general desire for the "unity" of the Jewish people, and you will immediately spot the difficulty in the state's efforts—whether through the Neeman and Nissim committees or by other means—to find an agreed upon solution to the conversion question. Unity requires uniformity, which is not suitable for flexibility. It requires state coercion. Moreover, since most models require the enforcers to be rabbis, this is perceived as religious coercion. Unity requires people to conform to broadly accepted criteria—that is, to strict criteria, which by their nature infuriate large swathes of the population and engender a sense of alienation.

A policy solution for the conversion question would place officials and politicians in territory once reserved for rabbis, who would obviously refuse to accept this interference. Conversely, a policy solution for the conversion question would impose rabbinic criteria on secular citizens, and sections of the public would refuse to accept such diktats. As MK Sofa Landver said in a meeting about the Neeman Committee's recommendations at the Knesset Immigration and Absorption Committee: "We understand life differently. What can you do? We do not feel that we are less Jewish."[132] That is, her mostly Russian-born supporters, whose Jewishness might be questioned by Orthodox rabbis, no longer accepted the authority of rabbis to decide who is and who is not Jewish. But in the absence of agreed upon authority, nobody has authority. Just as Landver doesn't recognize the authority of rabbis—her rivals don't accept the authority of bureaucrats.

\* \* \*

#IsraeliJudaism

So, we have returned to the question of who decides. Ostensibly, the State of Israel gets to decide. Just like it gets to decide the length of compulsory education. Like it gets to decide the design of the flag. Like it gets to decide the composition of its military. That said, Jews don't always respond well to diktats.

The state can decide to give the Jews Jerusalem Day, but it cannot compel them to rejoice. It can legislate a Chametz Law, but it cannot easily prevent them from eating bread. It can schedule national mourning on Tisha B'Av, but whoever does not feel sad will not feel sad. It can propose agreed pathways for conversion, but it cannot force a rabbi to recognize a conversion. And as the state comptroller has already proven: the state's attempts to convert hundreds of thousands of immigrants who arrived from the former Soviet Union under the Law of Return (but who are not Jewish in the eyes of the Rabbinate) have so far come to naught. Some believe that this is because immigrants were not offered a convenient and welcoming pathway to conversion. Others, because these immigrants do not need a kosher certificate from a religious authority to be welcomed into the group to which they already belong, in their own eyes and the eyes of many of their neighbors.

Moshe Nissim was concerned about the influence these immigrants were having on Israel's Jewish character: "Even in the State of Israel, in which we are one people, lurks assimilation," he wrote in his report. "We are talking about hundreds of thousands of non-Jews, who, according to estimates, will number 500,000 by 2035. This, as we have said, is while they are fully integrating and mixing with Jews in all walks of life. According to estimates, between 5-10% of couples who marry in Israel every year are mixed marriages."

Nissim's remarks contain an inherent contradiction. If these Israelis are "fully integrating and mixing with Jews in all walks of life," what makes them different from other Jews and renders their presence a catalyst for assimilation? The answer, clearly, is that the rabbis do not recognize them as Jewish. But perhaps this is insignificant, both to the individuals in question and the broader society around them. Around one-third of Jews in Israel (32%) say "it does not particularly matter" to them whether a close relative decides to marry a non-Jew; a few more Israeli Jews (4%) even say they would be happy.[133] So it is quite possible that the presumed problem of assimilation is not the problem of "the State of Israel." It is the problem of those who try to set conversion criteria that are incompatible with the circumstances of a state in which people can mix with Jews "in all walks of life" and thereby assimilate *into* the Jewish people, not out of it.

This is another of the ways in which the State of Israel is changing, sometimes unintentionally, the culture of the Jews. It is creating the conditions that allow anyone to feel Jewish by virtue of their surroundings. Without observing any particular customs, without needing a license from any particular authority, and without answering any particular criteria. Simply by living as a Jew in Israel, when being a Jew means whatever the Jews decide.

This is all consistent, of course, with the general message of this chapter. The state has tremendous power to direct new cultural currents. But the public retains its own tremendous power to go along with these currents or ignore them. Ultimately, even if it takes time, it is the Israeli public that shapes the Jewish culture of the state, not the state that shapes the Jewish culture of the public.

| The laws, the public | |
|---|---|
| I stand for the Yom Hazikaron siren, even at home | 81% |
| Jerusalem Day is a "regular day" | 72% |
| I don't eat pork[134] | 71% |
| I keep kosher-for-Passover | 64% |
| Tisha B'Av is a "regular day" | 55% |

# Chapter 7
# Who Loves Shabbat?

*In Israel, Shabbat is the primary catalyst of the so-called "religious-secular battles." It is the subject of legal disputes and the cause of political crises.*

Max Nordau, Herzl's right-hand man in the Zionist movement, pulled no punches when he described the Jewish predicament at the tail end of the 19th century and dawn of the 20th. He called the Jews "miserable dwarfs in a ghetto—helpless, skinny, gaunt, groaning, and coughing." At the Second Zionist Congress in 1889, Nordau said that Jews were "heavy of movement… comfortable standing crooked and curved." It was time, therefore, for the physical education of the young generation, who would "recreate for us the lost muscular Judaism." His speech spurred the Zionists to invest in the physical development of the Jews. The slogan "*Muskeljudentum*" ("Muscular Judaism"), as Hagai Harif explains in his book on the subject, was the parallel of "Muscular Christianity," which was prevalent in Britain at the time.[135]

But Nordau did not wish to copy from the Christians in every respect. When a proposal was made to move the Jewish day of rest to Sunday, in line with the Christian custom, he marveled:

"What is the purpose of this innovation? To abolish the distinction between Israel and the nations of the world and to assimilate into them? If so, let these innovators convert to another religion."

While Nordau wouldn't go so far as to change the day on which Shabbat is observed, he maintained that as a free thinker, he rested whenever he pleased. Zionist thinker Ahad Ha'am, however, described Nordau's blasé attitude about when to rest as "a chilly north wind" that "cast ice on the most sacred sentiments" of many Zionists. He responded to Nordau with an essay on the value of Shabbat, which many Israelis are still familiar with, thanks to one sentence, which has since become a common idiom: "One can say without any exaggeration that more than the Jews have kept Shabbat, Shabbat has kept the Jews."[136]

The debates of early Zionism are a suitable starting point for a discussion about Shabbat in the State of Israel. What was true then is true today, excepting one difference: back then, the debate was mostly talk—today, there is just as much action. Before Israel existed, Jews could make requests or recommendations, but today, in their own state, they can make decisions. The core questions of the matter, however, have stayed the same: Does Shabbat have intrinsic value in Jewish culture, and if so, what is it? From where does this value derive, and how should it be observed in the modern age? Should the state have a role in its observance? If so, what kind of role?

None of these questions are easily answered. Shabbat is the primary catalyst of the so-called "religious-secular battles" in modern Israel. It is the subject of legal and parliamentary wars and the cause of political crises.[137]

The first Yitzhak Rabin government collapsed after Israel's newly acquired F-15 jets landed just before the beginning of Shabbat. Rabin was correct when he stated in his Knesset speech, ahead of the no-confidence vote called by the (Haredi) Religious Torah Front, that the welcoming ceremony for the planes had ended *before* Shabbat. But this failed to satisfy the ministers from the National Religious Party. They abstained from the vote and were dismissed by Rabin in what was known at the time as "the brilliant ploy."[138] This led to new elections and the Likud Party's rise to power.

More than 20 years later, Ehud Barak's government was also thrown into crisis when Haredi MKs quit the coalition over a decision to transport turbine parts belonging to the Israel Electricity Corporation on Shabbat. The "Superheater Affair," named for the pieces of equipment being hauled, did not bring the government down but it did split the coalition and highlighted its instability. Barak's stormy rule was also short-lived.

What's the problem with transporting items on Shabbat? It counts as travel, and around one-third of Jews in Israel do not travel on Shabbat (35%). It also counts as work, and only one in ten Jews in Israel regularly works on Shabbat (13%).

Travel on Shabbat is a clear, well-known dividing line between Israelis who call themselves "Shabbat-observant" and those who don't. Almost all secular Israelis drive their cars on Shabbat. So do seven in ten traditionalists (67%). Religious and Haredi Jews, predictably, do not. The number of Jews who do not travel on Shabbat (35%) is roughly equal to the number of Jews who define themselves as "fully" or "largely" Shabbat-observant (33%).[139] As such, travel on Shabbat is a source of tension irrespective of F-15s and superheaters. In the 1980s, for instance, Haredi residents of Jerusalem's Bar-Ilan Street demanded the street be closed to traffic on Shabbat. Meanwhile, secular Israelis regularly demand that the state provide public transportation on Shabbat, which more than half of Israel's Jews support, but which is still largely unavailable.

The question of the character of Shabbat in the State of Israel is, in fact, three separate questions.[140]

The first concerns what Israeli Jews, as individuals, consider to be the desired character of Shabbat in Israel (and whether Shabbat even needs to have a "character"). Would it be better for there to be full or even limited public transportation on Shabbat, for the benefit of whoever cannot afford a car and wants to spend Shabbat at the beach? Would it be appropriate to shut down all commercial activity, for the benefit of whoever wants all workers to enjoy the day of rest? Should the state facilitate and even encourage theater on Shabbat, or should theaters be closed, and so forth?

The second question is not about the desired character of Shabbat, but the appropriate price for preserving this character. Would it be better, for example, for half of the country to be stuck in traffic on Sunday, if only for public works on Shabbat to be completely shut down? Would it be better for irascible and thirsty Israelis to be unable to buy popsicles on their way to the beach, if only for every supermarket and kiosk to be closed? Does the state have an interest in preserving a measure of the Shabbat spirit in the streets, to prevent religious groups from self-segregating into their own neighborhoods and towns? Nowadays, most Jews in Israel believe it would be undesirable to have mixed Haredi-secular communities. Three in four secular Israelis would not want this (78% of the totally secular), as well as half of the Haredim (49%).[141]

The third question is not actually about Shabbat at all, but about the desired level of state involvement in dictating the culture of its citizens (a matter we discussed in previous chapters). Should the state leave cultural matters to sort themselves out, perhaps even by separating religion and state, or should it be actively involved in encouraging a particular culture?

Each of these three questions is interesting in its own right, and each plays a distinct role in the overall conversation about Shabbat in Israel. The question of the Shabbat-ideal is chiefly a personal matter: How would *you* prefer Shabbat to look? The question of cost-benefit analysis is a public matter: How should the state balance the sometimes-contrasting ideals of individuals or groups? The question of the state's involvement is both ideological and practical: What is the role of the state as it relates to Jewish traditions and culture? Which policies will lead to the results that most closely approximate the individual ideals of each citizen?

One might expect a degree of consistency in the answers that citizens and leaders give to these three questions, but this is not always the case. For example, anyone who believes that the state mustn't force supermarkets to close on Shabbat must explain why the state *may* force cafés to close on the eve of Yom Hashoah. Are these not both instances of cultural coercion? Another example: Anyone who believes that there must be no public transportation on Shabbat must explain why hotels should not be similarly prevented from opening. Don't both operations employ workers on the day of rest? One final example: Anyone who supports opening theaters and closing malls on Shabbat (as proposed in the compromise known as the Gavison-Medan Covenant[142]) must justify why an hour's leisure at a classical music concert is inherently worthier than an hour spent window shopping with a friend. Is this not a distinction without a difference?

Perhaps these contradictions stem from the inability to find consensus on what constitutes the "ideal Shabbat." Most Jews in Israel spend Shabbat hiking or relaxing at the beach (59%). Around half will occasionally go shopping (51%). Almost all secular Israelis do so, whether they are totally secular or somewhat-traditional (around nine in ten go on hikes, and around three in four shop). Religious Israelis, of course, neither hike nor shop.[143] They go to synagogue (nine in ten men, and between one-third and one-half of women). The overwhelming majority of them self-report that they "keep Shabbat according to the rules of religious law."[144] They are limited in their movement and activities and are preoccupied with matters of Shabbat—long prayers, festive meals.

Across the board, most Jews are "resting" on Shabbat. Whether this amounts to the type of Shabbat rest practiced by religious Jews, or whether this amounts to secular recreation is a matter of who you ask. Here we stumble on the essence of the Shabbat dilemma. Nobody in Israel wants to cancel Shabbat, to abolish the day of rest, or to return to a seven-day working week. The substantive question regarding Shabbat, therefore, is this: Is Shabbat simply a day off, or does the Jewish Sabbath have a cultural value that transcends a regulatory day of rest?

\* \* \*

"It is clear that the legal day of rest in the Jewish State will be Saturday," wrote David Ben-Gurion in the "Status Quo Letter" he sent in the name of the Jewish Agency to Agudat Yisrael.[145] The purpose of the letter was to obtain Haredi society's support for the establishment of a new Jewish State while deferring a possibly heated discussion concerning the Jewish nature of this new state. Ever since, Israel has rested on Saturdays. But does it rest enough—or perhaps too much? This is a matter of debate. Whoever wants supermarkets open and public transportation running believes that Israel rests too much; whoever wants streets closed and commerce shut down believes that Israel does not rest enough.

Israeli law (Hours of Work and Rest Law—1951) does not determine the *nature* of the day of rest. The law simply prohibits employing anyone on their weekly day of rest, which for Jews is Saturday—Shabbat. The minister of the economy has the authority to permit work on Shabbat if he or she deems it necessary to protect the country's vital interests.[146]

For some, rest means disconnecting from the digital noise that pervades our lives. This idea was promoted by the "Shabbat Unplugged" campaign—an Israeli initiative advocating for a Shabbat without smartphone screens, without Facebook, and without Twitter. The founder of this initiative explained it thus: "We see in Shabbat an opportunity to disconnect from routine and connect to what is important to us: family, friends, community, nature. Each in their own way and according to their own way of life, and all of us together."[147] Some Israelis, however, strongly oppose the initiative, believing it to be a cunning ploy to undermine the legitimacy of a secular Shabbat. "This is undoubtedly the most sophisticated *Hadatah* initiative I have ever encountered," explained one opponent of the initiative. "It presents the secular family in a farcical manner, as if everyone is absorbed in their screens instead of each other."[148]

As one would expect, the debate over any particular initiative concerning Shabbat often spills into pettiness, spin, and squabbles enjoined with insults and anger. But this tone—which is unfortunately common in Israeli public discourse—must not obscure the importance of this discussion. Israel is the Jewish nation-state. Shabbat is a key Jewish symbol. How to behave in light of these two truths is a big question, and certainly worthy of argument.

Israel has indulged this argument numerous times. Jerusalem is a permanent flashpoint of Shabbat power struggles. The first demonstrations were protests against football matches adjacent to the neighborhoods of Mea Shearim and Beit Yisrael. Then came the struggles over traffic, first with the battle for the Ramot highway in the late '70s and early '80s, and later for Bar-Ilan Street in the '90s. In the '80s, there was also a notable power struggle over the Heikhal Cinema in Petach Tikva, which we shall return to later.

The battle lines in these culture wars are clearly drawn. We can call one side the observant side—it wants Shabbat to exist in a more traditional spirit and advocates for the state to enforce this in the public sphere. The other is the liberating side—it wants citizens to be allowed to do (almost) anything they want on Shabbat and wants the state to stay out of it. At each extreme, Israelis tend to exaggerate the current situation and its probable implications.

The observant side reasons thus: If we are completely liberal, Shabbat will retain neither a flavor of Judaism nor even a scent. It will be like a regular day, just without work—and in fact, no few Israelis *will* be forced to work, to serve those who wish not to work: shopkeepers, cinema cashiers, beach lifeguards, and so forth. Most likely, there's a kernel of truth to this, but it is also partly oblivious to the reality that has developed in Israel in recent decades. Many Israelis already shop on Shabbat, and many more support having the option of shopping on Shabbat. That does not mean their Shabbat has lost all flavor or scent of Jewish tradition.

On Shabbat in Israel, most homes light candles (65%[149]), including many homes whose members later go shopping. One in five totally secular Israelis lights candles for Shabbat (22%). Six in ten somewhat-traditional secular Israelis light candles (60%). A very large majority of traditionalist Israelis do so (85%). Perhaps even more Israelis make kiddush on Friday night—totaling almost seven in ten Jews in Israel (68%), including almost all the traditionalists (95%) and many of the somewhat-traditional secularists (65%). Even some of the totally secular homes make kiddush (20%). Clearly, traditional symbols are being preserved, as is the family experience. Four in five Jews (82%) have a family dinner on Friday night. That includes a majority of the totally secular (56%), a large majority of somewhat-traditional secularists (82%), and almost everyone else.

The liberating side, however, says this: If Shabbat is enforced, it will not be *our* Shabbat, nor will it be *our* day of rest. It will be a Shabbat that is imposed on us, leaving us no room to spend our day of rest as we see fit. Most likely, there's a kernel of truth to this as well. In Israel, one can find Jews who want to go to the beach but cannot because there is no public transportation. But this argument is also somewhat oblivious to the reality that has developed in Israel in recent decades. Israelis, all in all, do what they please on Shabbat. They rest as they please, spend time as they please, and entertain themselves as they please.

Nine in ten secular Israelis take advantage of the day for travel or to go to the beach. They seem to have found a transport solution to get them there. Between seven and eight out of ten secular Israelis occasionally go shopping on Shabbat. This means that they can not only find open shops but can also find a way to get there without much impediment. Many go to a cultural activity on Shabbat (42% of the totally secular, one-quarter of the somewhat-traditional secular). Some work—perhaps of their own volition, perhaps out of necessity. Around one-quarter of totally secular Israelis work frequently on Shabbat (26%). Despite this, most complaints about the inconvenience of Shabbat restrictions come from the secular population.

To summarize: On Shabbat in Israel, there is neither any difficulty in observing tradition, nor much difficulty in ignoring it. The battles that are so loudly waged—a recent example includes a fight over the so-called Supermarkets Law, which aims to shut down convenience stores—must not obscure this fact.[150]

\* \* \*

The Israeli public arena has seen multiple attempts at reaching compromises and agreements to avert battles over religion and state, including battles over the character of Shabbat. These include efforts at compromise, including the Religious Kibbutz Covenant, the Meimad Covenant, the Kinneret Covenant, and the Gavison-Medan Covenant. They also include public committees on specific issues: The Zvi Zameret Committee was formed after the battle over traffic on Bar-Ilan Street; the Yaakov Neeman Committee debated the question of conversion; and the Tzvi Tal Committee dealt with the matter of conscription among yeshiva students.[151]

Each of these attempts was notable in its own way. Some ended with festive, general declarations; others with detailed proposals for new arrangements. It is not difficult to see, however, what they all had in common: They lagged behind developments on the ground and failed to shape reality in accordance with the principles they advocated. There were always objectors from both sides of Israeli society. One side saw attempts to impose traditional practices on secular citizens; the other saw substantial concessions on core religious values. These arguments were compelling in theory. In practice, however, the public voted with their feet and decided with their own habits.[152]

Regarding commerce, the Gavison-Medan Covenant proposes: "Services and commercial establishments will be closed on the Sabbath. The prohibition against opening on the Sabbath will apply equally to urban areas, kibbutzim, and moshavim, and along the roads."[153] Whoever takes this covenant seriously, as worthy of implementation, must understand that it involves winding back the clocks and reversing the already settled reality of shopping on Shabbat—a reality shared by more than half of the Jewish population. Under such circumstances, it is difficult to see who might implement this proposal, and how. As Ruth Gavison explained, apropos this clause: "My consent, as a free person, to certain restrictions on Shabbat is not based on religious coercion. The reason for consenting—as a free Jewish woman, living in a state that wishes to preserve its Judeo-Hebrew public culture—is my independent desire for a clear and meaningful expression of the uniqueness of Shabbat in the Israeli public sphere. I accept, therefore, that there is a limitation on freedom here for cultural reasons."[154]

It is clear, however, that this covenant from the early 2000s no longer meets the definition of the country's "Judeo-Hebrew public culture." Israel's present culture includes shopping on Shabbat. No wonder, therefore, that most of those who wish to restore the covenant to public discourse come from the traditional end of Israeli society. These traditionalists realize that time is not on their side. They see the changes Israeli society is undergoing and understand where they lead. "The real alternative facing us at this time is not between 'Shabbat observance' and 'Shabbat desecrations,' but between limited desecrations of the Shabbat, by agreement, and even greater desecrations," wrote Professor

Amnon Shapira and Dr. Yohanan Ben Yaacov, both leaders in the Religious Kibbutz movement.[155]

Indeed, it is difficult to accept the claim that a status quo exists. "From the mid-1980s till today, the status quo on the matter of commerce on Shabbat has been increasingly eroded," wrote Dr. Shuki Friedman. He reports that "98% of cinemas in Israel, 65% of museums, 83% of the main cultural institutions, and some 20% of malls operate on Shabbat, and the supply is influencing citizens' purchasing habits."[156]

This causal relationship is well illustrated by the episode of the Heikhal Cinema in Petach Tikva in the mid-1980s. The story is simple: The elected mayor of Petach Tikva, Dov Tavori, promised to amend a municipal bylaw in order to allow the Heikhal Cinema to open on Shabbat. Many thousands took to the streets in protest over Tavori's announcement, demonstrating week after week. Some people were arrested, including the municipal rabbi. When the prime minister, Shimon Peres, searched for a solution, Haredi lawmakers threatened to topple his government. The issue wound up at the Supreme Court.[157]

For a whole summer, the conflict surrounding this cinema appeared very important. In hindsight, it was not important in the least. The cinema remained open, the protests died down, and what once seemed inflammatory (cinemas on Shabbat!) is now taken for granted.

What's true of Petach Tikva is also true of Jerusalem, where a battle brewed over cinema opening hours in the summer of 1987, three years after the disturbances in Petach Tikva. Secular protesters came on Fridays to defend the Beit Agron cinema. Barriers were erected in Haredi neighborhoods to prevent protests. There were clashes and tear gas. But three decades later, one can count dozens of cinemas, restaurants, and clubs in Jerusalem that open on Shabbat. Even in Jerusalem, with its high proportion of religious and Haredi residents, where a religious Shabbat atmosphere is so keenly felt, it is clear where the status quo has gone. When it comes to cinemas, writes the researcher Ariel Finkelstein, "the status quo is no more than a slogan."[158]

As with battles over road work, commercial centers, or the sale of non-kosher meat, the conflict over cinemas is powered as much by ideological aspirations as by personal and practical concerns.

An ideological aspiration is an attempt to influence the public sphere and the nature of Shabbat in Israel. It is the aspiration that *no Jew* should watch a film in a cinema on a Friday night. It is the aspiration for *all of Israel* to be a Shabbat-observant country. Practical concerns, on the other hand, intend simply to avoid offending particular communities that are troubled by violations of Shabbat. It is the aspiration that in *my* neighborhood, in *my* city, no cinemas should be open on a Friday night. Obviously, there is a significant difference between these two goals. In the terminology of Justice Barak-Erez, one concerns a "national symbol" and the other a "religious interest." She notes that prohibitions on the sale of pork, for instance, are increasingly interpreted as means to "protect religious sensibilities." Such an interpretation will necessarily limit the scope of the prohibitions.

Similarly, if the goal of Shabbat legislation is to protect Sabbath-observant citizens from having their sensibilities offended, one must take into account where particular cinemas are located, how far they are from the offended populations, and the seriousness of the offense.

Such an inquiry has its own implications for the character of Shabbat in Israel. Namely, that in the absence of an offended population, there would be no need to consider whether cinemas, roads, beaches, or malls should be open or closed on Shabbat. From this perspective, the nature of Shabbat is no longer a national matter, but rather a *group* matter, with specific stakeholders.

\* \* \*

| Israelis and their Shabbat | Family meals on Friday night | Work frequently | Light candles on Shabbat[159] | Outings or beach trips |
|---|---|---|---|---|
| Totally secular | 56% | 26% | 17% | 91% |
| Somewhat-traditional secular | 82% | 14% | 49% | 89% |
| Traditionalist | 95% | 8% | 71% | 62% |
| Liberal-Religious | 100% | 4% | 81% | 16% |
| National-Religious | 99% | 2% | 91% | 9% |
| Dati-Torani | 99% | 4% | 94% | 4% |
| Haredi | 99% | 1% | 95% | 4% |

# CHAPTER 8
# Who Is Secular?

*Around half of Israel's Jews self-identify as "hiloni," Hebrew for secular. But they should not be thought of as a single group. There are vast differences between "totally secular" Jews and "somewhat-traditional secular" Jews.*

What is secularism? We can start with what it is *not*. Israeli Jewish secularism is not atheism. Most secular Israelis believe in God,[160] including one-third (36%) of those who identify as "totally secular" and almost everyone who identifies as "somewhat-traditional secular" (85%). Only slightly more than one-quarter of totally secular Israelis "believe"—that is, are convinced—that God does *not* exist (29%). One-third (30%) say they do not believe in God "but sometimes think he might exist after all." Only a small minority of somewhat-traditional secularists (5%) "believe there is no God."[161] Secular Israelis believe in God less than religious and traditionalist Jews—but many of them *are* believers, or at least, are not *non*-believers.[162]

So where does that leave us on secularism? There are some areas where most secular Israelis behave or think like one group. For example, they almost all oppose religious legislation.[163] Moreover, few believe that being a good Jew means being fully religiously observant.[164] On other matters, however, there are differences—small and large—between different models of Israeli Jewish secularism. For example, some observe holidays; others don't. For some, being Jewish is very important; for others, less so.

Around half of all Jews in Israel identify as secular. They are generally not anti-tradition. They simply don't want their Jewishness defined for them by outside authorities (i.e., rabbis).[165] They don't see tradition as a binding halakhic framework, and so they shun the religious establishment and many religious practices. One characteristic that unites almost all secular Israelis, for example, is that they travel on Shabbat. They do not abstain from listening to music or going to parties during the Counting of the Omer. If they fast, it is only on Yom Kippur.

From time to time, headlines in Israel speak of an attempt to initiate a "secular revolution" of one kind or another. Prime Minister Ehud Barak, in the twilight of his growing political distress, proclaimed one such revolution. It was a Saturday night in late summer, only a few weeks before the Second Intifada would erupt and knock Barak's so-called civil-social agenda to the bottom of the list of priorities. Either because of the intifada or for other reasons, nothing came of Barak's "revolution." Still, twenty years later, it is interesting to examine the elements of his proposal.

At a ministerial meeting at his home, Barak shocked his guests when he announced that "within a few weeks, we shall see bus lines starting to operate on Shabbat from neighborhoods and suburbs of Tel Aviv to the beach."

Support for public transportation on Shabbat is still typical of secular Israelis. But Barak didn't stop there. He also promised a constitution (there is still none), civil marriage (there is still none), El Al flights on Shabbat (there are still none), the abolition of the Religious Services Ministry (it is still active), and Haredi conscription (this has not happened). The question of secular support for a constitution is a complicated one, because support depends, among other things, on what clauses it might contain. But most of the other promises made by Barak had (and have) the backing of secular Israelis.[166]

In the eyes of most secular Israelis, Judaism is not defined by the restrictions that Barak promised to lift. These are merely bothersome legal or institutional impositions. Secular Israelis observe many Jewish practices and rituals. Secular boys celebrate bar mitzvahs and even read from the Torah. Secular girls celebrate bat mitzvahs (but far fewer read from the Torah).[167] Secular Israelis do not don *tefillin* every day, nor do they recite blessings before eating, but on Yom Kippur many of them fast. They also light candles on Chanukah, even if not every night. They dress up in costumes to go to Purim parties.[168] They celebrate the Passover Seder. Most dip apples in honey on Rosh Hashanah.

Israeli secularism is generally a *Jewish* secularism. It is also a matter of *belonging* to a particular social group, which is connected to "ethnic origin and level of education and income."[169] Secular Israelis are better educated, are politically left-leaning (if not fully "left-wing"), are mostly Ashkenazi, have higher incomes than their traditionalist and religious peers, and have fewer children. They have a different worldview from non-secularists. Only among secularists do a majority see themselves first as Israeli, and only then as Jewish. As the sociologist Dr. Shlomo Fischer explained, for secularists, "being Israeli is the primary aspect of their collective identity, one might even say that being Israeli *is* their Jewish identity."[170]

\* \* \*

Secular Israelis are far from homogenous, and one could argue that the half of the population we call "secular" is not one but two groups. The size of one group is a little more than a quarter of Israeli Jewish society (28%); the other, a little more than one-fifth (21%).[171]

To understand the sometimes-vast differences between these two groups, we can examine the matter of the Women of the Wall.

It is a well-known issue, one which has preoccupied the Israeli legal and political systems for many years: A group of women is demanding the right to pray, wear prayer shawls, and read out loud from the Torah at the Western Wall in Jerusalem (the Kotel). The Rabbinate, whose representatives administer the site, oppose these requests on the grounds that they contradict Orthodox halakhic customs. The political establishment, for its own reasons, sides with the Rabbinate.

Most of the Israeli public would like the Women of the Wall to be permitted to pray at the Western Wall Plaza (58%), including a large majority of secular Israelis (88%). But when we dig deeper into secular Israelis' views on this issue, it becomes clear that secular Israelis are not a monolith.

In a survey, we asked: "Should the Women of the Wall be allowed to don *tefillin* at the Western Wall?" This question is slightly more provocative than a question solely about prayer because it forces respondents to contend with women who wear *tefillin*—a form of Judaism that is rarely seen in Israel. Most of the totally secular group (57%) see no problem with women donning *tefillin* at the Kotel. Another roughly one-fifth (18%) of them "somewhat" agree with this proposition. In contrast, the "somewhat-traditional secular" really are, well, somewhat traditional. Less than one-third of them (31%) agree that women should be allowed to don *tefillin* at the Western Wall. Half of them are resolutely against it.[172]

Here is another example of the clear attitudinal difference between totally secular and somewhat-traditional secular Israelis. We asked Jews whether the State of Israel "should enable Jews to marry non-Jews." According to Israeli law, legal marriages in Israel are conducted by religious authorities—Jewish, Christian, or Muslim—and hence Jews can only marry other Jews (as the Rabbinate is the sole institute through which legal marriage is conducted for Jews). Among the totally secular, an absolute majority (61%) answered that they "completely agree" that the state must allow legal marriages of Jews and non-Jews. Among the somewhat-traditional group, only around half of that proportion (31%) answered that they "completely agree" with this proposition. This is no coincidence. Members of the somewhat-traditional group feel much more Jewish than members of the totally secular group. In fact, almost everyone in the somewhat-traditional group feels strongly Jewish (80%), whereas only around half (55%) of the totally secular group feel the same.[173]

Not only do somewhat-traditional secular Israelis feel more Jewish, but their Jewishness is also more important to them. Being Jewish is "very important" for one-quarter (26%) of totally secular Israelis. The same is true for more than *half* of the somewhat-traditional group (57%). It is "very important" for one-quarter of totally secular Israelis (27%) that their children be Jewish. The same is true for almost two-thirds (60%) of the somewhat-traditional group.

The differences between the positions of secular Israelis are also evident in their actions. How many go to hear the shofar blown in synagogue on Rosh Hashanah (7% vs. 52%); how many sit in the sukkah on Sukkot (26% vs. 52%); how many join the *hakafot* dances on Simchat Torah (7% vs. 30%); how many read the *megillah* (the Book of Esther) on Purim (2% vs. 11%); how many read the whole Passover Haggadah (22% vs. 58%); how many fast on Tisha B'Av (1% vs. 13%[174]); how many light Shabbat candles (17% vs. 49%); how many keep kosher at home (12% vs. 59%); how many intend to recite Kaddish when their parents die (19% vs. 41%); and how many go to synagogue on some holidays (17% vs. 59%). Simply put, those cosmopolitan Jews you see lying on the beach or drinking espresso at the café may be far more traditional than they appear.[175]

The two secular groups differ in more than just matters of Jewish faith and practice. More than half of the totally secular group are Ashkenazi (54%), as opposed to one-third of somewhat-traditional secularists (33%). Almost half of somewhat-traditional secularists (43%) are Mizrahi (of Middle Eastern descent), while only a small minority of the totally secular (17%) are Mizrahi. Less than one-third of the totally secular identify politically as right-wing or center-right (29%). Half of the somewhat-traditional group are right-wing or center-right (50%). A significant minority of the totally secular are left-wing (15%). A negligible minority of the somewhat-traditional group are left-wing (3%).

Obviously, these differences influence the mindset and positions of secularists. When examining what secular Israelis think about "the contribution of the settlers to the success of the State of Israel," the answers divide along political lines—as expected—but also along a scale of traditionalism. Most totally secular Israelis believe that the settlers have a negative impact (63%); most of the somewhat-traditional group believe they have a positive impact (62%).[176] Similarly, when secular Israelis are asked whether being a good Jew means settling the whole Land of Israel, the answers are predictably distributed along both political and traditionalist lines. Only one-quarter (26%) of the totally secular believe that being a good Jew means settling the whole Land of Israel, in contrast to around half (49%) of somewhat-traditional secularists.[177]

The political differences between totally and somewhat-traditional secularists even pertain to attitudes towards festivals of a clear national nature. For example, a slightly smaller proportion of totally secular Israelis fly the flag on Independence Day compared to their somewhat-traditional peers (53% vs. 66%). The totally secular are less inclined to stand during the Yom Hashoah or Yom Hazikaron sirens if they are at home.[178] A higher proportion of them regard Jerusalem Day as a "regular" day (92% vs. 82%), and fewer think that being a good Jew means living in Israel (40% vs. 54%) or serving in the IDF (a 10 percentage point gap).

\* \* \*

Secular Israelis find themselves in conflict with "Judaism" when Judaism means the religious establishment of Israel. They are in harmony with "Judaism" when Judaism means holidays and key life cycle ceremonies.

Naturally, many secular Israelis are torn between the effects of their positions regarding the *religious establishment*—and their personal preferences regarding certain *practices*, which offer a sense of community, continuity, and wholeness. This conflict is more acute among the totally secular than the somewhat-traditional.

No issue brings this conflict to light more than "religious coercion."

"Religious coercion" is a vague concept with multiple possible interpretations. It can be interpreted stringently, as any attempt to introduce a Jewish symbol into the public sphere—say, stationing a Chabad Menorah at a roundabout. It can also be interpreted leniently, as attempts to invade individuals' personal space and impose a certain lifestyle on them—say, non-recognition of weddings conducted outside the Rabbinate. One can oppose coercion of any sort or one can oppose coercion and still support some forms of it for the sake of social cohesion and cultural appreciation.

In other words, the feeling of coercion is often more of a mental state than an indication of established facts.

Secular Israelis believe there is coercion in Israel more than members of other groups (as is to be expected).[179] But how coerced they feel depends on whether we're talking about the totally secular or the somewhat-traditional. Three in four totally secular Israelis (74%) believe there is religious coercion. But only two in four somewhat-traditional secular Israelis (44%) believe the same. Clearly, there is a tangible difference between the two secular groups: a clear majority of totally secular Jews believe there is coercion, whereas a majority of somewhat-traditional secular Jews *do not*—even though they all live in the same conditions, in the same country, and under the same laws. Simply put, something that bothers many totally secular Israelis does not bother many of their somewhat-traditional compatriots.[180]

This obviously leads to a "chicken and egg" question: Are totally secular Israelis less connected to Jewish tradition *because* coercion makes them feel a heightened sense of siege and revulsion? Or is it the other way around: Are totally secular Israelis less connected to Jewish tradition, *and therefore* any expression of Jewishness in the public sphere causes them to feel besieged and repulsed?

It is doubtful whether there can be an unequivocal answer to this question. Many Israelis presume that religious coercion, or the excessive stringency of the rabbinic establishment, drives secular Israelis away from Judaism. Marriage is a prime example. One poll discovered that a significant majority of the public (80%) are convinced that forcing Jewish Israelis to marry through the Rabbinate "increases the number of Israelis who choose to marry in civil ceremonies abroad." That is, institutional coercion is leading them to forgo a Jewish ceremony, which they might otherwise have had in circumstances involving less compulsion. Most Israelis (56%) also agree that "the scope of religious legislation in its present form is driving Israeli citizens away from Judaism."[181] A detailed position paper on marriage arrangements in Israel found that the religious monopoly "tends to alienate large sectors of the population from religion." The paper's authors reasoned that "for this reason, and others, we believe that altering the existing situation is also a religious interest."[182] For such reasons, many religious Israelis believe there is room for civil marriage in Israel.

So, most of the public believes that coercion begets alienation. Is this true? Not necessarily. In the United States, which is frequently cited as an example of a country that is deeply religious thanks to the complete separation of religion and state, there has been a discernibly sharp drop in recent years in religiosity levels among the young. The fastest growing population group are the "nones"—those of no religion.[183] That is, the avoidance of coercion does not necessarily lead to a religious-cultural renaissance, even if this has seemed to be the case for so long. Moreover, since Judaism is not purely a religion but a culture that also contains religious elements, it is not always clear what deserves to be defined as "religious" coercion and what can be defined as encouraging a national "culture."

Consider Bible classes and Jewish cultural studies. Should they be taught in public schools? For Israelis who place themselves on the religious spectrum, this question is easy to answer. For secular Israelis, it can be complicated. Should the Hebrew Bible be taught because it is a cultural asset of the Jewish people? Should it be taught despite containing, or perhaps because it contains, messages with religious significance? Can it be taught without a religious framing? What should be done about the God who splits the Red Sea, or the fortune-telling prophet Jeremiah, or Elijah who rises to heaven by fire? What should be done with the fact that the Biblical text was one of the factors that laid the ground for the Jewish people's return to the Land of Israel? Not to mention the patriarch Abraham's purchase of a field in the ancient city of Hebron? Or the connection to Shiloh, Givon, and Shechem (Nablus), all in Judea and Samaria—i.e., the "West Bank"?

The mainstream education system has had limited success walking on these eggshells. On the one hand—students should know the Bible. On the other hand—they should learn that the Bible was written by human beings. This pivot is not exactly a new challenge. Wars over education and the Bible are interwoven into the recent history of the Jewish people. In 1907, the Herzliya Hebrew Gymnasium high school in Jaffa experienced a revolution. Academic instructors from the University of Bern in Switzerland came to teach, including Benzion Mossinson, who was influenced by a school that dealt with Israelite culture and religion from a secular, historical perspective. According to Israel Brenner, when Mossinson came to teach the ten-year-old pupils of the Gymnasium, he "revised the original texts in the lessons. More than that, he would pick and choose from the sources. He skipped the laws in the Torah that 'have no place in modern society' and devoted most of his time to 'The Torah of the Prophets.'"

Of course, none of this passed quietly. A "Bible War" had begun. A war that has not entirely ended to this day—and might never end.

Almost one-third of parents in the public secular Jewish education system in Israel (30%) believe pupils learn "too much Jewish Studies."[184] In fact, around one-fifth of these parents oppose "any kind of Jewish Studies in the mainstream education system." In recent years, these feelings have been given a name and an ideological structure in the context of the battle against what is called "*Hadatah*" (religionization, which we have already addressed, mainly in Chapter 3). The numbers show that one-fifth of parents in the mainstream education system consider any Bible class, any lesson on the structure of the *siddur* (prayer book), any participation in a bar or bat mitzvah project, to be *Hadatah*. And since there is a mandatory curriculum of Jewish Studies in mainstream Israeli schools, we can easily surmise whether these parents think religionization is a problem in Israeli society. They do.

A poll of the education system conducted by the organization Panim, which works to promote Jewish pluralism in Israel, helps to make sense of the argument over Jewish Studies in schools. It makes it clear that while the argument purports to be about facts, it is really about *feelings, positions,* and *control.*

Here is the breakdown in more detail. *Feelings* pertain to questions like whether children are learning too much Judaism, or whether parents "fear that Jewish Studies at school will change [their] children's way of life." How many parents worry that this will happen? Around one-quarter (26%). It is difficult to argue with such feelings. One can argue they are unjustified, but this is not easy: Why are they unjustified? Because it's no big deal if the children are influenced? This is an ideological position. Because there is little chance that the children will be influenced? This opens up a new argument: What risks are parents willing to take in order for their children to learn a little Yiddishkeit?

Moving on to the argument about ideological *positions*. Some think there is no need for Judaism in schools at all. This is a position. As such, the details (whether they learn too little or too much, whether the approach is right or wrong) are irrelevant. The position is that there should be *no* Judaism in schools. The argument (with which 44% of the parents agree) that "Jewish Studies at school come at the expense of more important disciplines, like mathematics and English" is also a position. One cannot argue with what matters to the parents. Anyone who considers math lessons more important than Talmud can probably rationalize this stance, but this is also true of whoever thinks that Talmud is more important than math. From a factual standpoint, Jewish Studies must come at the expense of *something*. So do sports classes. So does Geography. Every hour that is dedicated to one discipline is not dedicated to another. It is impossible, therefore, to avoid making a choice with an ideological basis.

Feelings and positions are subjective. As with the ideal temperature for the thermostat, different people will have different opinions. But the bigger question, according to Michal Berman, director-general of Panim, is who gets to hold the thermostat remote.

Who has *control?* There are decision-makers at the national level—they decide how many hours are dedicated to certain curriculum. Others control the classroom, pupils, the principals, and the teachers. These two levels are obviously connected. Most parents in the mainstream secular education system (60%) do not want "anyone who is not from the school's permanent educational staff" to deal with "schoolchildren's Jewish Studies." In other words, they do not want any volunteers, activists, rabbis, or wheelers-and-dealers to get involved in teaching their children Judaism. We can guess why. The parents are suspicious. They believe there is religious coercion. They believe, often for good reasons, that many NGOs that wish to be involved in teaching Judaism in public schools have different ideological agendas from their own.

The argument over *control* lies at the core of any argument about Jewish Studies in the education system. Most secular parents

(56%) agree that children should learn some Jewish Studies because Jewish subjects "are important for my child's identity." If so, what are they worried about? They are worried about those who currently have *control*. They want someone else to decide. Someone who is on the same ideological page about what constitutes Jewish Studies.

This objective is very difficult to achieve because it is connected to politics. In Israel, the education system is *always* governed by a politician, who has an ideological outlook, which will always be acceptable to some and unacceptable to others. This is a familiar Israeli ritual: If the Education Ministry is headed by secularists, religious parents will cry secularization. If it is headed by leftists, parents will claim that civics lessons preach post-Zionism. If the ministry is headed by right-wingers, left-wing parents complain that the curriculum is nationalistic. If it is headed by religious Israelis, secular parents accuse them of religionization. And admittedly, in each of these complaints, there is a measure of truth. The Israeli education system is not value-free, nor is it free from considerations of other state interests. If the state needs engineers, it will exploit its education system to direct students to professions that plug this shortage. This is a national interest. If the state needs soldiers, it will rank schools by various criteria including enlistment rates and will incentivize them accordingly. And if the state believes that its students need a booster shot of Judaism—it will use the tools at its disposal: schools, teachers, charities, and budgets.

\* \* \*

As we have said, many secular Israelis find themselves in conflict with "Judaism," in the sense of the religious establishment. On the other hand, it is clear from their behavior that they are in harmony with "Judaism," in the sense of the comfortable observance of customs and traditions without compulsion or coercion. It is worth juxtaposing this reality with the analysis of two young

Israeli thinkers: two of the most prominent and brilliant writers of recent years, who enjoy tens or hundreds of thousands of interested readers.

Professor Yuval Noah Harari addressed the question of Jewish Studies in the education system when he recommended thus: "Instead of focusing on what should be removed from classrooms and textbooks, it would be better if secularists focused on what should be introduced." Harari sees a problem with Israeli secularism: a problem of self-confidence, and a lack of self-worth. He suggests overcoming it with a change of perspective: don't think about what secularists *do not* do, but what they *do*.

"Some people mistakenly believe that secularism is an empty cart, defined by what it's missing, not what it contains," he wrote. "Secularists are those who do not believe in God, do not keep Shabbat, and do not eat kosher. This is completely erroneous. Secularism is a positive, vibrant worldview, which gives individuals very broad freedom of choice but still demands their commitment to a certain code of ethics. This is a code that includes the values of truth, compassion, equality, freedom, courage, and responsibility. Secularists raise their children on this code of values, which form the foundation of the institutions of modern science and modern democracy—institutions that have liberated billions of human beings from the tyranny of despotic regimes, epidemics, famine, and ignorance."[185]

Dr. Micah Goodman also discerns a problem in Israeli secularism. This, too, relates to secular Israelis' self-confidence and sense of worth. This problem, he surmises, is causing confusion among "a growing number of secular Israelis." Israelis, he writes, are "yearning for intimate contact with the tradition, while sparing themselves from enslavement by that tradition." For Goodman, the crisis of secularism is that "there is a growing sense across the West that something is rotten in enlightened secularism, and that lurking in its folds are major threats to human beings' mental balance." He identifies a possible solution for this crisis in the Jewish tradition, which he says contains "ideas and lifestyle habits that can help people to cope."[186]

Both proposals are obviously good, but given the data we have presented, we can ask whether and to what extent either is needed. Do Israeli secularists really have a problem of self-confidence, or do the figures show that the opposite is true? Secular Israelis have not given up on Judaism, nor have they given up on secularism. They are quite happy to make kiddush and then drive on Shabbat; to read from the Torah at their bar mitzvah but not pray the next day; to call themselves secular while having doubts about God's existence; to keep a Hebrew Bible at home and debate whether their children should study it.[187]

Very many secular Israelis inhabit the sphere that we identify as "Israeli Judaism." It contains tradition, it contains nationality, and it contains a great degree of freedom of choice.

\* \* \*

| Do or don't Israeli secularists…? | Totally secular | Somewhat-traditional |
|---|---|---|
| On Yom Kippur, attend Kol Nidrei or Neila | 12% | 35% |
| On Chanukah, light candles every night | 40% | 71% |
| On Passover, read the whole Haggadah | 22% | 58% |
| On Shabbat, make kiddush | 16% | 54% |
| Prefer a religious burial | 23% | 65% |
| Eat only kosher at home | 12% | 59% |
| Believe that the settlers have a positive impact on Israel | 37% | 62% |
| Identify as politically left-wing | 15% | 3% |
| Consider it very important that their children be Jewish | 27% | 60% |
| Believe there is *no* God | 29% | 5% |

# CHAPTER 9
# Who Are the Haredim?

*Are the Haredim on their way to further separation from the rest of Israeli society? Alternatively, are they heading toward gradual integration into mainstream Israeli society? The signs point in both directions.*

Confronting the memory of the Holocaust is a difficult challenge for any Jew. It is particularly difficult for Jews who believe in God. Where was God during the Holocaust? This is only one of many questions that Jews ask, and there is no answer. Faced with the unfathomable, some believers have opted for "theological silence." Others have clung to a reclusive and defensive concept of faith.[188] Either way, for Haredi Jews, the Holocaust also marks a political crossroads. Ultra-Orthodoxy opposed Zionism, but "historical circumstances" led "the overwhelming majority" of Orthodox Jews to cooperate with the movement. The attempt to stand aloof from Zionism failed, wrote the scholar Menachem Friedman. The ultra-Orthodox public was a minority within the Jewish people even before the Holocaust, but "the Holocaust transformed Haredi society into a small minority with meager means." This minority was forced to compromise with the institutions of Zionism and integrate into the political life of the State of Israel.[189]

The Holocaust, along with integration into Zionism, presented Haredi society with a crisis of consciousness. Not only did the Holocaust seem to validate the "basic concepts of Zionism," but the Haredi world's rehabilitation increasingly appeared dependent on the secular State of Israel. One of the ways of escaping this challenge was to cast aspersions: Zionism was to blame for the Holocaust, so no matter how much it assisted this rehabilitation, it would never atone for its sins. What exactly was Zionism guilty of? Some made do with the claim that Zionism was the cause of divine rage, which unleashed catastrophe. Others went further, believing in baseless conspiracy theories that accused the leaders of the Yishuv of all sorts of malicious deeds: Zionist leaders supposedly sabotaged attempts to rescue the Haredi Jews of Europe out of hatred for the Jews of the Diaspora. Perhaps they even had an interest in seeing that what happened happened.[190] In harsh and bitter tones, these accusations even included comparisons between Ben-Gurion and Hitler.

In the years after the Holocaust, Haredi society was utterly "immersed in colossal trauma at all levels," as Michal Shaul has written. "Many inside and outside Haredi society had major doubts whether they would recover."[191] But they recovered. The yeshiva world was rehabilitated and is now bigger than ever. Probably even bigger than it was 2,700 years ago during the reign of King Hezekiah, when according to Talmudic legend, "they searched... and did not find an ignoramus" from the Dan region to Beersheba.[192] Everyone was a Talmudic scholar. Of course, not everybody in the State of Israel is a Talmudic scholar, but the country proved to be a convenient base for rapid demographic growth, relative economic security, and the construction of a vast education system. There are around one million Haredim in Israel, and according to the projections of the Israeli Central Bureau of Statistics, their numbers and share of the population will continue to rise.[193]

A conversation about the state of the Haredi world is an important component of any conversation about Israeli society. And it

## Who Are the Haredim?

must begin with the question: Who are the Haredim, or ultra-Orthodox, and what even *is* ultra-Orthodoxy? Some categorize the Haredim by self-definition (i.e., whoever calls himself or herself Haredi); others, by their educational institutions, voting patterns, or places of residence. Psychologist Reuven Gal proposed in a policy paper ten key traits that identify Haredim: absolute Jewish faith; intense religious observance; comprehensive societal supervision of lifestyles; Torah study as a supreme value; self-subordination to the authority of a Hasidic rebbe or respected rabbi; a conservative and puritanical worldview; a counter-cultural stance against non-Haredi society; faith in the coming of the Messiah and rejection of the Zionist vision; physical and spiritual communal seclusion; adherence to the community's special educational institutions; and external characteristics such as sidelocks, head coverings, and dress).[194]

That said, the Haredim are not a monolith. They must be divided into a minimum of three main groups: Yeshivish, Hasidic, and Sephardic. In parentheses, we must also add that the presence of the Haredi-Sephardic sub-sector as a part of the larger Haredi camp is already a distinctly Israeli novelty. In fact, it is an important example of the Israelification of Haredi society, which requires a separate discussion.[195]

In our survey, around one-tenth of respondents identified as Haredi (9%).[196] Politically, they are right-of-center (82%). The majority are Ashkenazi (58%). The large majority were born in Israel (88%). They live in cities (82%). Most (66%) have children and a majority (54%) have children at home under the age of five. For the sake of comparison, one in two Haredim has children under five at home, as opposed to one in five secular Israelis (22%). The marriage age among Haredim is low. The number of children is high. This is a very youthful society. Roughly half of its members are under 16.[197]

This is already the fourth, maybe fifth, generation after the Holocaust. A generation that has been exposed to a different narrative, a different tone, and a different approach. Like all Israelis, the Haredim still struggle with the Holocaust. But they are ready to hear more facts and fewer myths. They are "discovering Yad Vashem," as became clear at a seminar on Holocaust education in Haredi schools.[198] Professor Kimmy Caplan of Bar-Ilan University sees this as a process of habituation to the Zionist establishment, the Zionist story, and Zionist scholarship. There is "a rise in the numbers of Haredim visiting the Yad Vashem museum, especially in the intermediate days of Passover and Sukkot and during the yeshiva summer holidays."[199] In recent years, there is much talk of the growing Israelification of Haredi society. Does this increase in Holocaust education constitute Israelification? Perhaps. But it is important to note that alongside Israelification there also exist trends in the opposite direction, of alienation and argument.

The Holocaust is a highly charged subject, and it is interesting to observe how Haredim talk about the day commemorating it, Yom Hashoah. "For the Jews who have faith in the Torah, there is an order and there are rules about who is authorized to set days of remembrance for the People of Israel, and when it is permitted to set such days and when it is not," wrote the Haredi paper *Hamodia* a few years ago. "Torah sages, teachers, and halakhic authorities are the ones who are authorized to decide here." Yom Hashoah was set by the state, not the sages. More than that, the date was set for the month of Nissan, when it is not customary in Judaism to declare days of mourning. The date was also chosen to coincide with the Warsaw Ghetto Uprising. "The State of Israel makes a connection between its resurrection and existence and the destruction of Jewry by the Nazi oppressor," observed the Haredi writer Racheli Ibenboim in an article on Holocaust remembrance from a Haredi perspective. "In the girls' kindergarten where I learned and later at Bais Yaakov High School, our teachers instructed us not to stand during the memorial siren on Yom Hashoah," she wrote.[200] She's not alone. Every year one can find stories in the media about Haredim who are caught walking during the siren, or articles about Haredim who insist it is their right not to stand during the siren.

But reality does not always look like the conversation in the media. Two-thirds of the Haredim (66%) report that they *do* stand during the Yom Hashoah siren: less than other groups of Jews, but high enough to make one question commonly held notions about Haredim and Yom Hashoah. One in five Haredim (22%) lights a memorial candle on Yom Hashoah. As an expression of grief, memorial candles are more suited to Haredi language than sirens. But lighting memorial candles on a day of remembrance set by the *state* expresses a desire of some sort to participate in public grieving, not to ignore it or run away. Around one-quarter of Haredim (26%) stand during the siren even if they are at home and nobody can see them (and thus be offended by their reluctance to stand still).

Haredi society is not always characterized, as some assume, by a desire to provoke other Israelis. Only one-fifth of Haredim (20%) say that Yom Hashoah is a "regular day" for them. That is, the majority accept, at least to some degree, that it is not a day like any other, and that completely ignoring Yom Hashoah would be a crude provocation. They are willing to engage in a fierce debate with Israeli Jewish society on many matters: conscription for yeshiva students, financial support for Torah studies, the core curriculum in schools. But for Yom Hashoah—which they identify, quite rightly, as a line that fellow Israelis will not tolerate being crossed—they tend to lower the flames.

* * *

Israel's lively secular society does not particularly value the Haredi state of existence. "Haredim," together with "yeshiva students" (who are essentially the same people), come bottom in every ranking of the different sectors' perceived contributions to Israel's prosperity.[201] On average, Israeli Jews rank Haredim second from the bottom (outranked at the bottom only by Muslim Arabs). Totally secular Israelis rank Haredim last; somewhat-traditional secular Israelis rank them second from last; traditionalist Jews rank them fourth from last. Interestingly, even Israeli Arabs rank the Haredim very low on the scale of contributions to Israel.

These poor rankings are no great mystery, nor do they evince inexplicable prejudice. The Haredim rank low because of a realistic assessment of their actions: Their contribution (to what most Israelis consider important) *is* low. A substantial proportion of them do not serve in the IDF, and many are not integrated in the productive economy. Of course, Haredi leaders have a different view. They claim that Torah study is their community's major contribution to the existence of the Jewish people. But on this matter, they dissent from the rest of the Jewish public. What they consider a contribution, the rest of the Jewish public considers lazy and even somewhat parasitic.

Haredi society presents a challenge to Israel in three respects: economically (failing to integrate and contribute), militarily (dodging the burden of the IDF draft), and culturally (trying to enhance religious coercion in the public space).[202] But Israel also presents several challenges to Haredi society. For many years, the leaders of the Haredi public have successfully coped with their surroundings through the creation of socially isolated and culturally fortified communal spaces. It is precisely the success of this model that explains why Haredim resist attempts to impose change on them. If the model works, it is not worth revising: Any possible benefits to be derived from connecting to general society, integrating into the economy, or serving in the military are deemed unworthy of the risks.

That said, the external and internal pressures on Haredi society are mounting. The Haredi population is growing rapidly, and it is becoming increasingly difficult to provide for them on the backs of other taxpayers. The young generation, meanwhile, is pained by its estrangement from its Israeli Jewish surroundings. They are searching for a way to improve their living conditions and alleviate at least some of the tensions damaging their relations with other sections of society.

Obviously, none of this changes the fact that the Haredim are indeed distinct from the rest of the population in their lifestyles, customs, and beliefs. They are the only group in which a crushing majority believes that being a good Jew means "observing all the laws of halakha."[203] Accordingly, they observe rituals, customs, and festivals more than most others. The men don *tefillin* every day. They go to synagogue. Everyone recites a blessing before eating (99%). In the month of Elul, many attend *Selichot* every morning (37%). On Tisha B'Av, a clear majority abstain from wearing leather shoes (94%). Two-thirds of Haredi Jews participate in the *hillula* for Rabbi Shimon Bar Yochai, commemorating the anniversary of his death on Lag Ba'Omer (67%). A large majority do not listen to music during the mourning period of the Counting of the Omer (89%). They send *mishloach manot*—baskets of food to friends and family—on Purim (99%). They fast all day on Asara B'Tevet (85%), the fast commemorating the beginning of the Babylonian siege of Jerusalem. A significant proportion not only eat in the sukkah, but sleep there too (70% of men).

The Haredim stand out in their strict ritual observance, but also in their greater (sometimes much greater) social involvement relative to other groups: They give to the poor, donate to organizations and social charities (85%), and volunteer at higher rates than all other groups (49%). But this does not extend to reserve duty (14%). Most of them do not serve in the army. A majority do not think that being a good Jew means raising one's children to serve in the IDF (55%), or only think so to a small extent (29%). They have no interest in living anywhere but Israel,[204] but most do not see living in Israel as a meaningful expression of their Jewish identity.[205] When the Haredim say they are not Zionists, as the sociologist Shlomo Fischer wrote, they mean that "they emphatically reject the Zionist revolution in regard to collective identity and its ramifications. That is, they totally reject the idea that one can be Jewish simply by belonging to a Jewish political collectivity."[206]

The Haredim are most distinct in the arena of nationalism, not just from secular and traditionalist Israelis but also from other religious Israelis. On Independence Day, most Religious Zionist Jews recite the *Hallel* prayer to thank God for the establishment of the state. The large majority of Haredim do not (95%). Only one in ten Haredim flies the flag on Independence Day; around half say that for them it is a "regular day" (48%).

On Jerusalem Day, the gulf between Haredim and the Religious Zionists is even wider. The vast majority of Haredim (87%) say that for them, Jerusalem Day is a regular day. This is somewhat ironic. More than any other group, the Haredim take advantage of the ability to safely visit the Old City and the Western Wall, which only became possible when Jerusalem was liberated. Despite this, few fly the flag (5%), few recite *Hallel* (6%), and few join marches or ceremonies in honor of the occasion (8%). This is particularly glaring given that around one-third of Jerusalem's Jewish population is Haredi, as is a large proportion of those who live along the old seam line, or in neighborhoods like Ramat Shlomo, built on territory that was under Jordanian control before the Six-Day War.

*  *  *

"The Haredi Ghetto," as the scholar Joseph Shelhav described it, "is perhaps the sharpest territorial expression of the gulf between the Israeli world of culture and values and Haredi society."[207] His choice of words is somewhat antiquated for several reasons. First, the word "ghetto" grates on the ear. Second, he assumes that there exist separate "Israeli" and "Haredi" cultures. Haredi society is part of Israeli culture. Third, he hints at a majority-minority relationship, which is true *numerically* but not necessarily in substance. Haredim in Israel have long not been "a small and marginal minority, but a sizeable portion of Israeli society," as the law professor Yishai Blank has written.[208]

The "territorial expression" of Haredi segregation still exists, however, perhaps even more than in the past. The Haredim live in their own neighborhoods, and increasingly in their own towns as well. Mixed towns exist, but as soon as increasing numbers of Haredim move in, the non-Haredi population tends to pack up and leave. The town of Beit Shemesh is a clear example, which has also produced numerous headlines and widely reported skirmishes. There are also intentionally-built towns just for Haredim, such as Elad. A Supreme Court ruling concerning Elad reinforced a legal reality that sees no problem with zoning Haredi-only residential areas. Such a reality, wrote Justice Aharon Barak, "fits with the conception that recognizes the right of minority communities interested in preserving their distinctiveness in this way."[209]

Barak's reasoning forces us to return to the question of whether the Haredim merit the designation "minority community." Do they? We are not sure. But it is certainly a community with an interest in preserving its distinctiveness. Almost all the Haredim have predominantly Haredi friends (89%).[210] Virtually no Haredim want to send their children to mixed secular-religious schools, because such an education "might weaken their faith and religious observance" (63%) and because "every population needs its own specific education" (27%).[211] Haredim strongly disapprove of the possibility that a close relative might marry someone who is not Haredi (or at least religious). Almost half of them would be "dissatisfied" if this happened (46%), and around one-third would be deeply upset (35%). Only around half of the Haredim would want Haredi and secular Israelis to live together in mixed neighborhoods. But notably, on the question of coexistence, the Haredim are actually the more tolerant group: A very large majority of *secular* Israelis do not want to live in the same neighborhood as Haredim (78% of the totally secular). Nor are secular Israelis enthusiastic about marriages with Haredim or mixed schools with Haredim. Around one-fifth of totally secular Israelis fear this "may lead to people becoming religious." Another one-third (32%) fear there will be an overload of Jewish Studies in the schools.

In other words: Segregation is desired by all. Neither side wishes to live with the other, marry the other, or study with the other. Every section of society wants to safeguard a suitable space for its lifestyle, free from the influence of other groups. National-Religious Jews withdraw into their own neighborhoods or settlements. Secular Israelis try to stop religious and Haredi Jews from moving into their own neighborhoods. The Haredim build their own towns—Immanuel, Modiin Illit, Kiryat Sefer—which, thanks to their high natural growth rates, quickly fill up. These new towns help the government achieve various national objectives, such as building along the Green Line or moving the population south to the Negev (as with the construction of the future Haredi town of Kasif, near Arad).

Of course, the fact that citizens perceive segregation as desirable does not necessarily mean it is good for the state. Prof. Blank, who has thoroughly documented how the state "aggressively" encourages separation between different Jewish groups, believes that this policy is wrong for various reasons—from the damage to citizens' individual rights to live wherever they want, to concerns about strengthening stereotypes and structural discrimination. According to Blank and Issi Rosen-Zvi,[212] separation nourishes the "growing hostility between Arabs and Jews, secularists and Haredim, veteran citizens and immigrants." These are salient points, but one could also argue that separation prevents friction, obviates disputes, and enables communities to live homogeneous lives. When groups are separated on Shabbat, secular citizens need not feel uncomfortable lighting a barbecue in the yard, and Haredi citizens need not suffer the smell of smoke or the sound of cars. "Most people want to live somewhere they feel they belong, where they do not feel alien or threatened," claimed Ruth Gavison and Uri Schwartz when presenting a position that sided, at least partially, with the right of citizens to live segregated lives.[213]

More than any other group, according to the data, Haredim see religion as the main component of Judaism. More than any other Jewish group, according to our findings, it is important for them to be Jewish and that their children be Jewish. Connect these facts to the rest of the data, and the situation becomes clear: the Haredi community's guiding principle is the maximal preservation of an environment that facilitates the strictest religious observance. Segregation is the clearest path to achieving this goal.

*  *  *

There is no religious coercion in Israel. There is secular coercion. This may not be the position of the general public, but this is how the Haredim perceive things. Looking around themselves, they see the imposition of values they reject, of behaviors that upset them, of a public discourse they do not share.[214] One must admit, this position is not baseless. It rests on a realistic appraisal of reality in 21$^{st}$ century Israel, which is more secular, more permissive, and more open than it used to be. The Haredim have indeed gained considerable political power. They have indeed learned to leverage it to their great advantage. But the face of Israeli society—that, they cannot change.

The Pork Law has not stopped pork eaters. The Chametz Law has not stopped *chametz* eaters. Marriage laws have been undermined by marriages conducted outside the Rabbinate and public recognition of common-law marriages. The streets are full of billboards with scantily clad models. The television and internet are overflowing with sexual content. The radio broadcasts heresies. Bookshops sell titles that question the religious narrative. In this sense, it seems the Haredim are more finely attuned to Israel's social reality than others. Israel is not becoming Haredi. It is becoming secularized. And this places Haredi society in a dilemma.

The Haredim excel in erecting barriers to safeguard their way of life, but they do not see themselves as a separate group from the Jewish collective. A significant majority of them believe that Jews have an obligation "to care for other Jews, whoever they may be" (89%). An absolute majority (98%) feel "part of the Jewish people in the world." This sense of collective responsibility has practical implications: Very few Haredim support "a separation of religion and state." The large majority believe that the state should pursue a policy of promoting certain values and beliefs among the general public (82%). In fact, an overwhelming majority of Haredim would like halakha—Jewish law—to become the law of the land (86%).[215] In other words: the Haredim stand aloof from the rest of society in their separate residential areas and distinct lifestyles, but they still aspire to influence the character of Israeli society.

In the immediate run, this aspiration serves as a flashpoint between the Haredim and other groups in society. In the long run, it might pose a challenge to Haredi society itself. After all, it is very difficult to achieve contradictory goals simultaneously: to stand aloof and differentiate oneself; but also to get involved and have an impact. What will the Haredim choose? That will depend in part on what the State of Israel does (e.g., economic integration, IDF conscription). It will depend in part on whether other Israelis embrace Haredi integration or push the Haredim away. It will also depend in part on the Haredi leadership's risk assessments and projections in pursuit of its goals.

But if we may infer from the situation with other groups in Israeli society, there will be no uniform "Haredi" response. Some of them will choose one path, others will choose another, and yet others will choose to chart a middle course. There will be quarrels from without and within. And in Israel's ever-changing circumstances, it is doubtful whether the Haredim of tomorrow will be the same as the Haredim of today.

* * *

| What do the Haredim think? (1—not at all, 10—completely) | 1 | 2 | 3 | 4 | 5 | 6 | 7 | 8 | 9 | 10 |
|---|---|---|---|---|---|---|---|---|---|---|
| How Jewish do you feel? | 0% | 0% | 0% | 0% | 0% | 0% | 1% | 1% | 9% | 89% |
| How certain are you that your children will be Jewish? | 0% | 0% | 0% | 0% | 0% | 0% | 0% | 5% | 10% | 86% |
| Do you think that your grandchildren will be Jewish? | 0% | 0% | 0% | 0% | 0% | 0% | 1% | 8% | 8% | 82% |

CHAPTER 10

# Who Are the Religious Zionists?

*The Religious Zionist community is stronger than ever. It's also more vulnerable than ever. Is its trademark knitted kippah unraveling into the fabric of Israeli Judaism?*

Three out of every hundred Israelis who grew up in a mainstream National-Religious home, what Israelis call "*dati,*" are now totally secular. Seven are now somewhat-traditional secularists. Seventeen are traditionalists. In total, around half of all Israelis who grew up in National-Religious homes no longer identify as *dati*. A minority (16%) have moved to the more strictly observant camps, becoming Dati-Torani or Haredi. Most have moved to the less stringent camps, ending up somewhere between Liberal-Religious (5%) and totally secular.

These are eye-opening figures, but they don't tell the whole story. One could have just as easily begun this chapter by citing the very high share of National-Religious Jews who are certain their children will also be Jewish (96%).[216] Or one could mention the very low share of National-Religious Jews who are politically left-wing or center-left (1%). Why not point out the share of National-Religious men who participate in the beating of the willow branches on Hoshana Rabbah (73%), or the proportion of National-Religious Jews who eat Shmurah Matzah on the first night of Passover (86%)?

The community dropout rates paint a picture of a community in crisis. The rest of the data, on the other hand, shows a politically and spiritually coherent population. That said, we will attempt to justify our choice of opening by showing that National-Religious society (also known as knitted-kippah wearers, but simply *dati* in Hebrew) is in a protracted process of disintegration. The movement is both leaking and splintering—falling apart just as it seems to have reached the pinnacle of its cultural influence and political power. Furthermore, it is disintegrating at a time when many of its members aspire to national leadership roles and see Religious Zionism as a suitable model for the rest of Jewish society in Israel: "The spear tip of a historic development," as the rabbi Professor Benny Ish-Shalom defined it.[217]

Talk of the disintegration of Israel's National-Religious society is nothing new. Studies pointed to an exodus from the National-Religious tribe decades ago, and they continue to do so.[218] It is known that close to half of all National-Religious Jews leave Religious Zionism.[219] It is also known that the dropout rate is relatively high compared to other groups. This rate explains, as Tamar Hermann noted, why this community is in a state of "relative demographic stagnation."[220] Even though National-Religious Jews have many children, their share of the general population is not rising. Their children grow up, and many of them leave: so many that they are even recognized as a social group deserving of its own name: "*datlash*," or "*dati-le'sheavar*"—formerly religious.

This trend of abandonment has a clear impact on National-Religious society. It also has an impact on the social groups that embrace the dropouts. Around one-quarter of traditionalist Jews in Israel used to be National-Religious (23%). The same goes for roughly one-tenth of somewhat-traditional secular Israelis (10%). Religious Zionists are therefore making an interesting contribution to secular society's levels of traditionalism.

## Who Are the Religious Zionists?

How many Israelis belong to the entire Religious Zionist sector? That depends on the exact sector to which one refers, but before we proceed, a quick note on terminology: In this text we use the term "Religious Zionist" as the general name for this population sector and National-Religious as a sub-grouping of that sector (which also includes Liberal-Religious and Dati-Torani Jews). There are others who use these terms differently.

The Religious Zionist population can be counted in a variety of ways, producing a variety of different results. That said, if we go by what religious Israelis say about themselves, we are talking about slightly more than one in five Israelis.[221] Something close to twenty percent. Around half of them are simply "*dati*" (the mainstream National-Religious group, with the above-mentioned dropout rate). The rest are "Liberal-Religious" (5%) or "Dati-Torani," also known as National-Haredi (7%).[222] Yes, these nuances can be confusing, except for those who count themselves as part of the sector and know the subgroups inside and out.

Israelis who belong to each of the three Religious Zionist groups share many behavioral traits, though two in particular define the entire sector: They *do not* travel on Shabbat, and they *do* fly the national flag on Independence Day. That is, they observe more *religious* rituals than other Israelis, except for the Haredim; and they observe more *national* rituals than other Israelis, bar none.

A large proportion of religious Israelis (six in ten) watch the torch-lighting ceremony on Independence Day. A similar proportion observes the Counting of the Omer. They read the Passover Haggadah all the way to the end and eat kosher both at home and outside. They listen mainly to Hebrew music, more than members of other groups (around seven in ten). They believe in God, in most cases unquestioningly. For the overwhelming majority, the fact that they are Jewish is very important to them. It is even more important that their children be Jewish, which they tend to feel confident about. They also share a broad consensus on a number of political issues: They are almost all right-wing or center-right. And while not all of them live in the settlements (in fact, they are just slightly less urban than members of other groups),[223] they are more inclined than any other group to believe that being a good Jew means settling the whole Land of Israel.

What about their trademark knitted kippah? Most of the men wear one (82% of religious men).[224] But not everyone does. Between a quarter and a third of those who identify as Liberal-Religious do not wear a kippah;[225] neither do nearly one in ten of the National-Religious (8-9%).

Speaking of kippahs, for Religious Zionist Jews, one's kippah signifies one's identity and represents a certain sub-sector of the movement. Professor Kimmy Caplan has noted that "there is a very broad spectrum of knitted kippot." Some are very small, and others cover the entire head. Some are made of thin fibers, others of wool. "Some kippot are a single color, others are mostly one color with a rim of another color, and some are entirely crocheted in a range of different shades." This all points to the deep fragmentation within the religious world. So much so, that we can rightly ask whether the three Religious Zionist groups can even be considered a single community anymore.[226]

\* \* \*

Forget the different varieties of knitted kippot and take instead these distinguishing nuances between sub-groups of Religious Zionist Jews: There's a debate over military conscription for women,[227] conversion, the status of the Chief Rabbinate, and attitudes towards homosexuality.[228] Many of these profound debates touch the core question dividing religious society: the status of women. Like other matters of dispute in religious society (e.g., its relationship to the state, attitudes toward non-Jews, and rabbinic authority[229]), questions regarding the status of women make it difficult to define all Religious Zionist society as a single camp.

## Who Are the Religious Zionists?

The Kaddish prayer serves as a litmus test for this trend. In Judaism, children recite this prayer for a year after their parents are deceased. Traditionally, this responsibility falls to sons, not to daughters. In certain communities, however, this convention is changing. Among Liberal-Religious Jews, around half want both their sons and their daughters to recite Kaddish for them when they die. Among (non-liberal) religious Jews, far fewer say they would want this (18%). Among Dati-Torani Jews, the most conservative group among the three, even fewer (15%) would want their daughters to recite Kaddish for them. No doubt, many would oppose changing the custom.

Are women permitted to recite Kaddish? Are they obligated to recite Kaddish?[230] Many Israelis had to alter the way they thought about this issue when Rachelle Fraenkel recited Kaddish out loud for her son Naftali, who was kidnapped and murdered by Palestinian terrorists in the summer of 2014. His funeral was, as the reporter Yair Ettinger wrote, "a seminal moment" from "the heart of the National-Religious community, on the fringe of the Haredi Zionist community."[231] Fraenkel recited Kaddish in the presence of the Chief Rabbi of Israel, in front of the principal of the renowned Mercaz HaRav Yeshiva, and facing many other rabbis, political leaders, and emotional youngsters from the Religious Zionist community. She recited Kaddish as the whole nation stood dumbstruck by the kidnapping and murder of three teenagers, which later cascaded into war in Gaza.

On the matter of Kaddish, Liberal-Religious Jews are already moving towards a consensus favoring change. Other religious groups, less so. But this is only one of the many debates among those who hold the different poles of the Religious Zionist tent. Here is another example: one-quarter of Liberal-Religious Jews celebrate the wholly non-Jewish Valentine's Day (23%). They see no reason, it seems, not to seize the opportunity for a romantic evening. When Dati-Torani Jews are asked about Valentine's Day, however, one-quarter of them ask: "What's that?" Not only do they not celebrate this day, they don't even know what it is (27%). On the other hand, an absolute majority of Dati-Torani Jews observes the Fast of Esther (80%). National-Religious Jews, less so (58%). Liberal-Religious Jews, even less (24%).

Almost half of the Dati-Torani believe one must be fully religiously observant in order to be a good Jew (44%). Only one-fifth of National-Religious Jews agree (21%). Liberal-Religious Jews, in general, do not believe that religious observance is what defines being a good Jew (5%). It is no coincidence, of course, that Jews who are less observant also attach less importance to observance. Nor is it a coincidence that those who are more observant attach more importance to observance. In each case, the result is that Israeli Jews identify good Jews by whatever *they* do, or, if you want to give them more credit, do whatever *they* identify as good. Their associations correspond with their own lifestyles.

These are clear differences on matters of custom and principle and describing all the internal battles of the Religious Zionist camp would require a whole book, not a single chapter. Such a book must include a discussion about whether Religious Zionist women may serve in the IDF. Positions range from support for female service, as with the Religious Kibbutz, to stark opposition, as with Rabbi Yigal Levinstein of the Eli pre-military academy, who said the army "drives our girls crazy." Such a book must include a discussion about whether it is permissible to compete with the Chief Rabbinate on kosher certifications. Positions range from demanding that people "vote with their feet" against those who abandon the Rabbinate (a conservative group called Chotam rabbis), to saying it is time "to challenge the Rabbinate" (a more lenient group called Tzohar rabbis). Such a book must include a discussion about the clash over gay pride parades. Some call the phenomenon "a march of abomination," as Rabbi Zvi Tau said. Others, like Rabbi Benny Lau, say that "life in the closet is like death." The list goes on and on: from gender segregation, to attitudes about secular Israelis, to the importance of democracy, to respect for state institutions, to the sanctity of the state, to relationships with Arabs, and to religion in the public sphere.

## Who Are the Religious Zionists?

In light of this, one might wonder what, if anything, unites Religious Zionists? Here is one option, proposed by Professor Asher Cohen in his article on "the multiplicity of identities in Religious Zionism," which begins with this provocation: "Yigal Amir was a religious murderer."

Can this be so? Can the man who murdered Prime Minister Yitzhak Rabin in 1995 truly be considered *dati*—religious?

Cohen explains: "Amir is a murderer because he committed a murder; and he is religious because in his day-to-day behavior he observes a limited and defined set of religious commandments that are perceived by society as sufficient for defining someone as religious."[232] The man who murdered the prime minister wears a kippah. The man who murdered the prime minister does not desecrate the Sabbath. The man who murdered the prime minister dons *tefillin*. If he were to switch on the light in his jail cell on Yom Kippur, he would no longer be considered religious. But as for planning an assassination, lying in ambush, cocking his gun, and pressing the trigger in cold blood—none of these disqualify him from being considered religious.

And no, this is not an ideological statement about how this killer should be labeled. It is a sociological claim about the way in which society, including Religious Zionist society, labels him. Society sees him as religious because he observes a certain "limited and defined set" of customs. Anyone who observes these customs—a kippah, a religious education, Shabbat, a kosher diet—is tagged as religious. Whoever deviates from these norms is tagged as *"lo-dati,"* non-religious, or secular.

Since Cohen first confronted his (Religious Zionist) readers with this perspective, things have changed. What used to be a "defined set" of customs seems to have become somewhat less distinct. Some kippot have become smaller; the average marriage age has gone up; LGBT members have come out; synagogues have split; aspersions have been cast; and religious Jews who consider themselves "on the spectrum" have become more vocal. (For anyone who is unfamiliar, these are religious Jews who openly admit that they do not observe all the laws, only what suits them. They might surf Facebook on Shabbat and eat at non-kosher restaurants, and they are not strict about praying on weekdays, but they still consider themselves part of the Religious Zionist community.[233])

So, is there still something we can call Religious Zionism? Maybe. At least when one looks from the outside and sees a community whose members look quite similar. But it is worth looking on the inside. Because the insides of this community reveal commotion, soul-searching, and constant erosion under the millstones of Israeli Judaism.

\* \* \*

This is not a book about what is happening to religious Jews, or Haredi Jews, or secular Jews, or Reform Jews. This is a book about how a distinctly Israeli Judaism is taking shape, and about the transformations it is provoking among its members. In the case of Religious Zionist Jews, Israeli Judaism is a catalyst for internal arguments.

Yair Sheleg explained it thus: Faced with the "liberal extremism" of secular Israelis (his description), Religious Zionism must choose between "two different and effectively contradictory answers… switch to a growing alliance with the Haredi camp, and especially with its norms of seclusion… [or] we shall take at least a few steps towards [Israel's secular society]."[234]

This is a faithful description of the attitude of competing sections of religious society, but the attitude itself is based on a number of false assumptions: Secular society is not sailing towards some distant, universalistic horizon—it is creating a cultural-tribal Israeli-Jewish compound. Haredi society is not sailing towards a horizon of perfect isolation—it is being drawn, even if hesitantly, into an Israeli-Jewish consensus. Elites quarrel, thinkers sharpen their positions, politicians build careers on divisions, and marginal figures pretend to speak for the masses. But ultimately the public has the greater power to create an Israeli culture that suits its beliefs and habits.

Religious Zionists don't want to be cut off from this public and are slowly assimilating into it. Mainstream society is siphoning many religious Jews who are adrift "on the spectrum," some still in the territorial waters of religious society, others who have abandoned it. But mainstream society is attractive to so many religious Jews precisely because it is *not* their polar opposite; because it offers them an alternative that does not require them to abandon their culture. One can become secular and still make kiddush. One can be secular and fly the Israeli flag. In fact, one can relinquish labels altogether and affiliate with the broad category of "Israeli Jew," like most of the Jewish public. When given the option, the "Israeli Jewish" stream is the stream to which most Religious Zionist Jews say they belong. This is neither true of the Haredim, nor of the totally secular.[235]

This affiliation with an undefined stream of "Israeli Judaism" bears significance for the interface between religious Jews and the rest of Israeli society. It points to a feedback loop. Religious Jews are influenced by general society, and they influence general society in turn. The Dati-Torani Jews pose a challenge to the Haredim in the form of a religious lifestyle that is no less strict than theirs (and in some cases, even stricter) but which remains connected to the state, the army, society, and the Zionist vision. Religious Jews "on the spectrum," the new traditionalists, and the new somewhat-traditional secularists, are injecting fresh blood into a secularized society and loading it with tradition, customs, knowledge, and cultural cargo.

Consider, for example, the eve of Shavuot.

This is a one-day holiday without much to offer by way of customs or ceremonies. At home, it became the festival of dairy products. In the kibbutzim, it became the festival of first offerings. Is there anything else this holiday can offer? Recent decades have seen the flourishing, or at least so it seems, of a growing and vibrant culture of "tikkun leil Shavuot." Originally, this was a night of Torah study to mark the date of the giving of the Torah. In Israel, frequently, it is a jam-packed event that includes seminars, talks, workshops and even shows on a variety of themes, which lasts all night, often till dawn.

This is, as one report described it, "an all-Israeli event, in which tens of thousands of Israelis—religious, traditionalist, and secular—all participate… Non-religious communities create new gatherings that challenge the traditional format and breathe new life into it."[236] And why do so many Israelis turn up for tikkun leil Shavuot? Because of "the need of secular Jews in Israel to connect to Jewish sources, without observing Jewish law," explains Naama Tsabar Ben Yehoshua and Yona Sorek.[237]

"Is this a case of a deep, drastic change happening in Israeli Jewish culture?" wondered the author Dov Elboim.[238] We have no choice but to disappoint him and the others. There are no "tens of thousands" going to such events, there has been no change, and the people who do attend these events are not secular. Out of the general Jewish public, around one-fifth attend a "religious" tikkun leil Shavuot in a synagogue. As for the secular version of such events (held in places such as theaters or study halls), about 6% of the public attends, a fraction of the number who attend religious events in synagogues. More interestingly: Even these people—by a rough calculation, 300,000—are in many cases religious, not secular. In other words: Even the secular-Israeli style of tikkun leil Shavuot is still, in a certain sense, a religious tikkun leil Shavuot.

Our aim here is not to argue that Israeli-style tikkun leil Shavuot is a failure. These events are a relatively recent, intriguing, and growing phenomenon, even if they are still something of a bubble. Our aim is to focus on Religious Zionist participation in these events because it too points to the religious public's slide towards a meeting of minds with secular-Israeli culture. The religious Jews who come to Israeli-style tikkun events teach and learn, influence and are influenced, pose challenges and are challenged.

## Who Are the Religious Zionists?

It seems that the religious public has been the most keenly influenced, of all groups, by the emergence of Israeli Judaism. There is obviously a paradox here: On the one hand, Religious Zionism has always embodied an amalgam of Jewish nationality and tradition. In this sense, one might view Religious Zionism as a functional model of Israeli Judaism in and of itself. But on the other hand, it is precisely Religious Zionism which is most threatened by Israeli Judaism.

If the identity of most Jews in Israel rests on a combination of Jewish nationality and tradition, then nothing can be said to distinguish Religious Zionism. Made redundant, one must ask if this movement is still needed. As Yoav Sorek commented, "the Israeliness that is our common traditional infrastructure, for kippah-wearers and bare-headed Jews alike, is not secular—but by the same token neither is it religious."[239] Sorek came from the Religious Zionist community but later removed his kippah and became "a secular, observant believer." Even without statistical proof, he discerned this phenomenon early on, and did so well.[240] Israeli Judaism, he wrote, is "a new and natural fusion." It "subverts ideologies and places them on fresh footing."[241]

If there is anything to this analysis, then religious society faces some big questions and complex challenges.

There are questions of faith and Jewish law: Will religious society adapt its practices to this wide spectrum of "Jewish practice"? If so, how?

There are social questions: Will religious leaders and educators fight the fact that their society has become a kind of production line for Israeli Jews who then leave it? If so, how?

There are internal questions: Are these trends leading religious society towards a profound rupture, culminating in the loss of their common sectoral identity?

There are also external questions: Will these trends prompt sections within religious society to clash with the rest of Israeli society, out of a desire to preserve their own unique way of life?

#IsraeliJudaism

The biggest challenge of all is the gravitational pull of Israeli Judaism. And this challenge is well demonstrated by the numbers we presented at the outset of this chapter. If Israel were to become more estranged from Jewish tradition, to move towards an embrace of Western universalism and the rejection of tradition and customs, Religious Zionism would have a very strong argument for preserving its communal barriers. Whoever leaves gets cut off. Whoever defects is lost. But when Israel is on a path of consolidating an Israeli Jewish identity, it is less clear why the walls of a distinct Religious Zionism are needed. The choice is not between black and white—but rather between shades of gray. Indeed, there is room to "misread" the data and assume that "the Religious Zionist fantasy is coming true." But when the Jewsraeli majority decks itself out with different shades of nationality and tradition, that is not a victory for the Religious Zionist community—it is a challenge.

* * *

| Religious Zionist groups (% who answer yes) | Liberal-Religious | National-Religious | Dati-Torani |
|---|---|---|---|
| To be a good Jew, must one be fully religiously observant? | 5% | 21% | 44% |
| Do you make a pilgrimage to rabbis' tombs? | 34% | 42% | 63% |
| Do you fast every Fast of Gedaliah? | 25% | 53% | 79% |
| Do you feel sad on the anniversary of the assassination of Yitzhak Rabin? | 48% | 42% | 34% |
| Politically, are you right-wing? | 36% | 62% | 71% |

## Chapter 11

# Where Are the Non-Orthodox?

*Are there or are there not Reform and Conservative Jews in Israel? That depends on definitions—and expectations.*

There are quite a few Israelis—former MK Moshe Feiglin, for example—who think that there are almost no Reform Jews in Israel. On most days of the week, as Feiglin pointed out, Reform synagogues "lie empty."[242]

There are quite a few Israelis, however, who affirm the existence of Reform Jews in Israel. These would be the half a million Israeli Jews who define themselves this way. Another quarter of a million define themselves as Conservative Jews. These are the figures that emerge from our study, according to which 8% of the Jewish population is Reform and another 5% is Conservative.

Some pollsters found slightly fewer Reform and Conservative Jews than we did (11%), others much fewer (5%), and others roughly the same (12%). Perhaps, as researcher Dan Feferman has suggested, the discrepancy can be attributed to the fact that many more Israelis identify as Reform or Conservative than are active and official members of these movements.[243]

Both Feiglin and the polls, therefore, are correct. The question is what matters more: how Israelis identify or what they do? We can pose this question differently: What must Israelis *do* for their actions to imply *belonging* to the Reform or Conservative denominations? Some Jews will probably say that anyone who fails to go to synagogue every day of the week is not doing enough. But other Jews would argue for other options. Perhaps it is enough to go to synagogue only on Shabbat? Or for holidays? Or maybe not at all? Plenty Israelis see things this way: One-third of those who self-identify as Reform (30%) and one-tenth of those who self-identify as Conservative (10%) have not been to synagogue this year. Not even once.

Does this fact bother you? Does it bother *them*? It certainly does not bother us. As we have already said, we are not in the business of grading Jews on their behaviors. We only describe them and seek to understand them. And here is something that demands our understanding: On the one hand, these Jews identify with religious denominations that focus their activities, at least in theory, around the synagogue; on the other, they rarely go to synagogue. To refine the matter even further: Little more than 10,000 Israelis are registered members of the Reform and Conservative movements. The gap between progressive Judaism's 10,000 "members" and half a million "identifiers" demands an explanation.

\* \* \*

The Reform Movement was born in Europe and took hold in the United States. The Conservative Movement was born in the United States. Neither built a strong base in Israel, where responsibility for religious services was handed to representatives of Orthodox Judaism. There were a number of reasons for this arrangement. Historically, Orthodoxy is what existed in Mandatory Palestine when the rules were set. Ideologically, sections of liberal Jewry (particularly the Reform Movement) were not big fans of the Zionist project. Sociologically, a large share of those who immigrated to

## Where Are the Non-Orthodox?

Israel came from places where liberal forms of Judaism had no presence. In addition to all of that, Progressive Judaism was suited for communities with synagogues, and secular Zionists had no interest in synagogues.

One way or another, Israel introduced the concept of a "status quo," which gave political and budgetary power to the Orthodox establishment and helped it to obstruct attempts by other Jewish denominations to enter the playing field.

Over time, however, Israel started having to contend at different levels with the reality of multiple Jewish denominations with profound ideological differences. Relations with Diaspora Jewry, particularly in the U.S., force Israel to reckon with a large majority of Jews who identify with the liberal denominations.[244] There is also a growing demand, on both the political and legal fronts, to allow progressive Judaism to participate in the Israeli arena. Beyond that, progressive Judaism has had an undeniable intellectual influence on Israeli Judaism, including in the Orthodox world, primarily in the realm of gender equality.

The question of how successfully Israel has coped with these developments is debatable: Some will point to tense relations between Israel and Diaspora Jewry as proof that Israel has failed. Others will see this tension as evidence of a firm, principled insistence that whatever happens in Israel must be decided by the citizens of Israel. Some will conclude that since Reform synagogues are "empty," progressive Judaism's attempts to gain a foothold in Israel can be written off as a failure. Others will track the growing number of Israelis who identify with progressive Jewry and see it as the beginnings of a success.

There are several other indicators that are worth checking: for example, the number of Israelis who choose to celebrate their children's bar or bat mitzvahs in Reform or Conservative synagogues. Or who choose to marry under the auspices of Reform or Conservative rabbis (even though such marriages are not legally "marriage" in Israel). Life cycle events bring many Israelis, who would not necessarily have visited in other circumstances, to the synagogues of the progressive movements. Around one-fifth of Jews in Israel (19%) only went to synagogue last year when invited for a particular event. Among Israelis who self-identify as "Reform," almost one-third (31%) only went to synagogue when invited for an event. The more events are hosted in progressive synagogues, the more Israelis are exposed to their prayer services and style.

Here is one reason to treat the "empty synagogues" claim with skepticism. There is no point arguing that something is empty when there is no intention to fill it in the first place. In other words, there is no point measuring the power and influence of the progressive movements by the yardstick of Orthodox Judaism. The Orthodox want to fill their synagogues on weekdays. The Reform and Conservative movements focus on attracting the public for life cycle events. The potential for success is clear: More than nine in ten Israelis intend to celebrate their sons' bar mitzvahs (95%) and daughters' bat mitzvahs (90%). The vast majority (94%) also want their sons (but not yet their daughters) to read from the Torah (94%). This includes a very large majority of the totally secular (78%) and the overwhelming majority of the somewhat-traditional secular (98%). These individuals are the target audience of the progressive movements. Nowadays, however, they perform only a small fraction of all bar and bat mitzvahs: some 3,000 a year. If there are roughly as many bar and bat mitzvahs as boys and girls in each year group, this translates to scarcely 3%: Here too there is a clear discrepancy between potential and its fulfillment.

One in ten Jews in Israel was married, or intends to be married, in a Jewish ceremony outside of the Chief Rabbinate (9%). Here is another target audience for the progressive movements, one which is growing larger among young Israelis, and which has become a majority among young secular Israelis, 68% of whom vow not to marry through the Rabbinate.[245] This target audience has already been partially conquered: More than half of secular Israelis (56%) have attended a bar or bat mitzvah or wedding officiated by a Reform or Conservative rabbi,[246] as have more than one-third of traditionalists (38%), one-fifth of Religious Zionists (18%) and one-tenth of the Haredim (11%). But again, the number of guests does not attest to the actual number of weddings, which is still relatively low compared to those officiated by the Orthodox Rabbinate: around 2,000 a year compared to the Rabbinate's 40,000.[247]

Something, of course, is hindering these movements' efforts to increase the number of marriages conducted under their auspices. Legally speaking, marriage and divorce between Jews in Israel remain the exclusive purview of the Chief Rabbinate. In light of this, quite a few Israelis wouldn't even consider having a progressive Jewish wedding. On the other hand, this hindrance also serves as a great marketing tool. Many Israelis see the Rabbinate as an irritant. It is one of the least respected institutions in Israel. So, for progressive Judaism, the Rabbinate is both an obstacle and an asset. Simply put: If the Orthodox establishment is perceived as a fossilized, unpopular bureaucracy, progressive Judaism can play the part of the vibrant alternative. One is an institution of coercion; the other, a force for liberation.[248]

Whom does progressive Judaism liberate? Whoever dislikes the Orthodox establishment. This is the majority who do not go to synagogue every day. The majority who do not pray every day. The non-religious majority. Israelis who call themselves "*hiloni*" – secular. True, the Reform and Conservative movements are religious movements, but most of their Israeli supporters do not identify as "religious" in any fashion. They either identify as "totally secular" (one in ten in this group is Reform), or as somewhat-traditional secular (one in five is Reform or Conservative), or as traditionalist (one in four is Reform or Conservative). Only a small minority of progressive Jews self-identify as *dati liberali* ("Liberal-Religious," of whom one in ten are Conservative).[249]

\* \* \*

Let's rewind. Self-identified progressive Israeli Jews are generally either secular or traditionalist. They identify with progressive Judaism but are not members of progressive Jewish movements. They do not pay synagogue membership fees (a problem, especially as these organizations get less financial support from the state than the Orthodox establishment). They seldom attend synagogue. They seldom pray. They are not religiously observant. Nor do they translate their affections into political support.

Nevertheless, it is still worth discussing what they *do* do. First and foremost, secular Israelis who identify with the Reform or Conservative movements behave somewhat differently from secular Israelis who do not identify with any Jewish denomination. Let's pause to explain—this is important. We asked a variety of questions in our study. Some pertained to levels of religiosity (religious, traditionalist, secular); others, to denominational affiliations (Conservative, Chabad, Orthodox, non-denominational, etc.). We therefore collated more than one fact about each Jew we polled. For example, Jews can be both "secular" *and* "Reform," both "traditionalist" *and* "Chabad," or both "religious" *and* "non-denominational."

A quick note of explanation here: it's not paradoxical in Israel to speak of "Secular Reform Jews" or even "Secular Orthodox Jews." These somewhat oxymoronic designations simply refer to secular Israelis who "identify with" a particular Jewish denomination or movement more than the rest. This means that when they engage with tradition, on holidays or during life cycle events, they display fealty towards one denomination over the others.

By small but significant margins, Secular Israeli Jews who identified with a progressive Jewish denomination were more likely to take part in religious traditions than those who didn't identify with any denomination of Judaism. This is to say that for Israeli Jews, Reform and Conservative are more than just labels.

There are many examples that track a similar pattern: Secular Israelis who self-identify as Reform or Conservative make kiddush on Friday nights more than secular non-denominational Israelis. Traditionalist Reform or Conservative Jews are more likely to don *tefillin* than non-denominational traditionalists. They are more strongly inclined to believe in God. Around half of somewhat-traditional secular Reform Jews (52%) believe in God without doubt, compared to a smaller share (42%) of non-denominational secular Jews. In other words, there is indeed a practical meaning to Jews' self-identification as Reform or Conservative, which can be seen from their observance of customs and rituals. Secular Reform Israelis are more Jewishly engaged than secular non-denominational Israelis.

There are, of course, caveats.

First: Secular Israelis who say they belong to the Orthodox stream (around one-fifth of somewhat-traditional secularists) practice more Jewish traditions than secular Israelis who say they belong to Reform or Conservative Judaism. In other words, secular Reform and Conservative Jews are more engaged than secular non-denominational Jews but less engaged than the secular Orthodox.

Second: Israeli Jews tend to be inconsistent in the way they identify with denominations. There are Jews who might say in one survey that they are Reform and in the next that they have no denomination (but in both cases self-identify as secular). The meaning of this is quite clear: Most Israelis who self-identify as Reform or Conservative do not treat such identifications as a salient feature of their identity. In fact, when they have to choose between self-identifying as Reform *or* secular, a vast majority opt for secular.[250]

Third: Conservative and Reform Jews are more observant of Jewish tradition than non-denominational Jews, but when it comes to beliefs and opinions, the difference becomes small. Sometimes, the situation even reverses itself.

One example: Secular Reform Israelis are slightly *less* "shocked" (that's how the survey question was framed) than non-denominational secularists by the prospect of a close relative marrying a non-Jew.[251] Why? It is difficult to know. But some will certainly see here a sign for the identification of these Israeli progressive Jews with the predicament of progressive Jewish movements in the Diaspora, one of whose main challenges is the transmission of the tradition to the next generation, many of whom were born to mixed marriages.

\* \* \*

Reform Jews have something of an image problem in Israel. Conservative Jews, somewhat less. There are several reasons for this problem. The first is historical: The Judaism of the early Zionists was Orthodox. Some Zionists were religiously observant, most were *not* religiously observant, but nearly all identified with Orthodoxy.

The second reason pertains to Israelis' perceptions of reality: progressive Judaism has always been perceived as a phenomena of the assimilating Diaspora. Israel's first chief rabbi, Yitzhak Herzog, considered the State of Israel important for various reasons, including that it would save "masses of the People of Israel" from joining "the Reform Movement or the movement he derisively called 'the Fifty-Fifty Movement'" (i.e., the Conservative Movement).[252] The progressive movements have seemingly never been able to shed the image of a Judaism that belongs elsewhere.

The third reason is political: The progressive movements are on the frontline of multiple battles—sometimes on issues for which they can hope for widespread support (e.g., marriage), but other times with causes on which they are out of step with public opinion (e.g., asylum seekers). Sometimes they advocate for their causes by petitioning the courts (e.g., conversion); other times, by trying to influence government policies (e.g., the Western Wall Plaza).

For Israelis, therefore, progressive Judaism is often associated with disputes. The Orthodox disparage it, politicians use it as a term of abuse, and public thinkers warn against it. Many Israelis see progressive Judaism as a threat to Israel's Jewish identity. It is no coincidence that a large majority of Religious Zionist and

## Where Are the Non-Orthodox?

Haredi Jews in Israel say Reform Jews make a "negative" or "very negative" contribution to Israeli society. The Haredim rank Reform Jews last in perceived contributions to society. The other Religious Zionist groups rank them third from bottom.[253] But secular Israelis do not: Most secular Israelis believe that Reform Jews make a positive contribution to Israel. This is only natural: Most Reform Jews identify as secular; most secular Israelis do not disapprove of Reform Jews. Secular Israelis are progressive Judaism's target audience.

There is an unusual phenomenon at play here, of course, which distinguishes progressive Judaism in Israel from that in the Diaspora. In Israel, progressive Jewry does not necessarily answer the description of *religious* Judaism. True, it has synagogues, Torah scrolls, rabbis, prayers, prayer books, and festivals. But its target audience self-identifies as secular, and the range of its activities positions it as a supplier of Israeli Judaism, not of religious Judaism.

This all compels us to revise an old cliché. Secular Israelis used to be fond of saying that the synagogue *they don't attend* is Orthodox. In other words, despite not being religious, they saw Orthodox Judaism as the only authentic expression of Judaism. Nowadays, there are almost no totally secular Israelis who still self-identify as Orthodox (1%); and among somewhat-traditional secularists, the Orthodox share is almost identical to the proportion who are Reform or Conservative (20% and 19% respectively). Even among Jews who self-define as traditionalist, only a slightly higher rate are Orthodox (31%) than Reform or Conservative (24%).

Orthodoxy is losing its hold as the popular expression of secular Judaism in Israel. As a term, "Orthodoxy" no longer corresponds with true, authentic Judaism, but rather describes a very specific type of religious Jew, which is not necessarily agreeable to non-religious Jews. Reform and Conservative Judaism, which many have already written off as having "failed" in Israel,[254] have received a second chance: an opportunity to be the Israeli Judaism of those who do not wish to be religious. They have received a chance to be a logical alternative for those who find Orthodox religiosity too heavy, too alien, or too off-putting.

* * *

Are there Reform and Conservative Jews in Israel? An answer is beginning to take shape. There exist almost no Reform or Conservative Jews in terms of ideology, theology, thought, or philosophy. But there certainly do exist Reform and Conservative Jews in a practical, Israeli guise: Reform in the sense of preferring to celebrate bat mitzvahs in a synagogue with mixed seating; Conservative in the sense of believing that it does not matter if the rabbi is not a man with a beard.

Progressive Judaism may prove suitable for Israelis who are not interested in becoming strictly religiously observant but still want some form of kosher stamp: someone to tell them that their conduct is all right and that what they want can also be called Judaism. A large share of Jews in Israel want their Judaism to be relaxed. They do not need theology, only a pleasant and friendly practical code for festivals and rituals. These Israelis seek to blaze their own Jewish paths in line with their personal inclinations and priorities, even if these paths diverge from halakhic precedents set in distant centuries. Progressive Judaism could be a natural choice for them, but only so long as it makes no demands of them and places no expectations on them. Dispassionate support—in exchange for little expectation of commitment.

It is possible, therefore, though not certain, that Israel will have many more Reform Jews in the future —practicing an eclectic, uncoerced form of Judaism.

But this possibility confronts Israel's progressive Judaism with a dilemma: Does it wish to be a liberal form of Judaism as it is in the United States—with its own theology, rabbis, doctrines, and ceremonial styles designed in 19th-century Germany and 20th-century America—or does it wish to be a down-to-earth, forthright, unpretentious, popular and *Israeli* style of Judaism? Practically speaking:

## Where Are the Non-Orthodox?

Does it wish to be the Judaism of Liberal-Religious Jews, or does it seek to be the Judaism of non-religious Israelis?

This is not a simple choice. Progressive Judaism will need to consider what it must relinquish to become more Israeli. It will need to think about the ramifications of such a development on ties between progressive Jewry in Israel and progressive Jewry abroad—ties that also have political and economic consequences. It will need to correctly assess whether the potential is really that great. Do there exist enough non-religious Israelis who are sufficiently interested in their type of Jewish services to sustain a movement?

\* \* \*

| Israelis' denominational affiliations | Reform | Conservative | Orthodox | None |
|---|---|---|---|---|
| Which of the following definitions describes you? | 8% | 5% | 37% | 51% |
| Which synagogue have you been to this year? | 6% | 8% | 52% | 32% |
| I am politically left-wing or center-left. | 27% | 6% | 5% | 28% |
| I am completely certain my children will be Jewish.[255] | 52% | 67% | 81% | 47% |
| My daughter will read from the Torah at her bat mitzvah. | 33% | 19% | 4% | 12% |
| I fast the whole of Yom Kippur. | 62% | 82% | 97% | 45% |
| I would be shocked if a family member married a non-Jew.[256] | 10% | 24% | 66% | 12% |

# Chapter 12

# Are We One People?

*Israeli Jewish culture is developing in one way, and the Jewish culture of the other almost-half of the Jewish people—American Jewry—is developing in another. This creates a complicated challenge.*

Israel's former deputy foreign minister, Tzipi Hotovely, did not intend to cause a major furor when she said that American Jews do not understand Israel because they "never send their children to fight for their country." But she did. Such storms occasionally erupt when an important, or even semi-important, Israeli figure dares to complain about the attitudes of American Jews, or when an American figure dares to criticize the attitudes of Israeli Jews. "Most of them are having quite convenient lives," said Hotovely. "They don't know how it feels to be attacked by rockets." As if that were such a bad thing.[257]

It's hard to argue with Hotovely. These are facts. Nevertheless, Prime Minister Benjamin Netanyahu condemned his deputy minister's remarks. "The Jews of the Diaspora are dear to us and are an inseparable part of our people," he said.[258] These are also facts, which nevertheless have not stopped Netanyahu himself from infuriating those same dear Jews with several of his decisions.

As one poll demonstrated, however, many Israeli Jews agreed with Hotovely and felt that her comments weren't grounds for dismissal, as several American Jewish leaders demanded.[259] Hotovely made her remarks in a discussion about the extent to which Israel should take the views of American Jews into account when making decisions. Like Hotovely, most Jews in Israel see no particular reason to do so (55% according to the poll that also covered the incident with Hotovely). The columnist Chemi Shalev was right when he wrote: "Hotovely was simply representing the true attitude of many right-wing Israelis, including a majority of Netanyahu's governing coalition."[260] This is to say that she was representing the majority of Israelis.

Jews in Israel and the United States understand that their respective communities differ, but they frequently struggle to articulate their differences and so get dragged into exchanging insults, which mainly boil down to "why are they not like us?" The answer, of course, is that *they* are not *us*. Americans are Americans. Israelis are Israelis. The differences are inevitable.

What are these differences? First—the Jews of Israel are neither concerned about nor preoccupied with "Jewish continuity" in the Diaspora sense; they do not fear that the next generation will not be Jewish. Second—the Jews of Israel do not need to make an effort to feel Jewish or to be actively Jewish.[261] Third—the Jews of Israel are indeed active Jews, much more so than Americans, as this book has consistently proven. Fourth—for the Jews of Israel, Israeliness is a central element of their Jewish identity. Moreover, it is often difficult for them to separate Israeliness from Jewishness. So much so, that most of them agree with the (highly problematic) statement: "To be a real Israeli, you need to be Jewish."[262]

In short: Israel's Jews are relaxed, effortless, active patriots.

Obviously, these are generalizations. Every rule has an exception, and every sweeping statement is qualified with reservations. Nevertheless, we shall generalize and begin by explaining the most obvious, glaring difference: A little more than half of all Jews in

Israel believe that living in Israel is an important or very important part of being Jewish. Moreover, around half of the Jews in Israel (54%) believe that "being a good Jew" means supporting the settlement of the Land of Israel. It is no wonder, therefore, that around two-thirds of Jews in Israel believe that a Jewish life in Israel is more meaningful than a Jewish life elsewhere. It is not that they think it is impossible to live as a Jew in America. They understand and accept this reality. Still, in their eyes, it counts for less.

Jews in Israel believe that service in the IDF is an expression of Jewishness. Should we even ask Jews in the Diaspora whether they agree? And what if they say yes? Does this mean they are not-as-good Jews? There are quite a few such questions about the practices and beliefs of Jews, which there is no point even asking both Israelis and American Jews: What do Israelis do at Christmas? How many times a year do American Jews visit the Western Wall? But even with questions that everyone can answer, which allow us to compare the world's two biggest Jewish communities, there are often difficulties. For example, does being a good Jew mean being responsible for the welfare of other Jews? It is possible to pose such a question, but we must assume that when Israeli Jews answer, they are thinking of American Jews, and when American Jews answer, they are thinking of Israeli Jews (of course, both should be thinking mostly about smaller, usually needier, Jewish communities: the Jews of France, Hungary, or Sweden). So, again, it is not really the same question.

Three in four Jews in Israel (77%) believe that being a good Jew means "caring for other Jews whoever they may be." Here is an opportunity to begin thinking about the relations between Jews around the world, and their responsibilities towards one another. The question about "caring" refers to all Jews. Nine in ten Jews in Israel say they feel a strong bond with the Jewish people. This is also a general question about the entire Jewish "people." Two-thirds of American Jews (63%) say they have a responsibility to care for Jews in crisis around the world. Jews "in crisis" are of course a more specific group than "the entire people." This demands follow-up questions: What does "crisis" mean? What about caring for Jews who are not in crisis? The overwhelming majority of Jews in America say caring for Israel is a vital or important element of being Jewish (87%). Israel is also a specific target. We can assume that caring for Israel means something different than caring for the Jews of Ukraine. After all, Israel is the state of the Jewish people—a national project—whereas the Jews of Ukraine are a small and shrinking community. This clearly calls for another follow-up question: What does "caring for Israel" *mean* in practice? It obviously does not mean supporting Israel's every move. Still, we would like to assume that the overwhelming majority of American Jews, who feel that caring for Israel is an important element of their Jewishness, mean *something* by it.

Not all Jews in Israel feel equally connected to the Jewish people; likewise, not everyone feels the same degree of obligation for other Jews' welfare. This tendency is more glaring among right-wing and center-right voters and religious groups; less so among self-identifying secular Israelis. Nine in ten right-wing voters (87%) believe that being Jewish means caring for Jews whoever they may be, compared to only four in ten (41%) left-wing voters. Less than one-fifth of Israel's secular Jews believes that caring for Jews in other places is a very significant part of being Jewish. One in two religious and Haredi Jews believes so.

There is a similar distinction around the question of whether being a good Jew means living in Israel. One might detect a paradox here: It is precisely the Jews who most believe it is important for Jews *to live* in Israel who also tend to believe that it is important to care for the Jews who *do not live* in Israel. Consider another paradox: The Jews who have the biggest problem with the culture of Jewish America (which they associate with Reform Judaism and assimilation), express the greatest interest in the welfare of America's Jews. As Elan Ezrachi defined it in a report

## Are We One People?

he submitted to the Jewish Federation of New York: "The more Israeli Jews express views of belonging, unity, and responsibility to the Jewish Diaspora, the more they tend to be judgmental and critical of the core values of the largest Jewish community outside Israel."[263]

Circumstantial changes are transforming the relationship between Israel and Diaspora Jewry: chief among them, Israel's population growth relative to the rest of world Jewry; Israel's declining reliance on economic and political assistance from Diaspora Jewry for its survival; the passage of time since the seminal historic events that shaped the consciousness of the older Jewish generation (such as the Holocaust and the Six-Day War); and deepening political and cultural differences, owing to variations in life circumstances.

Israel has changed in recent decades, from being a small and intimate society to a burgeoning population encompassing multiple sub-groups, each with their own social and ideological agendas. It enjoys high birthrates and rapid demographic change; military might and political power; economic growth and the development of a Western-style society of abundance. Politically, the conservative right—relying on religious and traditionalist voters, many of them Jews of Middle Eastern descent—is dominant. Diaspora Jewry, meanwhile, is characterized by growing assimilation within Western society; diminishing group cohesion due to the waning of outside threats, among other things; the dwindling influence of organized communities; changing patterns of philanthropy; skyrocketing rates of intermarriage, with attendant changes in Jewish consciousness; a growing demand for change in the relationship with today's stronger Israel; opposition among some groups within the Jewish community to Israeli policies, especially regarding the peace process and matters of religion and state.[264] And of course, it is hard to avoid adding a more recent worrying development: the exposure of Diaspora Jews to antisemitic harassment and attacks.

When two groups of Jews differ in their lifestyles, beliefs, and relations with their surroundings, their forms of Judaism will also be different. This is not a matter of will or choice. This is simply reality. It is doubtful whether things could be otherwise.

*　*　*

Whoever invited Michael Chabon to deliver the commencement address at a ceremony for newly ordained Reform rabbis at the Hebrew Union College in the spring of 2018 certainly did not expect the controversy that followed. "I am for ambiguity, ambivalence, fluidity, muddle, complexity, diversity, creative *balagan* [chaos]," said Chabon, a prominent American novelist and extremely fierce critic of Israel's policies in the West Bank. Chabon, a Jewish man married to an Israeli woman, railed against endogamous marriages between Jews, calling them a "ghetto of two."

Chabon has a knack for speaking even when his remarks grate on the ear. As a young man, he admitted with a kind of suspiciously staged embarrassment, he had hoped that his children, young Jews, would eventually marry within the tribe. His position has changed. He now hopes that his children will "marry into the tribe that sees nations and borders as antiquated canards," not into the Jewish tribe. Of course, he was not blind to what would happen "if every Jewish parent thought that way." Judaism would likely disappear—so let it disappear, he told his young audience.[265] One audience member, Morin Zaray, stormed out of the hall, mainly over his fierce criticism of Israel. Others remained seated and listened.

The college management later defended its decision to invite Chabon to speak and compared his speech to the address delivered by the renowned American thinker Ralph Waldo Emerson at the Harvard Divinity School in 1838. In this famous address, revolutionary for its time, Emerson told a stunned audience that human morality trumped religious doctrine. Emerson, too, caused a storm. He, too, was attacked. So much so, he was called an "atheist"—about as harsh a derogatory term as there was.

# Are We One People?

We can debate Chabon's arguments at length. We can debate whether Chabon was the right choice of speaker for a rabbinical ordination ceremony. We can ask about the event's ramifications for the image of the Hebrew Union College. These are all important debates, but they are not our concern. Chabon's speech interests us because it is one of many examples that attest to differences between two communities. Jewish cultures develop in accordance with the circumstances of their time and place. The Jewish culture developing in Israel differs from Jewish cultures elsewhere, in particular from the largest Jewish diaspora community, in the United States: the home of six or seven million Jews, roughly as many as in Israel.

Chabon is not a spokesman for American Jewry. Presumably, many American Jews regard him as more radical, rejectionist, and scathing than most in their communities. That said, whether intentionally or not, Chabon's generation and the younger generation live largely in accordance with what he prescribed. Intermarriage, between Jews and non-Jews, is the default for most young American Jews. One recent study of Jews in the Washington metropolitan area found that almost two-thirds (61%) of young married Jews under 29 are married to non-Jews. Among married adults over 65, the figure is the inverse: Two-thirds (64%) are married to Jews. In effect, among non-Haredi Jews in the United States (nine-tenths of the community) aged 25-54, some 58% of those who are married are married to non-Jews. Since many American Jews are not even married, and those who *are* married have very few children (relative to Israel and also other groups in the United States), it would hardly be preposterous to suspect that the next generation of active Jews will be smaller than the last. Obviously, the question of exactly how much smaller (if at all) depends on various factors, including what you, the reader, consider to be the bar under which it is no longer reasonable to call someone "actively Jewish."[266]

Consider this significant difference between the United States and Israel, which we addressed earlier, under the title of "Jewish continuity." Israeli Jews are unfamiliar with the life circumstances and challenges of minorities living in an inclusive American society. Neither are they necessarily familiar with the exact intermarriage rates and their significance in the eyes of researchers and leading thinkers. Nevertheless, many have already formed a solid opinion about the predicament of American Jews. Nearly half of the Jews in Israel (46%) believe that in the next 10-20 years, most non-Orthodox Jews in the United States will assimilate.[267] Moreover, the greater the confidence Israeli Jews have that Jewish life is more meaningful in Israel than in the Diaspora, the more likely they are to assume that most of Diaspora Jewry is en route to disappearing. For those Israelis who heard him, Chabon's speech certainly convinced them that this is the situation.

This is no reason for the American reader to feel insulted or angry. Living as Jews in a non-Jewish majority country is a complicated challenge, which is harder to understand and discuss matter-of-factly in faraway Israel. That is because everyone's personal understanding is influenced by their views and beliefs: Jews in Israel tend to hold more conservative positions and so are more likely to disapprove of interfaith marriages. Jews in Israel are also unfamiliar with circumstances that lead to the formulation of such families. They have almost nobody to marry but Jews. They have little familiarity with interfaith families. They do not know that there is a difference between interfaith couples who raise their children Jewish and those who do not, and that there is no point generalizing about both using the same label.

What Jewish identity looks like, in the present and future, will be determined by social trends in the United States and Israel. But more than this, the future of Jewish identity depends on how future generations define terms like "Judaism," the criteria they set for being Jewish, and the importance they place on their own and their children's Jewish identities.

Regardless of their desires, American Jews today cannot be sure with any degree of certainty that their children will be Jewish. Even less so, their grandchildren. The numbers speak for themselves. Most young married American Jews are married to non-Jews. Of these, around half raise their children Jewish (some Jewish "by religion," and others Jewish "not by religion"—which we won't get into now). The other half do not raise their children Jewish. This situation drives some American Jewish activists in the United States to despair, but there is little point despairing. Better to look for ways to influence the flow of the current: chiefly, to cause more couples to raise their children Jewish. This effort raises questions of its own and its ultimate results remain unknown.

What is known is this: That which is a core challenge for Diaspora Jews is completely alien to the Jews of Israel. The overwhelming majority of Jews in Israel (86%)[268] are certain that their children will also be Jewish. A somewhat narrower majority (79%) believe their grandchildren will also be Jewish. Even totally secular Israelis, who have the least confidence about the next generation, are fairly certain (69%) that their children and grandchildren will be Jewish. This all means that the question of Jewish continuity, which many generations of Diaspora Jews have fretted about, is simply irrelevant to Israelis so long as they live in Israel.

Obviously, Jewish continuity is more important to some Jews than others. How important is it for the Jews of America to be Jewish? Here are the facts: It is very important for slightly less than half of American Jews (46%) and somewhat important for another one-third (34%).[269] Israeli Jews attach greater importance to being Jewish. This is very important for two-thirds of them (64%) and important for another one-quarter (23%). It is also important for Israelis that their children be Jewish: two-thirds even say it is very important indeed (67%).

\* \* \*

The Jews of Israel and the United States differ on matters of faith. Around one-third of American Jews are certain there is a God or higher power (34%). A similar proportion (38%) believe this but are not certain. In Israel, almost twice as many are certain—believe "with perfect faith" ("*b'emunah sh'leimah*")—that God exists (58%). Does this matter? It does if we assume that a strong sense of faith spurs believers to realize their Judaism more vigorously.

The two biggest Jewish communities also differ greatly in their observance of rituals and customs. Differences in faith might partly explain this. Over half of Israeli Jews light candles on Friday nights (57%). One-quarter of American Jews do the same (23%). Two-thirds of Jews in Israel fast for the whole of Yom Kippur (67%); under half of American Jews do the same (40%). Furthermore, Israeli Jews participate in Passover Seder night more often, make kiddush on Shabbat more frequently, and eat kosher in greater numbers. They even light more Chanukah candles than their brothers and sisters in the United States.

The statistic about Chanukah candles might seem surprising, considering that for Israeli Jews, Chanukah is just another festival, and not a particularly important one. During Chanukah, most businesses are open as usual. There is public transport. Employees don't get a day off. Chanukah is a children's festival, full of kids' shows. Nevertheless, three in four Jews in Israel (73%) light Chanukah candles every night, including all Haredi, religious, traditionalist, and even somewhat-traditional secular Jews. Among the totally secular, the split is roughly half-half between those who light candles every night and those who do so on some nights. Either way, Chanukah candle-lighting is common to Israeli Jews, almost without exception.

In the United States, the proportion of Jews who light Chanukah candles is also high. This isn't surprising. Chanukah is a very powerful festival in a place where around the same time (sometimes the exact same time) the majority of the population celebrates Christmas, with its trees, lights, songs, and presents. Over time, Chanukah has been integrated into the American landscape of winter holidays. It is a key holiday in the American-Jewish calendar. Two-thirds of Jews in the United States list it among the three most important festivals (compared to one-third in Israel).

Nevertheless, proportionally fewer American than Israeli Jews light Chanukah candles. In San Francisco, around 60%. In Washington D.C., around 80%, but it is unclear whether they do so every night. Around half of Las Vegas' Jews always light candles (53%). In Denver, Colorado, the rate is roughly the same (54%). In Orlando, it is almost two-thirds (64%). In Detroit, about the same (69%). In New York, slightly less (60%).[270]

Even Chanukah, what might be called the seminal festival of American Jewry, is celebrated more by Israeli Jews than American Jews. Why? More Israeli Jews consider themselves bound by halakha, but conditions in Israel also make it easier to observe Jewish rituals and customs. During Chanukah, schools are on vacation, there is an almost obligatory family get-together, and the Jewish majority means that Chanukah doesn't have to compete with any other festivals for attention.

Quite a few American Jewish leaders—rabbis, community leaders, activists—will speak of these palpable differences in the observance of Jewish rituals with subtle derision. Practices such as candle lighting are important, they will say, but there are other ways to express Judaism, which are no less meaningful, and are maybe even more so. As Steven Weisman has noted, as early as the 19th century, the Jews of America decided to transform their culture from being mainly ritual-based towards a primary focus on values and beliefs. Lighting candles would not change the world, but helping the needy, fighting for social justice, giving to charity, donating to the community, and waving the banner of morality and values *would*, and for the better. American Jews began to believe that such practices were more important expressions of Jewishness than rituals. And thus, the Jews of America began to excel in these fields.

And so, we need to talk about values. Those that Jews in America care about, and those that Jews in Israel care about. As well as the respective values both populations love to critique.[271]

The question of how to define Jewish values is a weighty one, and this is not the place for it. We shall suffice with the data at our disposal, as well as with the assumption that Jews know what they mean when they speak of values. The Jews know, for example, that Holocaust remembrance is important to them. Three in four Jews in the United States agree that "being a Jew means remembering the Holocaust" (73%), as do four in five Jews in Israel, most of whom agree "to a very great extent" (54%) or "to a great extent" (30%). The Holocaust still leaves a profound impression on the entire Jewish collective.

The key reason for this Jewish consensus is the colossal scale of that destruction of Jewish life. The Holocaust made a dramatic impact on the lives of the Jews in both the short term and long term. There are also two important subsidiary reasons for the shared sentiment. First: Both the State of Israel and Diaspora Jewish communities have invested enormous energies in entrenching the memory of the Holocaust. Second: Holocaust remembrance is uncontroversial. It encompasses the religious and secular, Orthodox and Reform, right and left, Israelis and Diaspora Jews. The Holocaust is a matter of consensus, and this is no trifling thing in the modern Jewish world. Of course, we can ask whether, and to what extent, reliance on this tragedy as a cornerstone of modern Jewish culture has a positive impact on Jews and the future direction of their cultural development. This question crops up from time to time in various contexts, such as Israeli high school trips to the death camps in Poland.[272] But there are facts not to be ignored: The memory of the Holocaust allows the Jews to strengthen the next generation's Jewish identity, to instill in it a desire to safeguard the Jewish people, and to bind it to the fate of the Jews. Holocaust remembrance is a value that unites Jews.

That said, the very purpose of Holocaust remembrance is a source of divisions. While some Jews see a call to Jewish solidarity and security, others see a warning about racism, tribalism, and nationalism in any form. Roughly speaking, most Israeli Jews incline to the first vision; most American Jews, to the second.

## Are We One People?

\* \* \*

We wanted to talk about values; we must talk about politics. It is very difficult to separate between the two. Here is an example.

Forty thousand asylum seekers were enough to demonstrate the difference in worldview between the Jews of Israel and the Diaspora. They confronted them with "a dilemma between Jewish humanitarian values on the one hand and Israel's raison d'être as the nation-state of the Jewish people on the other," in the words of Dan Feferman and Dov Maimon.[273] Every Israeli knows the story, which is also controversial in Israel: Several tens of thousands of migrants have entered Israel illegally, demanding redress. The overwhelming majority want to be recognized as refugees, which Israel is not willing to do. They all need employment, housing, education, and health services. Although the number of migrants is not particularly high, it is a source of concern to Israel for two reasons. The first, less important, reason: The large concentrations of migrants in certain neighborhoods are a nuisance for the local population. The second, more important, reason: The world is riding the crest of a large wave of migration, which many believe will grow stronger in the future, and Israel is located at a junction that will likely render it a relatively convenient destination for millions in search of a better life. Israel's leaders believe that in order to prevent a "deluge" and to hint to potential immigrants that they have nothing to look for in Israel, it is necessary to deport the tens of thousands of migrants who entered Israel illegally.

The debate over the fate of the settled foreigners and the arrangements for evicting them or leaving them in place was a standard policy debate, which raised questions about laws and procedures, enforcement capacity and political motivation, responsibilities and authorities. But there were clearly value judgments, often contradictory ones, at its core. "We share a deep hope that Israel, as a nation founded and settled by refugees, will protect victims of persecution who have fled their countries seeking safety," wrote a group of American Jewish leaders to the Israeli prime minister, requesting that he reconsider his intention to expel the migrants.[274] In Washington, a small protest was held opposite the Israeli embassy. American rabbis preached against Israel's policy. American donors expressed their unease. Various organizations seized the opportunity to mobilize supporters and resources and launch campaigns. In the United States, there is a fierce and bitter debate about immigration, which sometimes seems to have been transplanted, without regard for the different context, to Israel.

How many American Jews opposed Israel's migration policy? It is hard to count them. But its opponents were clearly more vocal and energetic than its supporters (if there were any), who chose to keep silent. Major Jewish organizations received phone calls from important donors, demanding they do something. The leaders of these organizations delivered the message to Israel, but they hit a brick wall.

There were some Israelis who agreed with the dissenting Americans and also cited their Jewish values in support of their positions: Meretz Party lawmaker Ilan Gilon called the policy "an inhumane, un-Jewish, and immoral act," as if there were consensus on what constitutes a "Jewish act." Obviously, there is no such thing, as was proved by the fact that a majority of Jews in Israel disagreed with Gilon. A significant majority of Israeli Jews supported the decision to expel the foreigners.

Our data may help us understand the vast discrepancy of opinion on this issue between Israeli Jews and American Jews. Compare, for example, the attitudes of Israeli and American Jews on whether "living a moral and ethical life" is an essential part of being Jewish. A large majority of American Jews (69%) say it is. A significantly smaller proportion of Israeli Jews say the same (47%). Without getting into whether or not it is more moral to leave the migrants than to expel them (a question on which we, the authors, are divided), this disagreement attests to Jews' different priorities in describing their respective cultures' basic values.

Jews in the United States rank ethical living right after Holocaust remembrance, followed by "activism for justice and equality" (56%). In contrast, only one-quarter of Jews in Israel believe that justice and equality are significant elements of Jewishness (27%). Does this mean that Israeli Jews do not want to be moral or to make the world a better place? Of course not. In many cases, the wording of the question determines people's answers. When we asked Jews in Israel whether "to be a good Jew, one must work to improve the situation of the whole world," most of them said yes (57%). An even larger majority agreed that "to be a good Jew, one must be a good person" (88%). So the debate, to the extent that one exists, is not about *whether* one must be a good person but *how*.

The typical American Jew, who is exposed to debates about immigration in the United States and whose worldview is shaped by the feeling of being a minority in their own country, will say that the moral thing to do is to offer shelter and security to anyone in need.

The typical Israeli Jew, whose worldview is shaped by the feeling of being a majority fighting to remain a majority, and who considers it a key moral imperative to safeguard Israel's security and character, will say that there are plenty of places in the world where refugees and migrants can be absorbed, but only one Jewish state, which is obligated to first take care of its own.

As we have emphasized, this is not just about values but also politics, which neither in Israel nor the United States can be separated from Jewish identity. In Israel, the majority lean to the right politically, are more religious or traditionalist, tend towards conservative positions, and are more hawkish on matters of security and diplomacy. In the United States, the Jews lean in the other direction: Most are Democrats (70%), half are liberal (49%), and only a minority are conservative (19%). In both groups, political positions must match Jewish identity.

These differences create two challenges, both conscious and practical.

# #IsraeliJudaism

The practical challenge is less interesting but more widely discussed. American Jews often oppose the policies of the Israeli government, because *it* is conservative and *they* are not. They (again, a generalization) disagree with most Israelis on matters of security and peace, settlements and occupation, religion and society, immigration and education. They voted for Barack Obama and are appalled by Israeli Jews' appreciation of Donald Trump. They are used to a political system that steers clear of matters of religion and find it hard to accept Israel's system of a state Rabbinate with a monopoly on Jewish marriage.

This, as we have said, is the less interesting challenge. The real challenge relates to Jewish consciousness: in effect, to what Judaism *is* and what Jewish values *are*. Most Israelis might answer: settling the whole Land of Israel. Most Americans might retort: partitioning the land and creating a Palestinian state. Most Israelis might say: safeguarding Israel from non-Jewish immigration. Most Americans might say: welcoming asylum seekers with open arms.

To simplify, we're looking at the difference between "tribal" and "universalist" worldviews. Israeli Jews look inwards; American Jews, outwards. But it is important to understand that this is not a party-political difference. This is a profound question, which touches the very roots of Jewish identity. Just as most Israeli Jews consider the settlement of Judea and Samaria a Jewish act, most American Jews would consider a withdrawal a Jewish act. It is not that they do not share the same politics—they do not understand Judaism in the same way.

Obviously, none of this means that two interpretations of Judaism cannot coexist. The Judaism of Maimonides and the Judaism of the Kabbalists rested on theological bases that are hard to reconcile, but the *Guide for the Perplexed* and the *Zohar* can still be found on the common Jewish bookshelf. The Judaism of the Hasidim and the Judaism of the Misnagdim struggled to coexist for a while until they learned to get along as parts of a single Jewish nation. Even Orthodox and Reform Jews, with all their quarrels, have been practicing different types of Judaism in parallel for over 200 years. Not to mention Beit Shammai and Beit Hillel, or hundreds of more disputes over hundreds of Jewish generations.

When sage Rabbi Yirmeya, who lived in the Land of Israel, was told about the Babylonian sage Rabbah's answer to a halakhic question, he replied with a bluntness that might be more readily accepted nowadays: "Foolish Babylonians! Because they live in a dark, low land, they speak darkened *halakhot*, devoid of logic."[275] This is a fitting way to conclude this chapter: Who are the fools of today and who are the sages? Which community lives in the dark and which is enlightened? The fact is that nowadays, Jews still study both the Talmud of Babylonian Rabbah and the Talmud of Israel's Rabbi Yirmeya.

There must be a lesson in this somewhere.

\* \* \* \*

| American Jew, Israeli Jew | Israeli | American |
|---|---|---|
| Do you believe in God without a doubt? | 58% | 34% |
| Are you right-wing/conservative? | 60% | 19% |
| Are you Orthodox? | 37% | 10% |
| Is it very important for you to be Jewish? | 64% | 46% |
| In your eyes, is the main component of Judaism "religion"? | 43% | 15% |
| Do you light candles every Friday night? | 57% | 23% |
| Do you only eat kosher at home? | 64% | 22% |
| Is observing the laws of the Torah an essential part of being Jewish? | 35% | 19% |
| Are you married to a Jew (or are you certain you will marry one)? | 98% | 56% |
| Do you have children? | 53% | 39% |

# Afterword

# The Essential Debate

*If almost all the Jews in Israel feel Jewish, why won't they stop arguing?*

"Do you fast on the Seventeenth of Tammuz?"

What can a Jew learn about another Jew by asking this question?

Is whoever fasts on the Seventeenth of Tammuz (to commemorate the breach of the walls of Jerusalem before the destruction of the Temple) more Jewish than whoever does not? Perhaps those who do *not* fast are more Jewish than those who do? Simply asking about the Seventeenth of Tammuz fast, or flag-waving on Independence Day, or Purim alcohol consumption, or Friday night kiddush, is already a statement: that the commission or omission of these acts *matters*. That they are worth measuring. That the results will teach us something about the Jews.

"Does being a good Jew mean being a good person?"

Let's ask again: What is the purpose of this question? Is someone who thinks that being a good Jew means being a good person right or wrong? And whether they are right or wrong, does this make them a better or worse Jew than someone who thinks otherwise? What about the question: "Do you believe in God?" What about: "Is it important for you that your children be Jewish?"

Again, we see that questions can be a form of statement: These beliefs *matter*. They are worth measuring. The results will teach us something about the Jews.

There are many ways of asking questions. For example, we could ask Jews whether they do this or that on Yom Kippur. We could also ask a more general question: "What do you do on Yom Kippur?" We could take Yom Kippur out of the equation: "What do you do as a Jew?" The first question is closed: It presents a series of actions that characterize Yom Kippur and explores which of them characterize which Jews. The second question is open: It assumes that Jews experience Yom Kippur in diverse ways, not all of which are known in advance. Perhaps by asking an open question, we might discover some of these ways. The third question provides unlimited space for answers: Someone might even say that as a Jew, he paves roads. Israeli novelist A.B. Yehoshua once suggested that paving a road in Israel is a Jewish act—a compelling answer. Someone else might say that as a Jew, she volunteers with a charity to help the elderly, associating compassion and morality with Jewishness. Of course, this throws up new questions: What about Christians or Buddhists who also volunteer to help the elderly? Are they also performing a *Jewish* act?

The research for this book is based on questions that almost all offered a very wide range of possible answers. They were mostly about what Jews in Israel do as expressions of their culture. *This*, to a great extent, is what makes this research distinct. When it came to questions about Yom Kippur, for example, we did not just ask about fasting—but also about partial-day fasting, abstaining from food but not water, cycling, and watching television. We did not just ask about Passover Seder attendance—but also about Shmurah Matzah consumption, *kitniyot*, and reading the Haggadah till the end. We did not just ask about Yom Kippur and Passover—but also about Mimouna, Sigd (an Ethiopian Jewish holiday), and the anniversary of the assassination of Yitzhak Rabin. We asked about listening to Hebrew music, reading Hebrew books, volunteering, and participating in protests. And we asked not just about ancient holidays but also modern ones, like Independence Day.

We also asked about beliefs and positions, to see how these correspond with the activities that Israeli Jews perform. After all, some people told us during our preparations that *their* Judaism is not about celebrating festivals but about values: respecting one's parents, being socially engaged, wanting the world to be a better place. Of course, this too is an interesting idea: Perhaps some Jews express their Judaism by celebrating festivals, and others do so by helping the weak? Our numbers give reasons to doubt such a theory. In many cases, the same groups who engage in more "Judaism" in the sense of traditional practice are also the ones who give more to charity, and volunteer more frequently.[276]

The more we examine what makes Jews in Israel Jewish, what keeps them aware of their Jewishness, and what connects them to the rest of the Jewish people, we find this almost always involves *action*. Customs or rituals, daily routines, or annual calendars. Judaism almost always finds expression in the real world—not just in Jews' heads, and not only or necessarily in their consciousness or sense of belonging. A robust Jewish sense of self almost always comes together with action: Jews study, celebrate, and congregate; they get involved, and they rejoice; they also give to charity.

It takes no effort for Israeli Jews to meet up with other Jews because they meet up all the time. It takes no effort for Israeli Jews to provide their children with a Jewish education. The state will make the effort. There always have been and always will be arguments about how much and in what spirit Jewish Studies should be present in the schools. But the State of Israel is unlikely to give up on Jewish education in the broad sense of the term: culture, ethics, history, rituals, and heroes. From Samson to Prime Minister Ariel Sharon, from the prophet Ezekiel to the visionary Herzl, from the leadership of Joshua to the leadership of Ben-Gurion. Jews in Israel hear all this, absorb their stories, become familiar with their history, and grapple with their shortcomings.

It takes no effort for Israeli Jews to engage with Jewish tradition. It is always there, flooding one's senses, hardwired into the calendar. Commercials for cheesecakes mean Shavuot is around the corner. Flags sold at the junction mean it's Independence Day. Discounted honey on the shelves means Rosh Hashanah is coming. Newspapers brimming with supplements herald Passover. On Friday night, you can hear the Shabbat siren from Bnei Brak. On Lag Ba'Omer, close your windows—there is smoke outside. And before Tu Bishvat, your daughter will come home from kindergarten with dry leaves stuck to a piece of paper, which will fall all over your living room carpet.

Israel makes things easy, and therefore pleasant, and therefore popular. Anyone who insists on having arguments—as everyone does, at least occasionally—will obviously find reasons to do so. And when Israelis quarrel, they increasingly believe that there is no common denominator between them, and that their society is torn. But this is worth closer inspection: Can a society be torn when 87% of its members think it is important for them to be Jewish? Can a society be torn when 88% of its members say they feel Jewish to a very great extent?[277]

It seems to us that the biggest difficulty with the book we ended up with—which we suspect will be the same for some of our readers—is the need to reconcile what we have written with what people feel. In other words: The facts do not always match what Israelis (and non-Israeli Jews) feel in their guts. The conclusions do not always match the angry posts on their Facebook feeds. The relative harmony described in this book does not always correspond with the sense of unrest that characterizes the Israeli public sphere, or with what happens every day in the wrestling ring of Israeli society.

If almost all the Jews in Israel feel Jewish, why do they not stop arguing? If almost all of them want their children to be Jewish, what are they fighting over?

They are fighting over precisely this. They almost all want their children to be Jewish—they simply cannot agree on what that means. And since what is at stake is something that is important to them—their children—the arguments are conducted in raised voices.

They almost all want Israel to be a Jewish state, but what is the proper role of a Jewish state? To provide a refuge for Jews? To fulfill the national and religious ideals of the Jewish people (assuming we have a clue what these "ideals" purportedly are)? To sustain a modern Jewish existence in a secular state with Jewish cultural characteristics (assuming we have a clue what these "cultural characteristics" are)?

Around one-fifth of Israeli Jews say one thing ("refuge"), one-third or so say another ("ideals"), and another roughly one-third say yet another ("culture").[278] Israel, a state with a Jewish majority, with a Jewish ethos, has solved one difficulty. Some things, thanks to Israel, have become easier. But Israel also made some things more difficult. Having ingathered so many Jews, it forces them to articulate together what they have in common. Having united so many Jews, it compels them to live together: bound as neighbors in friction and compromise.

This is why Israeli Jews debate so much.

It can be infuriating and alarming. But it is also necessary.

# Appendixes

## 1. The Survey and the Statistical Analysis

The survey that serves as the base of this book is one of the largest and most detailed surveys to map the religiosity and national sentiments of the Jewish population of Israel.

It included 3,005 participants who were questioned in two rounds conducted a month apart. During the first round of data collection (December 2nd – 7th, 2017), 2,004 participants were asked 300 questions regarding their beliefs, emotions and daily behaviors.

During the second round of data collection (January $5^{th}$ – $7^{th}$, 2018), 1,001 participants were asked 100 questions, some of which were identical to those asked during the first round.

Both rounds were conducted over the internet using an online panel of participants (conducted by the Midgam Project, led by Dr. Ariel Ayalon).

The choice of an online survey was a conscious one, based on its merits against other survey methods, such as phone, face-to-face, or mail.

The large scope of this study made a phone survey unfeasible because of the amount of time that would be required from both the pollster and the answerer. Beyond this, a group of people willing to answer 300 questions over the phone are unlikely to be a representative sample of the Jewish Israeli population.

There were also a number of advantages to conducting the survey this way. Using an already existing panel of respondents, for instance, allows us to use in the quota sampling the important demographic information provided by each participant when registering to be part of the panel.

There was information about age and gender, and if the participant was willing to give it, information about religiosity level, education, ethnicity and more.

Another advantage of conducting the survey online concerns touchy questions. It is known that the absence of a pollster reduces the phenomena of social desirability—i.e., the tendency of some respondents to report an answer in a way that they deem to be more socially acceptable than their "true" answer.

Of course, online questioning has its disadvantages. The online panel is characterized by the fact that its participants are volunteers. They sign up for the panel and agree to answer questionnaires that are occasionally sent to them.

One could make the claim that even if the panel participants are identical to the general population in terms of gender, age, and religiosity level, their willingness to sign up and become members of the online panel may indicate that the distribution of their opinions is not identical to the general population. This is a claim that concerns pollsters, but phone surveys are equally vulnerable to this criticism, especially when it is commonly known that the rate of people who agree to participate in phone surveys is not considerably high.

Most importantly, wide-ranging studies show us that when it comes to surveys which seek to gather data about people's beliefs, internet surveys may have a higher rate of precision compared to other methods of surveying.[279]

## 2. The Participants: Demography, Gender, Age, and Religiosity

The demographic information we had on the panel members allowed us to use the technique of quota sampling. The next table shows the sample distribution by age groups, and within those age groups, the distribution by gender. The distribution of data gathered by us matches the data published by the Israeli Central Bureau of Statistics (CBS).

|  | Gender Within an Age Group | |  |
|---|---|---|---|
|  | Female | Male | The Entire Sample |
| 24-18 | 49% | 51% | 16% |
| 34-25 | 49% | 51% | 22% |
| 44-35 | 51% | 49% | 21% |
| 54-45 | 53% | 47% | 19% |
| 64-55 | 56% | 44% | 14% |
| +65 | 52% | 48% | 8% |
| Overall | 51% | 49% | 100% |

Another demographic item of data concerns the level of religiosity among the Jewish panel members. The panel defines four levels of religiosity: secular; *masorti*; religious, and Haredi. The following table shows the distribution of the panel according to these four levels:

| Secular | 44.1% |
|---|---|
| Masorti | 27.5% |
| Religious | 19.4% |
| Haredi | 9.1% |

Data from the Israeli CBS breaks Jewish Israeli religiosity into five levels: secular; traditional who are not very religious; religious traditionalist; religious and Haredi. This is the distribution of the panel according to these five levels:

| Secular | 44% |
|---|---|
| Traditional who are not very religious | 24% |
| Religious traditionalist | 12% |
| Religious | 11% |
| Haredi | 9% |

The difference between the two tables derives from the different number of categories (four and five) used in each one. Were one to divide the members of the extra CBS category into the four groups of religiosity that were shown to the panel, the resulting distribution would be very similar to that of the panel. This could be done by categorizing one-fourth of the respondents who identified as "religious traditionalist" as "*masorti*" and three-fourths as "religious."

For our own purposes, we needed an even more precise categorization, so we asked the participants to redefine their level of religiosity on a seven level scale: Totally secular; somewhat-traditional secular; Traditionalist (*masorti*); Liberal-Religious; National-Religious, National-Haredi (Dati-Torani); and Haredi.

## 3. The Questionnaire

Both rounds of the questionnaire were focused on two main axes of Jewish living in Israel:

- The Jewish religion and tradition.
- Jewish nationhood and the feeling of belonging to the Jewish state.

Using these two axes, our survey focused on:

- Demographic information, personal background—including religious background, and personal religiosity (traditionalism).
- Everyday habits, including some which have a direct correlation to Jewish observance and others which do not.
- Behavior and adherence to tradition on national and religious holidays.
- Attitudes towards different aspects of Judaism and Israel as a Jewish state.

As we said before, some of the questions were asked only in one of the survey rounds and naturally, our analysis is solely based on the data that we have available.

In cases where the same question received significantly different response distributions (mostly in cases of a small but significant change in the wording) we will present only data that is based on one of the rounds, and we do of course specify that. In cases where we have answers from all 3,005 participants, we will use them.

Most of our questions were phrased in a dichotomous manner ("agree" or "disagree"). In other questions, participants had to choose one answer from four possible options ("to a very great extent," "to a great extent," "to a small extent," or "not at all") or ten possible options ("On a scale of 1-10, how much does your Jewishness matter to you?").

A small number of questions had participants choosing one of multiple options, or, in even rarer cases, choosing all relevant answers (such as the question about which stream of Judaism participants feel represents them).

And now we will review both questionnaires according to our study's four main subjects:

**Demographic information, personal background—including religious background, and personal religiosity (traditionalism).**

To obtain general demographic information, participants were asked about:

- Gender and age group
- Family background and number of children (second round of questioning)
- Ethnicity, place of residence, and political orientation (first round of questioning)

To obtain information about Judaism, participants were asked about:

- The level of importance they ascribe to their and their children's Judaism (first round of questioning)
- Their level of "feeling Jewish"
- Their sense of confidence in their children being (or remaining) Jewish
- Their sense of confidence in their grandchildren being (or remaining) Jewish (second round of questioning)

Level of religiosity (traditionalism) was ascertained by asking about:

- Personal level of religiosity on a scale from 1-7
- Personal level of religiosity in the participant's childhood home (first round of questioning)

Jewish stream was ascertained by asking participants about:

- Type of synagogue participants choose to attend

- Type of synagogue participants feel describes them best (from a list of possible Jewish streams, including the option of "do not belong to any stream"). The lists were different in both rounds of questioning.

Belief in God was ascertained by asking participants about:

- Belief in God's existence as a dichotomous (yes or no) question and also as a question which allowed us to understand the variable layers of belief or lack thereof (second round of questioning)

**Everyday habits, including some which have a direct correlation to Jewish observance and others which do not.**

Attitudes and behaviors surrounding Jewish life cycle events were ascertained by asking participants about:

- Habits and preferences surrounding weddings (including one's children's weddings), such as whether they prefer to marry through Israel's Chief Rabbinate
- Attitudes and habits surrounding childrearing including questions about brit milah, pidyon ha'ben, and bar mitzvah
- Attitudes towards burial (religious or civil); and Kaddish (yes or no).

A series of 19 "yes or no" questions were asked regarding different aspects of everyday life such as:

- Tradition and religion ("I visit the Tombs of the Righteous," "I only eat kosher, even when I am outside of my home")
- The Jewish people and the State of Israel ("I donate to social organizations," "I believe in greater Israel")
- Home life ("I read Hebrew literature regularly," "I often travel within Israel")

**Behavior and adherence to tradition on national and religious holidays.**

Participants were asked about their behavior on holidays from the first day of Rosh Hashanah through the month of Elul (including Rosh Chodesh and Shabbat).

# Appendixes

Most of the questions in our survey dealt with this subject. For each holiday several activities (from three to ten) were offered. Participants had to select those which they "usually do."

The first questionnaire included questions about 36 holidays and occasions, most of them from the Hebrew religious calendar but some of them national, such as Israeli Independence Day, Yom Hashoah, Yitzhak Rabin Memorial Day, and more. For each holiday or occasion, participants could choose to mark that the day was, for them, "a completely ordinary day." For some of the lesser known occasions (such as "Novi God" or "the Fast of Gedaliah"), we also added the option of "what is that?"

Five occasions (including Shabbat) were asked about in both rounds, with slightly different wording each time.

**Attitudes towards different aspects of Judaism and Israel as a Jewish state.**

Participants were asked what it means, to them, to be a Jew.

In both rounds of the survey, participants were presented with ten statements beginning with the words "for me, being a Jew is…" For each of these statements, they had to respond with their level of agreement by choosing one of four options ("do not agree at all," "slightly agree," "highly agree," or "very strongly agree").

The statements were the same for both rounds, with a small but important distinction. In the second round, the question was phrased: "for me, being **a good Jew** is…"

The statements touched on religion, tradition, state, nationality, and universal qualities (such as "being a good person").

Our participants' stances on different aspects of Judaism and Israel as a Jewish state were ascertained by asking questions about essential elements in Judaism, Jewish customs and the State of Israel. The questions were the following:

- What is the most essential part of Judaism? Culture, ethnic origin, religion, or nationhood?
- What is the main justification for the existence of Israel? A safe haven for the Jewish people, the fulfillment of the nation's national and religious spirit, a civil state with some cultural Jewish aspects, or a civil Israeli (not Jewish) state?
- What is the main reason to adhere to Jewish customs? The words of the Torah, the passing of customs from generation to generation, cultural reasons, social cohesion? Participants could also answer that they don't adhere to Jewish customs.

There is no doubt that these are heavy questions. The next appendix presents our findings about the personal background of our participants, and then our analysis of the correlations between these findings and the participants' demographic data.

## 4. Being and Feeling Jewish

### How important is being a Jew?

In the first round of the questionnaire, 64% out of the 2,004 participants reported that it is "very important" to them to be Jewish, and another 23% reported that being Jewish is "important" to them.

Overall, an 87% majority claimed that they find it "very important or important" to be Jewish. Another 8% claimed that being Jewish is of "little importance" to them and a minority of 5% said that it is "not important at all" for them to be Jewish.

| very important | 64% |
| important | 23% |
| little importance | 8% |
| not important at all | 5% |

And what about the next generation? How important is it to the survey participants that their children be Jewish? Apparently, it matters quite a lot. To be precise—it matters about as much as their own Jewishness matters to them.

In the relevant survey question, the percentage of those who stated that their Jewishness is "very important" to them is similar to the percentage of those who stated that their children being Jewish is "very important" to them, or even a bit higher (67% versus 64%).

It looks like there is a high (and natural) correlation between the two. The next table presents it. In it, 75% of those who stated that their Jewishness is of "little importance" to them, are also those who state that it is of little importance to them that their children remain Jewish.

On the other side of the scale, among those who stated that their Jewish identity is "very important" to them, 98% also stated that it is "very important" that their children remain Jewish. This cross-generation correlation is extremely high (0.905).

| Is it important for you that your children be Jewish? | | | | | |
|---|---|---|---|---|---|
| | | not important at all | little importance | important | very important |
| Is it important to you that you are Jewish? | not important at all | 87% | 9% | 3% | 1% |
| | little importance | 11% | 75% | 11% | 3% |
| | Important | 2% | 7% | 76% | 15% |
| | very important | 0% | 0% | 2% | 98% |

**How Jewish do you feel?**

We asked our participants to rate how Jewish they feel on a scale from 1 to 10.

Out of all 3,005 participants, 54% chose the number "10" to describe how Jewish they feel, 14% chose "9," and 12% chose "8." Overall, a majority of 80% chose numbers within the range of 8-10 to describe how Jewish they feel.

| Not at all | 2 | 3 | 4 | 5 | 6 | 7 | 8 | 9 | The maximum |
|---|---|---|---|---|---|---|---|---|---|
| 1% | 1% | 2% | 2% | 3% | 4% | 8% | 12% | 14% | 54% |

The generational transitions are relevant for this question too. The research included two additional questions, one about the generation of the participants' children and one about the generation of their grandchildren. We asked (also on a scale from 1 to 10) two questions – "how confident are you that your children will be Jewish" and "to what extent do you believe that your grandchildren will be Jewish?"

The results were quite surprising. If we set the participant's answer to the question "how Jewish do you feel" as the reference bar – then on average, the percentage of participants who gave a **higher score** than the bar to the question of children's Jewishness is **significantly higher** than the average of participants who gave a **lower score** than the bar to the question of their grandchildren's Jewishness.

That and more: on average, the percentage of participants who gave a score **higher than the bar** to the possibility of their grandchildren being Jewish is **significantly higher** than the percentage of those who gave a **lower score than the bar** to the possibility of their grandchildren being Jewish.

The two transitional matrices present the empirical proof of such claims. For example, among those who answered 8 when asked how Jewish they feel, 37% answered 8 to the possibility of their children being Jewish. 49% gave a score higher than 8 to their children's prospective Jewishness and only 14% gave a score lower than 8 to their children's prospective Jewishness.

| | | On a scale from 1 to 10, when 1 is "not at all" and 10 is the maximum, please indicate how certain you are that your children will also be Jewish: | | | | | | | | | | |
|---|---|---|---|---|---|---|---|---|---|---|---|---|
| | | Not at all | 2 | 3 | 4 | 5 | 6 | 7 | 8 | 9 | The maximum | Overall |
| On a scale from 1 to 10, when 1 is "not at all" and 10 is the maximum, please indicate how Jewish you feel: | Not at all | 33% | | | | | | | | | 67% | 3 |
| | 2 | 22% | 33% | | | | | | | | 44% | 9 |
| | 3 | | 17% | 33% | | | | | | | 50% | 12 |
| | 4 | | | 23% | 15% | | | | | | 62% | 13 |
| | 5 | | | | 13% | 32% | | | | | 55% | 31 |
| | 6 | | | | | 17% | 20% | | | | 63% | 30 |
| | 7 | | | | | | 21% | 19% | | | 60% | 84 |
| | 8 | | | | | | | 14% | 37% | | 49% | 131 |
| | 9 | | | | | | | | 15% | 50% | 35% | 136 |
| | The maximum | | | | | | | | | 11% | 89% | 552 |
| | Overall | 9 | 8 | 10 | 11 | 26 | 30 | 46 | 103 | 149 | 609 | 1001 |

| | | On a scale from 1 to 10, when 1 is "not at all" and 10 is the maximum, please indicate how certain you are that your grandchildren will also be Jewish: | | | | | | | | | | |
|---|---|---|---|---|---|---|---|---|---|---|---|---|
| | Not at all | Not at all | 2 | 3 | 4 | 5 | 6 | 7 | 8 | 9 | The maximum | Overall |
| On a scale from 1 to 10, when 1 is "not at all" and 10 is the maximum, please indicate how Jewish you feel: | Not at all | 33% | | | | | | | | | 67% | 3 |
| | 2 | 44% | 22% | | | | | | | | 33% | 9 |
| | 3 | | 25% | 25% | | | | | | | 50% | 12 |
| | 4 | | | 31% | 15% | | | | | | 54% | 13 |
| | 5 | | | | 26% | 29% | | | | | 45% | 31 |
| | 6 | | | | | 33% | 10% | | | | 57% | 30 |
| | 7 | | | | | | 32% | 23% | | | 45% | 84 |
| | 8 | | | | | | | 27% | 40% | | 32% | 131 |
| | 9 | | | | | | | | 33% | 41% | 26% | 136 |
| | The maximum | | | | | | | | | 22% | 78% | 552 |
| | Overall | 13 | 7 | 15 | 15 | 46 | 36 | 76 | 153 | 134 | 506 | 1001 |

There is a low correlation (0.673) between how Jewish participants felt personally and how confident they were in their children being Jewish. There was an even lower correlation (0.638) between how Jewish participants felt personally and how confident they were in their grandchildren being Jewish. That said, there was a higher correlation (0.867) between the confidence in one's children being Jewish and the confidence in one's grandchildren being Jewish, indicating that when it comes to their offspring's Jewishness, the participants judged the next generation's prospects as similar to those of the subsequent generation.

## 5. Religiosity and Secularism

After the analysis of the participants' Jewishness level, let us now examine their level of traditionalism—religiosity. We will begin by describing the current situation: out of all 3,005 participants, **49%** described themselves as "secular," including those who are "totally secular" **(28%)** as well as those who are "somewhat-traditional secular" **(21%)**.

19% described themselves as traditionalist and 5% as Liberal-Religious. 10% self-described as National-Religious and 7% as Dati-Torani. The final **9%** self-describe as "Haredi."

| Totally secular | Somewhat-traditional secular | Traditionalist | Liberal-Religious | National-Religious | Dati-Torani | Haredi |
|---|---|---|---|---|---|---|
| 28% | 21% | 19% | 5% | 10% | 7% | 9% |

Much like the previous case, this one also analyzes the change in religiosity within a generation. But unlike the previously studied case, this one researches the transition between the past generation and the current one.

Each person interviewed was asked about the level of religiosity in his or her childhood home, so that we could compare two different time periods for each participant.

The results reinforce the findings from previous studies, which show that level of religiosity tends to decrease between generations.

This transition matrix below shows, for example, that out of those who grew up in traditionalist households, 27% identify themselves as somewhat traditional while 9% identify as totally secular. The level of religiosity increased only for 17% of the participants.

In other words, level of traditionalism is decreasing. We can see all the results in the table below, where the diagonal marked in gray presents the percentage of those whose religiosity level as adults is the same as that practiced in the house that they grew up in.

|  |  | Previous generation | | | | | | |
|---|---|---|---|---|---|---|---|---|
|  |  | Totally secular | Somewhat-traditional secular | Traditionalist | Liberal-Religious | National-Religious | Dati-Torani | Haredi |
| Current generation | Totally secular | 75% | 38% | 9% | 7% | 3% | 8% | 1% |
| | Somewhat-traditional secular | 15% | 42% | 27% | 14% | 9% | 7% | 4% |
| | Traditionalist | 3% | 12% | 47% | 31% | 19% | 7% | 5% |
| | Liberal-Religious | 2% | 2% | 5% | 34% | 9% | 8% | 1% |
| | National-Religious | 1% | 3% | 7% | 9% | 40% | 16% | 5% |
| | Dati-Torani | 2% | 2% | 2% | 3% | 15% | 46% | 8% |
| | Haredi | 2% | 1% | 3% | 3% | 5% | 10% | 77% |

The next transition matrix details the percentage of those whose level of traditionalism-religiosity decreased, those who remained the same, and those whose level of traditionalism-religiosity increased across generations.

|  |  | Previous generation | | | | | | |
|---|---|---|---|---|---|---|---|---|
|  |  | Totally secular | Somewhat-traditional secular | Traditionalist | Liberal-Religious | National-Religious | Dati-Torani | Haredi |
| Current generation | Totally secular | 75% | 38% | | | | | |
| | Somewhat-traditional secular | | 42% | 36% | | | | |
| | Traditionalist | | | 47% | 52% | | | |
| | Liberal-Religious | 25% | | | 34% | 40% | | |
| | National-Religious | | 20% | 17% | | 40% | 45% | |
| | Dati Torani | | | | 14% | | 46% | 23% |
| | Haredi | | | | | 20% | 10% | 77% |

When level of Jewishness and level of religiosity are explored through a multigenerational lens, an interesting picture comes about: while the participants are confident in their Jewishness and its grasp on their offspring, the level of multi-generational religiosity decreases.

## 6. The Axis of Nationalism and the Axis of Traditionalism

More than 3,000 participants, more than 300 questions. One of the most extensive surveys on the subject ever conducted. The participants were asked about their views on a variety of subjects, and about their habits during holidays and everyday life. For most questions, participants were presented with two options—yes and no. Do I agree or disagree with what is being presented to me?

Overall, the survey questions touched on the two major axes of Jewish life: nationalism and traditionalism. Some questions touched on both axes, but most of them clearly deal with one more than the other.

The book's chapters are centered around discussions of certain elements in Judaism and Jewish life in Israel. In our research, we attempted to define some aggregative indices that would help us place the participants on a two-dimensional matrix of nationalism and traditionalism. Even more, given that we ascertained the level of nationalism and religiosity for all of our participants, could we map the two-dimensional distribution of the entire Israeli population? Or at least estimate it?

We can, and we did, and it can be seen in the first chart of this book. A reminder: the chart has two axes. The X-axis (horizontal) maps nationalism, and ranges from "Less Nationality" on the left to "More Nationality" on the right.

The Y-axis (vertical) maps traditionalism, and ranges from "More Tradition" at the top to "Less Tradition" on the bottom. Based on the values of the two axes, one can be broadly categorized in one of four boxes: "Jews" in the upper left, "Israeli Jews" in the upper right, "universalists" in the lower left, and "Israelis" in the lower right.

If we define those two axes as having a zero value, the values placed to the left of the Y-axis are negative and the ones to the right of

# Appendixes

the Y-axis are positive. Similarly, values above the X-axis line are positive, and under the X-axis line are negative (mathematically, not ideologically). In the chart that opens our book, one can see the percentage of participants who "fit" each box: 17% (Jews), 55% (Jewsraelis), 13% (universalists) and 15% (Israelis). How did these values come about?

As a first step towards building these indices, two groups of questions were formed: the "traditional" group, where every question addresses the subject of traditionalism and religious habits; and the "national" group, where each question deals with participants' sense of nationalism.

For every question, we determined which answers signify more traditionalism and which signify less. For example, the answer "yes" to the question "do you partake in a kiddush on Shabbat?" falls on the side of more traditionalism, whereas the same answer to the question "Yom Kippur is a day to watch TV at home" falls on the side of less traditionalism. Respectively, for every question that was chosen in the "nationalism" group, it was determined whether the answer "yes" meant more or less nationalism.

Responses which signified more traditionalism and nationalism received a score of +1, while those which signified less traditionalism and nationalism received a score of -1. We decided to give the same weight to every question and answer (so as to avoid the discussion of what we consider more "worthy"—"making a kiddush" or "waving a flag of Israel." After that, we simply defined the "tradition index" as the sum of all marks in its group, and the "nationality index" as the sum of all marks in its group.

On questions where more than two choices were presented, we grouped answers. For example: in the question "how important is it to you that your children will be Jewish?" we presented four possible answers: "very important," "important," "of little importance," and "not important." For the purpose of building the indices, we grouped the two first answers ("important" and "very important"), both of which would signify "more tradition"; and the two final answers ("of little importance" and "not important"), both of which would signify "less tradition."

The two indices define a point on the two-dimensional graph, which allows us to map those points by the pair of indices of all participants and get a distribution of the entire Jewish population in Israel.

The chart in the opening chapter is based on the "tradition" group and "nationality" group—16 questions in each category. The questions are presented in the rest of the appendix.

Here is the mapping of 2,003 index points of participants from the survey's first round:

|   |   |   |   | 1 |   |   | 1 |   | 1 | 1 | 2 | 2 | 5 |   |
|---|---|---|---|---|---|---|---|---|---|---|---|---|---|---|
|   |   |   |   |   |   | 4 |   | 3 | 3 | 6 | 7 | 9 | 10 | 12 |
|   |   |   | 1 |   | 1 | 3 | 2 | 6 | 2 | 9 | 8 | 14 | 17 | 28 | 20 |
|   |   |   | 1 |   | 2 | 6 | 9 | 4 | 8 | 13 | 15 | 16 | 25 | 20 | 23 | 34 |
|   |   | 2 | 2 | 2 | 9 | 6 | 12 | 15 | 16 | 24 | 26 | 31 | 21 | 25 | 23 | 25 |
|   | 1 | 1 | 3 | 6 | 5 | 21 | 17 | 14 | 17 | 26 | 25 | 27 | 29 | 28 | 24 | 35 |
|   |   | 2 | 4 | 10 | 13 | 17 | 18 | 23 | 22 | 18 | 26 | 24 | 15 | 26 | 15 | 17 |
| 1 |   | 10 | 6 | 14 | 13 | 20 | 22 | 17 | 22 | 15 | 16 | 14 | 15 | 14 | 17 | 17 |
|   | 1 | 3 | 9 | 21 | 9 | 17 | 16 | 10 | 13 | 17 | 10 | 16 | 10 | 15 | 12 | 15 |
| 1 | 3 | 2 | 9 | 8 | 13 | 10 | 11 | 5 | 12 | 9 | 6 | 6 | 8 | 6 | 15 | 14 |
| 2 | 1 | 4 | 3 | 5 | 10 | 10 | 5 | 2 | 10 | 6 | 7 | 3 | 3 | 13 | 13 | 11 |
|   | 1 | 2 | 10 | 9 | 6 | 7 | 1 | 5 | 5 | 2 | 1 | 4 | 1 | 11 | 9 | 14 |
|   |   | 1 | 4 | 4 | 8 | 3 | 2 | 4 | 2 |   |   | 3 | 2 | 2 | 6 | 7 |
|   |   | 2 | 3 |   | 2 | 4 | 1 | 1 | 1 | 1 |   |   | 3 | 5 | 6 | 7 |
| 1 | 2 | 2 | 1 | 3 | 5 | 3 |   |   | 1 |   |   |   | 4 | 2 | 1 |
|   | 2 |   |   | 1 | 2 | 2 |   |   |   |   |   | 1 |   |   |   |
|   |   |   |   | 1 |   |   |   |   |   |   |   |   | 1 | 1 |   |

The percentage of points in the four boxes are:

| 17% | 56% |
|---|---|
| 12% | 15% |

You can, of course, chose a different collection of questions to reflect the tradition and nationality groups. We did so in several compositions. The mapping that resulted from these alternative question groupings came out similar or very similar. For example, we tested the program 16 times using the "leave one out" method. In every round, we dropped one of the 16 original questions from the two groups. These were the results (for each of the four boxes) received in each round.

| 1 | | 2 | | 3 | | 4 | | 5 | | 6 | | 7 | | 8 | |
|---|---|---|---|---|---|---|---|---|---|---|---|---|---|---|---|
| 16% | 60% | 17% | 60% | 20% | 56% | 17% | 59% | 15% | 58% | 16% | 58% | 16% | 57% | 17% | 57% |
| 10% | 13% | 10% | 13% | 11% | 13% | 10% | 13% | 11% | 16% | 11% | 15% | 12% | 16% | 11% | 15% |
| 9 | | 10 | | 11 | | 12 | | 13 | | 14 | | 15 | | 16 | |
| 17% | 55% | 18% | 53% | 15% | 56% | 17% | 53% | 17% | 52% | 17% | 52% | 17% | 51% | 18% | 51% |
| 13% | 15% | 12% | 17% | 12% | 16% | 14% | 16% | 14% | 17% | 14% | 17% | 14% | 17% | 14% | 18% |

Additionally, we present the mapping that we got for two additional groups, where each had nine questions. The two groups shown here, both tradition and nationality, were chosen **by a completely random** set of nine questions (out of the original 16). As the number of questions decreased, the mapping became more precise because the indices received values between -9 and +9 instead of -16 and +16. But still, the overall image that we got was the same.

| | | | | | | | | | |
|---|---|---|---|---|---|---|---|---|---|
|   | 2 | 1 | 6 | 3 | 5 | 10 | 6 | 21 | 26 |
|   | 3 | 6 | 10 | 11 | 23 | 43 | 40 | 44 | 39 |
|   | 19 | 31 | 31 | 43 | 64 | 72 | 66 | 46 | 55 |
| 3 | 39 | 52 | 47 | 40 | 57 | 76 | 48 | 46 | 42 |
| 4 | 53 | 47 | 37 | 44 | 44 | 46 | 31 | 36 | 32 |
| 7 | 35 | 31 | 27 | 27 | 21 | 19 | 15 | 19 | 18 |
| 5 | 24 | 12 | 10 | 13 | 13 | 4 | 10 | 10 | 11 |
| 2 | 9 | 20 | 5 | 6 | 4 | 3 | 5 | 8 | 16 |
| 4 | 4 | 7 | 2 | 1 | 1 | 2 | 3 | 4 | 5 |
| 1 | 1 | 4 |   |   |   |   | 2 | 3 |   |

#IsraeliJudaism

Mapping the population by the sum of all the answers is not the only way to map. For example, one study about Jewish involvement in Washington state used a statistical analysis of latent variables in order to define five groups—each representing a different level of involvement in the community. In our study, we used some known statistical models (such as factor analysis, including latent variables and cluster analysis). With the kind help of Dr. Tal Galili from Tel Aviv University, we used another method of cluster analysis called Heatmap. All of these models divided the sample into only two groups, which, in our opinion, did not reflect the complexity of the Jewish Israeli experience.

Here are the 16 questions from the "tradition group." The questions that were sampled in the group of nine are written *in italics*.

| |
|---|
| *Visits synagogue every week* |
| *Rosh Hashanah: attends all prayers* |
| Prefers a secular burial |
| *The main component of the Jewish state is religion* |
| Tisha B'Av: a completely ordinary day |
| *Participates in Hakafot during Simchat Torah* |
| Shabbat: partakes in a kiddush |
| *First day of Passover: eats kosher-for-Passover food* |
| *Chanukah: lights candles every night* |
| *Being Jewish means upholding customs and traditions (true, very true)* |
| Shabbat: goes shopping |
| *Yom Kippur: watches TV at home + goes to the beach/park + riding bike* |
| how important is it to you that your children will be Jewish? (important, very important) |
| What is the Tenth of Tevet? |
| The secular new year: feels like real New Year's Eve |
| *Does not uphold traditions or commemorated events* |

Appendixes

And here are the 16 questions sampled for the "nationality group." The questions that were sampled in the group of nine are written *in italics*.

| |
|---|
| *Memorial Day: visits graves* |
| *Jerusalem Day: waves the Israeli flag* |
| *The main component of the Jewish state is nationality* |
| Jerusalem Day: a completely ordinary day |
| Self-identifies as an Israeli Jew |
| *Being Jewish means living in Israeli: (true, very true)* |
| *Mainly listens to Israeli music* |
| Independence Day: waves the Israeli flag |
| Being Jewish means serving in the IDF: (true, very true) |
| *Being Jewish means caring about all Jews: (true, very true)* |
| *Yom Hashoah: stands during the siren when in a public space* |
| Memorial Day: stands during the siren |
| Being Jewish means remembering the Holocaust: (true, very true) |
| Memorial Day: feels sad |
| Independence Day is a completely ordinary day |
| Main justification for Israel: a civil Israeli state |

## 7. The Jewish Streams

The participants had no difficulty identifying their religiosity, from the "totally secular" on one side to "Haredi" on the other.

However, the definition of one's religiosity/traditionalism is anything but simple.

Those who identify as "totally secular" are still likely to visit a synagogue, for reasons such as celebrations or sometimes even prayers.

Traditional and religious individuals can identify themselves and their synagogue as a sub-category from a wide range of options.

In the second round of the survey, participants were asked to choose the definition that "feels like it describes them best" between the three main streams of Judaism. They also had a fourth option of claiming that they "do not belong to any stream." The results of the entire survey were as follows:

| Do not belong to any stream | Orthodox | Conservative | Reform |
|---|---|---|---|
| 51% | 37% | 5% | 8% |

By the way, 8% out of those who identified as "totally secular" and 13% out of those who identified as "somewhat-traditional secular" responded that the Reform stream is the one that suits them best.

The findings from the first round of the survey showed a complex picture. We asked two questions regarding Jewish streams: in the first question, we asked participants to categorize the synagogue that they attend "in the event that they visit a synagogue." We further specified that this question does not refer to the synagogue one attends as an invitee to a bar mitzvah or someone's wedding. We asked the participants to choose the "most relevant" option out of these eight choices: Orthodox, Ashkenazi Orthodox, Sephardic Orthodox, Chabad

Orthodox, Conservative, Reform, secular Judaism, Orthodox with mixed seating (men and women). We added two categories for those who generally refrain from visiting synagogues: "does not visit a synagogue" and "I do not know which synagogue—whichever one comes up."

This was the distribution:

| Reform | secular Judaism | Orthodox with mixed seating (men and women). | "I do not know which synagogue—whichever one comes up | does not visit a synagogue |
|---|---|---|---|---|
| 3% | 2% | 1% | 11% | 27% |
| Orthodox | Ashkenazi Orthodox | Sephardic Orthodox | Chabad Orthodox | Conservative |
| 9% | 14% | 30% | 2% | 1% |

On the second question, we presented all eight streams and asked the participants to mark **all** the options that they feel represented by. We also added the option of "does not belong to any stream."

Here are the results:

| Reform | Conservative | Orthodox | Hasidic | Misnagdim | Chabad | Israeli Judaism | Egalitarian Orthodox | Does not belong to any stream |
|---|---|---|---|---|---|---|---|---|
| 6% | 3% | 28% | 5% | 5% | 3% | 55% | 5% | 27% |

It is easy to see that the sum of percentages comes up higher than 100%, because of the option of multiple answers. Here is the distribution of number of answers per person:

219

# #IsraeliJudaism

| Number of answers | 0 | 1 | 2 | 3 | 4 | 5 |
|---|---|---|---|---|---|---|
| percentage | 23% | 55% | 17% | 4% | 1% | 0% |

Indeed, in 22% of the cases, more than one answer was chosen. A more detailed analysis of the data brings up an interesting finding: a high percentage of participants who chose one of the streams, added the option of "Israeli Judaism." Not just a high percent, a very high percent. Here is the percentage of people who chose to select the option of "Israeli Judaism" in addition to another stream:

| Reform | Conservative | Orthodox | Hasidic | Yeshivish | Chabad | Egalitarian Orthodox |
|---|---|---|---|---|---|---|
| 57% | 60% | 49% | 42% | 21% | 59% | 73% |

Pretty impressive. Forty-nine percent of those who mentioned "Orthodox" as one of their options also chose "Israeli Judaism"; 57% of those who chose "Reform" and 60% of those who chose "Conservative" also chose Israeli Judaism. The smallest (yet still impressive) percentage was 21% of Misnagdim (Haredi, Yeshivish) who also chose Israeli Judaism.

One final somewhat surprising fact: 48% of those who identified as "totally secular" mentioned that the denomination of "Israeli Judaism" also defines them.

When it comes to Israel, it looks like "Israeli Judaism" is the most common denomination.

# 8. Belief in God

In the first round of the survey, we asked a number of questions regarding life cycle events. One of them presented the statement, "I believe in God," for which participants had to check "yes" or "no." Seventy-eight percent of participants replied "yes" (as in many previous surveys). However, what exactly do they mean when they claim to believe in God? On the second round of the survey, the participants had to choose from a set of options that was presented to them. The distribution of the answers was as follows:

| I do not believe in God. | I do not believe in God, but I sometimes think God may exist. | I want to believe in the existence of God. Sometimes I can and other times I cannot. | I believe in God but I sometimes doubt it. | I believe in God but do not believe in divine providence. (Meaning: I do not think that God is interested in every single human personally) | Yes, I fully believe in the existence of God. |
|---|---|---|---|---|---|
| 9% | 12% | 8% | 8% | 6% | 58% |

Fifty-eight percent of participants answered that they fully believe in the existence of God (*be'emunah sheleimah,* "with complete faith"). A relatively small percentage of 6% chose the alternative of a belief in God without a belief in divine providence. Sixteen percent believe infrequently and with some doubts. Out of them, 8% mentioned that they believe with caveats and the remaining 8% would like to believe but only succeed irregularly. Twenty-one percent do not believe in God.

The fact that different groups of participants responded to the "yes or no" and the multiple-choice versions of the question makes it hard to formulate a precise comparison. Overall, it looks as though the people who responded "yes" to one of the first four options presented in the second round (79%) are those who identify as "believes in God."

It is interesting to compare our data to the data from surveys that were conducted among American Jews. In a 2013 Pew survey, 37% of participants answered "yes" to the question of belief in God; 27% said that they are "pretty sure" of the existence of God. Of the remaining participants, 15% were "unsure," and 14% stated that they "[do] not believe in God."

In a 2018 Pew survey, only 33% of American Jews claimed to believe in "the God that was represented in the Bible" and 56% of them claimed to believe in a "higher power." In comparison, 80% of American Christian participants claim to believe in "the God that was represented in the Bible."

# 9. Political Beliefs and Ethnicity

It is a known fact that in Israel, the way one identifies politically is highly correlated with one's level of religiosity. Is this belief confirmed by our survey, and if so, is it correct for the whole spectrum of Israeli Jews?

Yes and no. A yes to the first question and a no to the second.

The two-dimensional table below tells us the story. The data are from the first round of the survey. Overall 34% of the participants identified themselves as "right wing" and only 5% identified themselves as "left wing". However, among those who identified as "totally secular," only 14% identified themselves as "right wing" (versus 34% in the entire sample). On the other side of the spectrum, 15% of those who identified as "totally secular" have also identified as "left wing" (versus 5% in the entire sample).

Generally speaking, The the level of "right wing" is positively correlated with religiosity level. Within the "traditionalist" group 42% identify as "right-wing (and an extra 30% identify as "center-right-wing"). The highest correlation is among the "Dati-Torani," from which 71% identify as "right wing" (with an extra 24% who identify as "center-right wing," for a whopping 95% overall).

The percentages drop for those participants in the last religiosity level group. Only 50% of Haredim identify as "right wing" (and an extra 32% identify as "center-right wing").

|  | overall | Totally secular | Somewhat-traditional secular | Traditionalist | Liberal-Religious | National-Religious | Dati-Torani | Haredi |
|---|---|---|---|---|---|---|---|---|
| Right wing | 34% | 14% | 22% | 42% | 36% | 62% | 71% | 50% |
| Center-right wing | 26% | 17% | 28% | 30% | 38% | 26% | 24% | 32% |
| Center | 23% | 30% | 33% | 22% | 21% | 10% | 4% | 14% |
| Center-left wing | 11% | 24% | 14% | 6% | 4% | 1% | 0% | 3% |
| Left wing | 5% | 15% | 3% | 1% | 1% | 0% | 0% | 1% |

#IsraeliJudaism

Unlike the correlation between religiosity and political alignment, the one between religiosity and ethnicity is much smaller. Still, it is important to note some of the differences.

Thirty-nine percent of the participants are Ashkenazi, which are mostly represented in the extreme groups. They are 54% of the "totally secular" and 58% of the Haredi. Mizrahi Israelis are more likely to be positioned in the center of the table.

Forty-one percent of the participants are Mizrahi and the highest percentage of them are among the "traditionalist" group (62%), the "Liberal-Religious" group (50%) and the Dati-Torani group (55%).

An extremely low rate of "mixed" ethnicity is noted within the Haredi community. 4% compared to the 16% of the survey.

|  | overall | Totally secular | Somewhat-traditional secular | Traditionalist | Liberal-Religious | National-Religious | Dati-Torani | Haredi |
|---|---|---|---|---|---|---|---|---|
| Ashkenazi | 39% | 54% | 33% | 18% | 29% | 34% | 39% | 58% |
| Mizrachi | 41% | 17% | 43% | 62% | 50% | 55% | 45% | 37% |
| mixed | 16% | 19% | 20% | 17% | 17% | 9% | 15% | 4% |
| Russian | 4% | 9% | 4% | 2% | 2% | 2% | 1% | 1% |
| Ethiopian | 0% | 0% | 1% | 1% | 1% | 0% | 0% | 0% |

Appendixes

# The Jewish People Policy Institute

**Partners and Members of the General Meeting:**

Sandy Baklor and Arlene Kaufman

David Breakstone
as Deputy Chairman of JAFI

Lester Crown and Charles Goodman
on behalf of Crown Family Philanthropies

William Davidson Foundation

Diane & Guilford Glazer Fund

Nathan and Frances Kirsh
on behalf of the Kirsh Family Foundation

Robert Kapito and Jeffrey Schoenfeld
on behalf of UJA Federation of New York

Mike and Sofia Segal

Michael Siegal
as Chairman of the JAFI Board of Governors

The Ratner Family

Isaac Herzog
as Chairman of the JAFI Executive

Beth Kieffer Leonard
as Chairman of the JAFI Budget
and Finance Committee

**Special thanks to**
UJA Federation of New York,
The Jewish Federations of North America,
The Jewish Federation of Metropolitan Chicago,
The Jewish Federation of Cleveland,
Sandy Gottesman, Mitchell Julis, Art Samberg,
Paul Singer, Wilf Family Foundation for
their kind support,
and with fond memories of Alex Grass z"l
and Jack Kay z"l

**Board of Directors and Professional Guiding Council:**

Co-Chairs
Stuart Eizenstat
Dennis Ross

Members of the Board
Elliott Abrams
Yohanna Arbib
Sandy Baklor
Irwin Cotler
Wendy Fisher
Sami Friedrich
Misha Galperin
Eric Goldstein
Dan Halperin
Steve Hoffman
Alan Hoffmann
Vernon Kurtz
Bernard-Henri Lévy
Glen Lewy
Judit Bokser Liwerant
Sallai Meridor
Isaac Molho
Miriam Naor
Steven Nasatir
Jehuda Reinharz
Doron Shorer
Michael Steinhardt
James Tisch
Marc Utay
Aharon Yadlin

**President and Founding Director**
Avinoam Bar-Yosef

**Projects Coordinator**
Ita Alcalay

**Founding President (Emeritus)**
Yehezkel Dror

# Bibliography

### JPPI Sources

Sylvia Barack Fishman and Steven M. Cohen, "Family, Engagement, and Jewish Continuity among American Jews," JPPI, accessible at: http://jppi.org.il/new/wp-content/uploads/2017/06/Raising-Jewish-Children-Research-and-Indicators-for-Intervention.pdf

Dan Feferman and Dov Maimon, "An Integrated Jewish World Response to Israel's Migrant Challenge," JPPI (03.08.2018), accessible at: http://jppi.org.il/new/en/article/english-an-integrated-jewish-world-response-to-israels-migrant-challenge/

Dan Feferman, "Rising Streams: Reform and Conservative Judaism in Israel," JPPI (2018), accessible at: http://jppi.org.il/new/wp-content/uploads/2018/10/RisingStreams.pdf

Shlomo Fischer, "2018 Annual Assessment of the Situation and Dynamics of the Jewish People," JPPI, accessible at: http://jppi.org.il/new/wp-content/uploads/2018/06/AA2018-GovEnglish.pdf

Shlomo Fischer, "JPPI Annual Assessment 2016," JPPI, accessible at: http://jppi.org.il/new/wp-content/uploads/2016/JPPI_2016_Annual_Assessment.pdf

Shlomo Fischer, "Who are the 'Jews by Religion' in the Pew Report?" JPPI (2013), accessible at: http://jppi.org.il/new/en/article/english-who-are-the-jews-by-religion-in-the-pew-report/

Avi Gil and Einat Wilf, "2030: Alternative Futures for the Jewish People" (2010), accessible at: http://jppi.org.il/uploads/2030%20ENG.pdf

Shmuel Rosner and Camil Fuchs, "Who Reads the Haggadah Until the End?" JPPI (March 2018) [Hebrew].

Shmuel Rosner and Dov Maimon, "The Haredi Challenge," JPPI (21.02.2013), accessible at: http://jppi.org.il/new/en/article/english-the-haredi-challenge/#.XJ-v0-szYxc

Shmuel Rosner and John Ruskay, "Jerusalem and the Jewish People: Unity and Division," JPPI (2017), accessible at: http://jppi.org.il/new/wp-content/uploads/2017/Jerusalem-Dialogue-Report-English.pdf

Shmuel Rosner and Avi Gil, "Israel as a Jewish and Democratic State: Perspectives from World Jewry," JPPI (2014), accessible at: http://jppi.org.il/uploads/jewish_and_democratic-eng.pdf

Shmuel Rosner and John Ruskay, "70 Years of Israel-Diaspora Relations: The Next Generation," JPPI (2018), accessible at: http://jppi.org.il/new/wp-content/uploads/2018/07/Dialogue-at-70-English.pdf

JPPI Pluralism Indexes

## Hebrew Books

Maoz Azaryahu, *State Cults: Celebrating Independence and Commemorating the Fallen in Israel 1948-1956* (Sde Boker: Ben-Gurion University, 1995)

Guy Ben-Porat, *In Practice: The Secularization of Contemporary Israel* (Haifa: Pardes, 2016)

Meir Buzaglo, "The New Traditional Jew and the Halakha: A Phenomenology" in Moshe Orfali and Ephraim Hazan (eds.), *Progress and Tradition: Creativity, Leadership and Acculturation Processes Among the Jews of North Africa* (Bialik Institute: Jerusalem, 2005)

Meir Buzaglo, *A Language for the Faithful: Reflections on Tradition* (Jerusalem: Keter, 2009)

Kimmy Caplan, *The Internal Popular Discourse in Israeli Haredi Society* (Jerusalem: Zalman Shazar Center, 2007)

Asher Cohen, "Orthodox Halakhic Commitment and the Challenge of Jewish Sovereignty: The Leibowitz-Neria Polemic in the Early 1950s" in Yedidia Z. Stern and Yair Sheleg (eds.), *Zionist Halakha* (Jerusalem: Israel Democracy Institute, 2017)

Asher Cohen, *The Tallit and the Flag: Religious Zionism and the Vision of the Torah State in the Early Years of the State* (Jerusalem: Ben Zvi Institute, 1998)

Yuval Cherlow, *Jewish Ethics: The Slippery Slope (2)* (21.08.2018), accessible on Tzohar website [Hebrew].

Uri Dromi, *Brethren Dwelling Together: Orthodoxy and Non-Orthodoxy in Israel – Positions, Propositions, and Accords* (Jerusalem: Israel Democracy Institute, 2005)

Chana Eden et al., *Being Citizens in Israel: A Jewish and Democratic State* (Ministry of Education, 2001)

Ariel Finkelstein, *The Sabbath in Israel: The Full Picture* (Jerusalem: The Institute for Zionist Strategies, 2016)

# Bibliography

Menachem Friedman, *The Haredi Ultra-Orthodox Society: Sources, Trends, and Processes* (Jerusalem: The Jerusalem Institute for Israel Studies, 1991)

Reuven Gal, *Ultra-Orthodox ('Haredi') Jews in Israel's Society: A 2014 Status Report* (Haifa: Samuel Neaman Institute, 2015)

Yitz Greenberg, "Theology After the Holocaust" in Dan Michman (ed.), *The Holocaust in Jewish History: Historiography, Consciousness, Interpretations* (Jerusalem: Yad Vashem, 2005)

Naomi Gutkind-Golan, "The Heikhal Cinema Issue: A Symptom of Religious-Non-Religious Relations in the 1980s" in Charles Liebman (ed.), *Religious and Secular: Conflict and Accommodation Between Jews in Israel* (Jerusalem: Keter, 1990)

Yaron Harel, "The Chief Rabbinate and Twentieth Century Fox Present: No Movies on Saturday: An Episode in the Struggle for Public Sabbath Observance in Jerusalem, 1930-1945," *Cathedra* 157

Haggai Harif, *Muscular Zionism* (Jerusalem: Yad Ben-Zvi, 2011)

Avner Holtzman (ed.), *Micha Josef Berdyczewski: Studies and Documents* (Bialik Institute, Jerusalem: 2002)

Tova Ilan and Batya Kahana-Dror, *Covenants in Israel: Attempts to Regularize Relations between Secular and Religious: Presented to the President of Israel, Mr. Moshe Katsav* (Jerusalem, 2005)

Assaf Inbari, "In the Ranks of Gershom Scholem's Zionism" in Avihu Zakai et al. (eds.), *Fields in the Wind: A Tribute to Avraham Shapira, in Friendship and Appreciation* (Jerusalem: Carmel, 2005)

Lee Kahaner, Gilad Malach, and Maya Hoshen, "The Yearbook of Ultra-Orthodox Society in Israel 2017" (Jerusalem: Israel Democracy Institute, Jerusalem Institute for Policy Research, 2017)

Yosef Kaplan, *From New Christians to New Jews* (Jerusalem: Zalman Shazar Center, 2002)

Yeshayahu Leibowitz and Aviezer Ravitzky, *Dialogue on Faith and Philosophy* (Tel Aviv: Ministry of Defense, 2006)

Nissim Leon, "Soft Ultra-Orthodoxy: Religious Renewal in Oriental Jewry in Israel" (Jerusalem: Yad Yitzhak Ben-Zvi, 2010)

Avraham Leslau and Mordechai Bar-Lev, *The Religious World of State Religious Education Graduates* (Ramat Gan: Bar-Ilan University, 1993)

Avraham Leslau and Yisrael Rich, *Research Report: Religious State Education, Survey of 12th Graders* (Ramat Gan: Bar-Ilan University, 2001)

Yagil Levy, *The Divine Commander: The Theocratization of the Israeli Military* (Tel Aviv: Am Oved, 2015)

Charles Liebman, "The Culture Wars in Israel: A New Mapping" in Anita Shapira (ed.), *State in the Making: Israeli Society in the First Decades* (Jerusalem: Zalman Shazar Center, 2001)

Yaakov Lupo, "Shas: Historical Depth" in Aviezer Ravitzky, *Shas: Cultural and Ideological Perspectives* (Tel Aviv: Am Oved, 2006)

Moshe Zvi Neria, *The Contours of the Debate*, 1951

Haim Nirel, *The Haredim and the Holocaust: Ultra-Orthodox Accusations of Zionist Responsibility for the Holocaust* (Jerusalem: Carmel, 1997)

Uri Orbach, *Religious as Normal* (Rishon Lezion: Yediot Books, 2018)

Ari Paltiel et al., *Long-Range Population Projections for Israel: 2009-2059* (Jerusalem: Central Bureau of Statistics, 2012) [Hebrew], accessible at https://www.cbs.gov.il/he/publications/DocLib/tec/tec27/tec27.pdf

Yochanan Peres and Eliezer Ben-Rafael, *Cleavages in Israeli Society* (Tel Aviv: Am Oved, 2006)

Malka Puterkovsky, *Following Her Halakhic Way* (Tel Aviv: Yediot Aharonot, 2014)

Yoel Rafel, *The Prayer for the Welfare of the State of Israel* (Tel Aviv: Kinneret-Zemora-Bitan, 2018)

Yisrael Rosen, "Shabbat in an Independent Jewish State" in Yedidia Z. Stern and Yair Sheleg (eds.), *Zionist Halakha* (Jerusalem: Israel Democracy Institute, 2017)

Shmuel Rosner, *The Jews: Seven Frequently Asked Questions* (Tel Aviv: Dvir, Museum of the Jewish People, 2016)

Shmuel Rosner, *Shtetl, Bagel, Baseball* (Jerusalem: Keter, 2011)

Amnon Rubinstein, *Tribes of the State of Israel: Together and Separately; Liberalism and Multiculturalism in Israel* (Hevel Modiin: Dvir, 2017)

Moshe Sicron, *Demography: The Israeli Population – Characteristics and Trends* (Jerusalem: Carmel, 2004)

Ilana Shamir, *So They Shall Not Be As If They Had Not Been: Establishing Commemorative Patterns—The Unit for the Commemoration of Fallen Soldiers* (Tel Aviv: Ministry of Defense, 2003)

Rachel Sharabi, *The Mimouna Holiday: From Periphery to the Center* (Tel Aviv: Hakibbutz Hameuchad, 2009)

Michal Shaul, *Beauty for Ashes: Holocaust Memory and the Rehabilitation of Ashkenazi Haredi Society in Israel 1945–1961* (Jerusalem: Yad Vashem and Yad Yitzhak Ben-Zvi, 2014)

Yosef Shilhav, *A Town in a City: The Geography of Separation and Integration* (Jerusalem: Jerusalem Institute for Israel Studies, 1991)

Hizky Shoham, *Let's Celebrate! Festivals and Civic Culture in Israel* (Jerusalem: Israel Democracy Institute, 2014)

# Bibliography

Zvi Shua, *History of the Kibbutz Haggadah* (Beit Hashita: Shitim, 2011)

Daniel Sperber, *Minhagei Yisrael: Origins and History*, vol. 1, 8 vols. (Jerusalem: Mossad Harav Kook, 1998–2007)

Joseph Tabory, *The Passover Ritual Throughout the Generations: Chapters from the History of Seder Night* (Tel Aviv: Hakibbutz Hameuchad, 1996)

Gadi Taub, *What Is Zionism* (Tel Aviv: Yediot Aharonot and Hemed Books, 2010)

Yaron Tsur, *A Torn Community: The Jews of Morocco and Nationalism 1943-1954* (Tel Aviv: Am Oved, 2001)

Shay Zarchi, "Reflections on Bialik's Conception of Halakha" in Avraham Shapira (ed.), *The Heart's Furrow: A Tribute to Muki Tzur* (Tel Aviv: Hakibutz Hameuchad, 2006)

## Hebrew Articles and Reports

Ari Alon and Yona Arazi, "Secular Judaism According to Bialik," *Deot* 79 (2017)

David Aronovsky and Gideon Sapir, "The Position of the Halakhic *Poskim* on the Matter of the Activity of the Security Forces and Vital Services on Shabbat," *Dine Israel* 31 (2016)

Dana Blander, "Old and New Cleavages in Israeli Society—a Perspective from Public Opinion Polls," *Parliament (Journal of Israel Democracy Institute)* 81 (2017)

Yishai Blank, "Islands of Pluralism: Segregation and Integration between Secular and Religious Jews," *Haifa University Law Review*, 6 (2011)

Yishai Blank and Issi Rosen-Zvi, "The Municipalities Bill: Present Without Past, Reform with No Future," *Hukim 1: Journal of Legislation*, 49 (2009)

Yisrael Brand, "The Argument Over Bible Study in Recent Generations", *Hemdaat*, 1 (2011)

Chaim Burgansky, "Zionist Halakhah in the Rulings by Rabbi Herzog" in Yedidia Stern and Yair Sheleg (eds.) *Zionist Halakha* (Jerusalem: Israel Democracy Institute, 2018)

Kimmy Caplan, "The Scholarly Study of Jewish Religious Society in Israel: Achievements, Missed Opportunities, and Challenges," *Megamot* 51:2 (2017)

Shlomo Deshen, "The Religiosity of the Mizrahim: Public, Rabbis, and Belief," *Alpayim* 9 (1994)

Shuki Friedman, "The Erosion of the Status Quo in the Religion-State Relationship," *Parliament (Journal of the Israel Democracy Institute)*, 81 (2018)

Ruth Gavison, "Constitutional Anchoring of Israel's Vision: Recommendations Submitted to the Minister of Justice" (2014)

Ruth Gavison and Uri Schwartz, "Segregated Housing as an Element in Discrimination: The American Experience," *Iyunei Mishpat (Tel Aviv University Law Review)* 25 (2001)

Tamar Hermann et al., "The National-Religious Sector in Israel 2014" (Jerusalem: Israel Democracy Institute, 2014)

Benjamin Ish-Shalom, "External and Internal Challenges on the Agenda of Religious Zionism," *Akdamot* 6 (1999)

Asher Cohen, "The Knitted Kippah and What's Behind It," *Akdamot* 15 (2004)

Rani Jaegar, "Bialik's Halakha and Aggadah: From Reading to Reading," *Bein Hashmashot, A*, Hartman Institute (2013)

Aryeh Kasher, "Jerusalem as a 'Metropolis' in Philo's National Consciousness," *Cathedra* 11 (1979)

Rafi Mann, "How Were Yom Haatzmaut and Yom Hazikaron Invented?" *Footnotes to History* blog (23.04.2012)

Daniel Mishori and Daniel Robinson, "The Israeli Yom Kippur: An Opportunity for Introspection about the Environment and Public Space," *Ecology and Environment* 4 (2011)

Moshe Nissim, "Conversion in Israel: Report and Recommendations" (2018)

Michal Shaul, "The Regeneration of Ultra-Orthodox (Haredi) Society after the Holocaust: Starting with the Old," *Iyunim Bitkumat Israel (Studies in Zionism, the Yishuv, and the State of Israel)* 20 (2010)

Yair Sheleg, "The Split in Religious Zionism—Past, Present, Future," *Deot* 46 (2010)

Eli Silver, "The Jewish Identity Card: Beliefs, Religious Observance, and Values of Jews in Israel, 2000," *Tzohar* 11 (2002)

Amnon Shapira, "Religious Zionism between Ultra-Orthodoxy and Modernity," *Akdamot* 26 (2011)

Anita Shapira, "Berl Katznelson's Conception of Culture," *Kesher* 35 (2007)

Yoav Sorek, "The Emergence of the Israeli Tradition," *Hashiloach* 10 (2018)

Avrum Tomer, "No Tribes, and No Forest," *Hashiloach* 3 (02.2017)

Yaacov Yadgar and Charles Liebman, "Jewish Traditionalism and Popular Culture in Israel," *Iyunim Bitkumat Israel (Studies in Zionism, the Yishuv, and the State of Israel)* 13 (2003)

Michael Zalba, "The Demography of Religiosity," *Chotam* (undated)

Michael Zalba, "Demography of Religiosity: Secularization in the Orthodox and Traditionalist Publics," *Chotam* (undated)

# Bibliography

## Hebrew Press

Shmuel Avneri, "Bialik and the cultural and religious emptiness; in the Land of Israel," *Haaretz* (07.07.2011)

Michael Avraham, "On the 'Decree' of Kitniyot: Conservatism and Hilul Hashem (Column 2)," published on https://mikyab.net (2016)

David Bar-Haim, "Whence Kitniyot from the Torah?" published on Machon Shilo website (www.hip.machonshilo.org) (2009)

Yehuda Brandes, "The Price of the Spectrum," *Makor Rishon* (04.08.2018)

Noam Buksbaum, "There are two states here: of universities and hi-tech—and everything else," *TheMarker* (07.08.2016)

Merav Crystal, "'Crazy Shopping Day': A Map of the Businesses Open on Shabbat in Israel," *YNet* (31.12.2017)

Yehuda Eisenberg, "Yibbum and Redemption in the Book of Ruth," *Daat*, accessible at: http://www.daat.ac.il/daat/tanach/megilot/yibum.htm

Tsur Ehrlich, "The First Post-Orthodox Jew: With Yoav Sorek on the Renewal of Judaism and the Removal of the Kippah," *Makor Rishon* (22.01.2010)

Dov Elboim, "The Real First Offerings of Our Generation," *YNet* (17.05.2018)

Racheli Ibenboim, "Fearful of the Holocaust: Holocaust Remembrance from a Haredi Perspective," *Tzarich Iyun* (23.04.2017)

Moshe Ifergan, "The Post-Zionist Shift of President Rivlin," *Mida* (31.12.2015)

Shahar Ilan, "Voting with their Rings," *Hiddush* (21.08.2014)

Shmuel Faust, "The Freedom to Know," *Makor Rishon* (04.2012)

Yael Freund Avraham, "The Death of the Atheist Kibbutz," *Makor Rishon* (06.12.2015)

Shuki Friedman, "Wage Jihad, IDF," *Haaretz* (14.12.2016)

Yuval Noah Harari, "The Secular Truth," *Yediot Aharonot* (31.08.2017)

Uri Heitner, "Collaborative-Innovative," *Shavim* (06.01.2008)

Rabbi Shmuel Holstein, "Bicycle Riding on Yom Kippur," *Yeshiva* (06.10.2008)

Micah Goodman, "An Encounter of the Perplexed on Both Sides," *Makor Rishon* (26.10.2015)

Ruth Kabbesa-Abramzon, "An Answer for Anyone Afraid of the Shabbat Unplugged Initiative," *Haaretz* (31.05.2018)

Neria Knafo, "Ashkenazi Men: Don't Take Over My Mimouna and Culture," *Kippa* (2017)

See Racheli Malek Boda, "Shabbat Shalom, Awake? Meet the New Orthodox," *Makor Rishon* (25.07.2013)

Uri Misgav, "The Religionization War: Have We Reached the Turning Point?" *Haaretz* (02.08.2018)

Shmuel Rosner, "The Status Quo is Not Even Relevant: Five Observations about the Supermarkets Law," *Maariv* (02.01.2018)

Shmuel Rosner, "The Debate Over the Character of Shabbat Has Become Righteous and Inconsistent," *Maariv* (08.09.2016)

Shmuel Rosner, "New Poll of Parents: Is There Religionization in the Israeli Education System?" *Maariv* (26.09.2017)

Shmuel Rosner, "In Constant Flux: The Great Challenge of Reform Jews in Israel," *Maariv* (27.07.2015)

Tamar Rotem, "The Haredim are Discovering Yad Vashem," *Haaretz* (22.02.2005)

Amnon Shapira and Yohanan Ben Yaacov, "The Issue of Shabbat in Israel: Not to Force—to Regularize," *Makor Rishon* (26.10.2018)

Noa Shpiegel, "From Cowshed to Synagogue: Kibbutzim Compromise on Secular Identity in Bid to Survive," *Haaretz* (03.05.2016)

Avraham Tenenbaum, "On the Wisdom of the Public and the Determination of Halakha," *Daat*, accessible at: http://www.daat.ac.il/mishpat-ivri/skirot/338-2.htm

Ron Tira, "In his Tribes speech, President Rivlin turned Hebrewness into a relic of a forgotten civilization," *Maariv* (27.10.2016)

Benny Toker, "No Reform Jews in Israel, Synagogues are Empty," *Arutz Sheva* (02.07.2018)

Naama Tsabar Ben Yehoshua and Yona Sorek, "Tikkun Leil Shavuot: Renewal of Secular Judaism," *YNet* (11.05.15)

David Tversky, "We Can Still Repair," *Davar Rishon* (10.06.2016)

Ram Vromen, "The Empty Cart is Full of Screens," *Haaretz* (29.05.2018)

"Upheaval: Dining Hall of Kibbutz Ein Harod in the North Made Kosher," *Yom Leyom* (2016)

"Ask the Rabbi: Bicycle Riding on Yom Kippur," *Kippa* (01.09.2010)

"1,150,000 flags will be flown in Israel on Independence Day" *Srugim* (20.04.2015)

"The Restaurants That Will Open and Those That Will Close," *Time Out Tel Aviv* (July 2017)

"Attention Tel Avivians (and Inspectors): These Are the Places Open Tonight, Tisha B'Av," *Haaretz* (31.07.2017)

"For the Revolution, Against the Revolutionary," *Globes* (13.09.2000)

"Barak: Buses on Shabbat within Two Weeks," *Walla* (09.09.2000)

"Barak Presents: The Secular Reformation," *YNet* (20.08.2000)

"Poll: Rabbinate Weddings Drive Israelis away from Religious Marriage," *YNet* (09.08.2016)

# Bibliography

## English Books

Hannah Arendt (Jerome Kohn and Ron H. Feldman, eds.), *The Jewish Writings* (New York: Schocken Books, 2007)

Daphne Barak-Erez, *Outlawed Pigs: Law, Religion and Culture in Israel* (Madison: University of Wisconsin Press, 2007)

Guy Ben-Porat, *Between State and Synagogue: The Secularization of Contemporary Israel* (Cambridge: Cambridge University Press, 2013)

Shaye J. D. Cohen, *The Beginnings of Jewishness: Boundaries, Varieties, Uncertainties* (Berkeley: University of California Press, 1999)

Eliezer Berkovits, *Faith After the Holocaust* (New York: KTAV Publishing House, 1973)

Haim Nahman Bialik (trans. Leon Simon), "Halacha and Aggadah" in Haim Nahman Bialik, *Revealment and Concealment: Five Essays* (Jerusalem: Ibis Editions, 2000)

Shlomo Hasson (trans. Eetta Prince-Gibson), *State and Religion in Israel: Possible Scenarios* (College Park, MD: The Joseph and Alma Gildenhorn Institute for Israel Studies, 2015)

Menachem Friedman, "The State of Israel as a Theological Dilemma" in Baruch Kimmerling (ed.), *The Israeli State and Society: Boundaries and Frontiers* (New York: SUNY Press, 1987)

Yosef Gorny, *Converging Alternatives: The Bund and the Zionist Labor Movement, 1897-1985* (New York: SUNY Press, 2012)

Ahad Ha'am, "The Jewish State and the Jewish Problem" in Arthur Hertzberg (ed.), *The Zionist Idea: A Historical Analysis and Reader* (Philadelphia and Jerusalem: The Jewish Publication Society, 1997)

Gideon Katz, *Pale God: Israeli Secularism and Spinoza's Philosophy of Culture* (Boston, MA: Academic Studies Press, 2011)

Rabbi Shmuel Katz, "Establishing a Holiday: The Chief Rabbinate and Yom HaAtzma'ut" in Rabbi Moshe Taragin et al. (eds.), *The Koren Maḥzor for Yom Haatzma'ut and Yom Yerushalayim* (Jerusalem: Koren Publishers, 2015)

Berl Katznelson, "Revolution and Tradition" in Arthur Hertzberg (ed.), *The Zionist Idea: A Historical Analysis and Reader* (Philadelphia and Jerusalem: The Jewish Publication Society, 1997)

Dan Michman, "The Impact of the Holocaust on Religious Jewry," in Yisrael Gutman (ed.), *Major Changes Within the Jewish People in the Wake of the Holocaust* (Jerusalem: Yad Vashem, 1996)

Amos Oz (trans. Nicholas de Lange), *Judas* (London: Chatto & Windus, 2014)

Dina Porat, "'Amalek's Accomplices': Blaming Zionism for the Holocaust: Anti-Zionist Ultra-Orthodoxy in Israel in the 1980s," *Journal of Contemporary History*, vol. 27, no. 4 (1992)

Stephen Prothero, *God Is Not One: The Eight Rival Religions that Run the World* (New York: Harper One, 2011)

Itamar Rabinovich and Jehuda Reinharz (ed.), *Israel in the Middle East: Documents and Readings on Society, Politics, and Foreign Policy, Pre-1948 to the Present* (2nd ed.) (Waltham, Mass.; Brandeis University Press, 2008)

Steven R. Weisman, *The Chosen Wars: How Judaism Became an American Religion* (New York: Simon and Schuster, 2018)

James Emery White, *The Rise of the Nones: Understanding and Reaching the Religiously Unaffiliated* (Grand Rapids, MI: Baker Books, 2014)

Alexander Yakobson, "Is Israeli Society Disintegrating? Doomsday Prophecies and Facts on the Ground," in Fania Oz-Salzberger and Yedidia Z. Stern (eds.), *The Israeli Nation-State: Political, Constitutional, and Cultural Challenges* (Boston: Academic Studies Press, 2014)

Phil Zuckerman, "The Rise of the Nones: Why More Americans are Becoming Secular, and What that Means for America" in Anthony Pinn (ed.), *Theism and Public Policy: Humanist Perspectives and Responses* (New York: Palgrave Macmillan, 2014)

## English Articles and Reports

Asher Ariann et al., "A Portrait of Israeli Jews: Beliefs, Observance, and Values of Israeli Jews, 2009" (Jerusalem: Israel Democracy Institute, 2009), accessible at: https://en.idi.org.il/media/5439/guttmanavichaireport2012_eng-final.pdf

Yoav Artsieli, "The Gavison-Medan Covenant: Main Points and Principles" (Jerusalem: Israel Democracy Institute, 2004), accessible at: https://en.idi.org.il/media/5308/gavisonmedancompact-mainprinciples.pdf

Steven Cohen et al., "Together and Apart: Israeli Jews' Views on Their Relationship to American Jews and Religious Pluralism, Findings from UJA-Federation's Survey of Israeli Jews 2017," accessible at: https://www.ujafedny.org/api/assets/789241/

Elan Ezrahi, "Israelis, American Jewry, and American Judaism: Analysis of Israeli Attitudes, Mapping of Interventions, and Reflections," 2018.

Aviezer Ravitzky, "Is a Halakhic State Possible? The Paradox of Jewish Theocracy," *Israel Affairs* 11:1 (2005)

Uzi Rebhun and Gilad Malach, "Demographic Trends in Israel" (Jerusalem: Metzilah Center for Zionist, Jewish, Liberal and Humanist Thought, 2009), accessible at http://www.metzilah.org.il/webfiles/fck/file/Demo%20eng%20final_pdf-%20%D7%A0%D7%95%D7%A1%D7%97%20%D7%A1%D7%95%D7%A4%D7%99.pdf.

# Bibliography

Jonathan Sarna, "The Cult of Synthesis in American Jewish Culture," *Jewish Social Studies* 5:1-2 (1998-99)

Alex Weinreb and Nachum Blass, *Trends in Religiosity Among the Jewish Population in Israel* (Jerusalem: Taub Center for Social Policy Studies in Israel, 2018), accessible at: http://taubcenter.org.il/wp-content/files_mf/trendsinreligiosity.pdf.

Avishalom Westreich and Pinhas Shifman, "A Civil Legal Framework for Marriage and Divorce in Israel" (Jerusalem: The Metzilah Center for Zionist, Jewish, Liberal and Humanist Thought, 2013), accessible at: www.metzilah.org.il/1153

Arthur J. Wolak, "Ezra's Radical Solution to Judean Assimilation," *Jewish Bible Quarterly*, 40:2 (April 2012)

Israel's Religiously Divided Society," Pew Research Center (2016), accessible at: http://www.pewforum.org/2016/03/08/israels-religiously-divided-society/

"A Portrait of Jewish Americans: Findings from a Pew Research Center Survey of U.S. Jews," Pew Research Center (2013), accessible at: http://www.pewresearch.org/wp-content/uploads/sites/7/2013/10/jewish-american-full-report-for-web.pdf.

"Being Christian in Western Europe," Pew Research Center (2018), accessible at: https://www.pewforum.org/2018/05/29/being-christian-in-western-europe/

"America's Changing Religious Landscape," Pew Research Center (2015), accessible at: https://www.pewforum.org/2015/05/12/americas-changing-religious-landscape

Report of the Neeman Committee on Conversion Proposals (11 February 1998), accessible on the website of the Israeli Ministry of Foreign Affairs: https://mfa.gov.il/MFA/ForeignPolicy/MFADocuments/Yearbook12/Pages/17%20Report%20of%20the%20Neeman%20Committee%20on%20Conversion%20Pr.aspx

"The Peace Index—October 2017," *Israel Democracy Institute*, accessible at: http://www.peaceindex.org/files/Peace_Index_Data_November_2017-Eng.pdf

## English Press

Anti-Defamation League, et al., "Letter to Prime Minister Netanyahu Concerning the Safety and Future of African Asylum Seekers" (05.04.2018), accessible at: https://www.adl.org/news/letters/letter-to-prime-minister-netanyahu-concerning-the-safety-and-future-of-african-asylum

Shmuel Avneri, "Spending Shabbat With Bialik," *Haaretz* (17.07.2011), accessible at: https://www.haaretz.com/life/books/1.5367403

Michael Chabon, "Those People, Over There," *Tablet Magazine* (23.05.2018), accessible at: https://www.tabletmag.com/jewish-arts-and-culture/262965/michael-chabon-commencement

Chaim Eckstein, "Yom Kippur bike rental – secular fanaticism," *YNet* (09.06.2012), accessible at: https://www.ynetnews.com/articles/0,7340,L-4277660,00.html

Yair Ettinger, "Four Surveys Yield Different Totals for Haredi Population," *Haaretz* (21.04.2011), accessible at: https://www.haaretz.com/1.5002201.

Yair Ettinger, "When Rachelle Fraenkel Recited the Kaddish, the Chief Rabbi Said 'Amen'," *Haaretz* (02.07.2014), accessible at: https://www.haaretz.com/.premium-the-chief-rabbi-said-amen-1.5254214

Amos Harel, "Israeli Government Panel Decides to Keep God out of IDF Memorial Prayer," *Haaretz* (03.08.2011), accessible at: https://www.haaretz.com/1.5039402

Liam Hoare, "Reform and Conservative Judaism Have Failed in Israel. And It's Their Own Fault," *The Tower* (March 2015), accessible at: http://www.thetower.org/article/reform-and-conservative-judaism-have-failed-in-israel-and-its-their-own-fault/

Kobi Nachshoni, "Poll: Majority of Israelis stringently define Jews," *YNet* (18.09.2014), accessible at: https://www.ynetnews.com/articles/0,7340,L-4572269,00.html

Shmuel Rosner, "Rebels in Uniform: Why More Young Orthodox Women are Serving in the IDF," *Moment Magazine* (10.05.2018), accessible at: https://www.momentmag.com/rebels-in-uniform/

Shmuel Rosner, "Do Israeli Students Need to Visit Auschwitz?" *New York Times* (14.02.2018), accessible at: https://www.nytimes.com/2018/02/14/opinion/israel-poland-holocaust-auschwitz.html

Shmuel Rosner, "How Israel's Modern-Orthodox Jews Came Out of the Closet," *New York Times* (06.08.2016), accessible at: https://www.nytimes.com/2016/08/05/opinion/how-israels-modern-orthodox-jews-came-out-of-the-closet.html

Shmuel Rosner, "The Challenge of Counting Israeli Reform Jews," *Moment Magazine* (May 2019)

Shmuel Rosner, "The Lazy Jew—Keeping Jewishness Alive," *RealClearPolitics* (27.12.2018), accessible at: https://www.realclearpolitics.com/articles/2018/12/27/the_lazy_jew_-_keeping_jewishness_alive_139025.html

Shmuel Rosner, "Sukkot, the holiday of appropriate balance," *Jewish Journal* (09.10.2017), accessible at: https://jewishjournal.com/rosnersdomain/225528/sukkot-holiday-appropriate-balance/

Sigal Samuel, "Atheists Are Sometimes More Religious Than Christians," *The Atlantic* (31.05.2018), accessible at: https://www.theatlantic.com/international/archive/2018/05/american-atheists-religious-european-christians/560936/

Chemi Shalev, "Haaretz Poll for Rosh Hashanah, a Picture of Israel's Muddled Jewish Soul," *Haaretz* (09.09.2018), accessible at: https://www.haaretz.com/israel-news/.premium-for-rosh-hashanah-a-picture-of-israel-s-muddled-jewish-soul-1.6462847

Chemi Shalev, "Israelis Support Equal Rights for Reform and Conservative Jews—but Want U.S. Jews to Keep Their Mouths Shut," *Haaretz* (04.07.2017), accessible at: https://www.haaretz.com/israel-news/.premium.MAGAZINE-israelis-support-non-orthodox-jews-but-want-u-s-jews-to-shut-up-1.6242552.

# Bibliography

Chemi Shalev, "Haaretz Poll for Rosh Hashanah, a Picture of Israel's Muddled Jewish Soul," *Haaretz* (09.09.2018), accessible at: https://www.haaretz.com/israel-news/.premium-for-rosh-hashanah-a-picture-of-israel-s-muddled-jewish-soul-1.6462847

Chemi Shalev, "Netanyahu Owns Hotovely's Arrogant, Hypocritical anti-Semitic Attack on U.S. Jews," *Haaretz* (23.11.2017), accessible at: https://www.haaretz.com/israel-news/.premium-netanyahu-owns-hotovelys-hypocritical-anti-semitic-attack-on-u-s-jews-1.5626735

Stuart Winer, "Netanyahu bashes deputy FM for saying US Jews have it easy," *The Times of Israel* (23.11.2017), accessible at: https://www.timesofisrael.com/netanyahu-bashes-deputy-fm-for-criticizing-us-jews/

"58% of Israel's Jews fast on Yom Kippur," *YNet* (07.10.2011), accessible at: https://www.ynetnews.com/articles/0,7340,L-4132382,00.html

"Tel Aviv Yom Kippur bicycle rental irks Katz," *Globes* (02.09.2012), accessible at: https://en.globes.co.il/en/article-1000781612

"Tel-O-Fun offers free Tel Aviv bicycles on Yom Kippur," *Globes* (01.10.2014), accessible at: https://en.globes.co.il/en/article-tel-o-fun-offers-free-tel-aviv-bicycles-on-yom-kippur-1000975676

"With end of Passover, Israelis celebrate Mimouna," *The Times of Israel* (17.04.2017), accessible at: https://www.timesofisrael.com/with-end-of-passover-israelis-celebrate-mimouna/

"67% of Jewish Israelis support freedom of choice in marriage," *Hiddush* (07.08.2017), accessible at: http://hiddush.org/article-23232-0-67_of_Jewish_Israelis_support_freedom_of_choice_in_marriage.aspx

i24NEWS interview with Tzipi Hotovely (22.11.2017), accessible at: https://www.youtube.com/watch?v=MZ-ELTSytuc

# *Endnotes*

### Notes for the Introduction

1. See Gadi Taub, *What Is Zionism* (Tel Aviv: Yediot Aharonot and Hemed Books, 2010) [Hebrew]; Shmuel Rosner, *The Jews: Seven Frequently Asked Questions* (Tel Aviv: Dvir, Museum of the Jewish People, 2016) [Hebrew].
2. Ahad Ha'am, "The Jewish State and the Jewish Problem" in Arthur Hertzberg (ed.), *The Zionist Idea: A Historical Analysis and Reader* (Philadelphia and Jerusalem: The Jewish Publication Society, 1997), 267
3. This figure includes Jews who, on a scale of 1-10 for the question "how Jewish do you feel?" gave answers from 7 to 10.
4. Based on the same scale (see the previous footnote). The questions were "How certain are you that your children will be Jewish?" and "To what extent do you think your grandchildren will be Jewish?" In both cases, 87% of respondents gave answers between 7 and 10 inclusive.
5. Information about the institute and its other publications can be found on its website: http://jppi.org.il/new/en/about
6. Hannah Arendt (Jerome Kohn and Ron H. Feldman, eds.), *The Jewish Writings* (New York: Schocken Books, 2007), 378
7. Ibid., 378

### Notes for chapter 1

8. The removal of the shoe in the Book of Ruth, according to most commentators, is not evidence of a *halitza* ceremony but of a different type of property transfer ritual; but it has become settled in popular memory as an example of *halitza* because of the description by Flavius Josephus, among other reasons. See for example, Rabbi Abraham ibn Ezra on

Ruth 4:7; see also Yehuda Eisenberg, "Yibbum and Redemption in the Book of Ruth," *Daat*, accessible at: http://www.daat.ac.il/daat/tanach/megilot/yibum.htm [Hebrew].

The rest of the discussion on this matter is based on Deuteronomy 25:9; Babylonian Talmud Tractate *Yevamot* 102:a; Jerusalem Talmud Tractate *Pe'ah*; Daniel Sperber, *Minhagei Yisrael: Origins and History*, vol. 1, 8 vols. (Jerusalem: Mossad Harav Kook, 1998–2007), introduction [Hebrew]; Avraham Tenenbaum, "On the Wisdom of the Public and the Determination of Halakha," *Daat*, accessible at: http://www.daat.ac.il/mishpat-ivri/skirot/338-2.htm [Hebrew]; Babylonian Talmud Tractate Avoda Zara 36:1; Yuval Cherlow, *Jewish Ethics: The Slippery Slope (2)* (21.08.2018), accessible on Tzohar website [Hebrew]; Maimonides, *Mamrim* 2:6 [Hebrew].

9. Babylonian Talmud, *Yevamot* 102a:3, translated by William Davidson, available from the Sefaria Library at Sefaria.org.
10. Babylonian Talmud, *Eruvin* 14b, translated by William Davidson, available from the Sefaria Library at Sefaria.org.
11. This statistic applies to men alone. Women were asked in the survey about daily prayer.
12. This statistic refers to those who answered "to a small extent" (30%) and "not at all" (36%).
13. 36% "to a very great extent," 32% "to a great extent." This figure is an aggregation of data from two iterations of the survey, which produced similar but not identical results.
14. See Shlomo Fischer, "Jewish Identity in Israel Today" in the Jewish People Policy Institute report "2018 Annual Assessment of the Situation and Dynamics of the Jewish People," JPPI, accessible at: http://jppi.org.il/new/wp-content/uploads/2018/06/AA2018-GovEnglish.pdf
15. Stephen Prothero, *God Is Not One: The Eight Rival Religions that Run the World* (New York: Harper One, 2011), 307. See also the chapter "What Is Judaism?" in Rosner, *The Jews: Seven Common Questions* [Hebrew].
16. Yosef Kaplan, *From New Christians to New Jews* (Jerusalem: Zalman Shazar Center, 2002) [Hebrew]
17. Aryeh Kasher, "Jerusalem as a 'Metropolis' in Philo's National Consciousness," *Cathedra* 11 (1979) [Hebrew]
18. On *tikkun olam* as the main cultural motif of American Jewry, see: Shmuel Rosner, *Shtetl, Bagel, Baseball* (Jerusalem: Keter, 2011), especially the chapter "*Shibbutznikim*" [Hebrew]. See also Jonathan Krasner, "The Place of Tikkun Olam in American Jewish Life," *Jewish Political Studies Review* (2013), vol. 25, no. 3-4: 59-98.

19. Jonathan Sarna, "The Cult of Synthesis in American Jewish Culture," *Jewish Social Studies* 5:1-2 (1998-99): 52-79
20. "Israel's Religiously Divided Society," Pew Research Center (2016), accessible at: http://www.pewforum.org/2016/03/08/israels-religiously-divided-society/. See also "Jewish Identity in Israel Today" in "2018 Annual Assessment of the Situation and Dynamics of the Jewish People," 18-22.
21. According to data from the Israeli Central Bureau of Statistics, the proportion of traditionalists in Israel has fallen from 42% at the start of the 1990s to a little over 35% in recent years.
22. Yaacov Yadgar and Charles Liebman, "Jewish Traditionalism and Popular Culture in Israel," *Iyunim Bitkumat Israel (Studies in Zionism, the Yishuv, and the State of Israel)* 13 (2003) [Hebrew]
In our writing about traditionalist Jews in Israel, we also used the following sources: Meir Buzaglo, "The New Traditional Jew and the Halakha: a Phenomenology" in Moshe Orfali and Ephraim Hazan (eds.), *Progress and Tradition: Creativity, Leadership and Acculturation Processes Among the Jews of North Africa* (Bialik Institute: Jerusalem, 2005), 187-204 [Hebrew]; Meir Buzaglo, *A Language for The Faithful: Reflections on Tradition* (Jerusalem: Keter, 2009) [Hebrew]; Eli Silver, "The Jewish Identity Card: Beliefs, Religious Observance, and Values of Jews in Israel, 2000," *Tzohar* 11 (2002): 89-96 [Hebrew]; Israel Central Bureau of Statistics Social Survey 2009.
23. Micha Josef Berdyczewski, "Paths," accessible through the Ben Yehuda Project [Hebrew].
24. Amos Oz (trans. Nicholas de Lange), *Judas* (London: Chatto & Windus, 2014), 183
25. Gideon Katz, *Pale God: Israeli Secularism and Spinoza's Philosophy of Culture* (Boston, MA: Academic Studies Press, 2011)
26. Oz, *Judas*. The quotations are from Shealtiel Abravanel, a fictionalized member of the Provisional Government, who opposes Ben-Gurion's intention to declare independence.
27. See "Jewish Identity in Israel Today" in the Jewish People Policy Institute report "2018 Annual Assessment."

## Notes for chapter 2

28. Haim Nahman Bialik (trans. Leon Simon), "Halacha and Aggadah" in Haim Nahman Bialik, *Revealment and Concealment: Five Essays* (Jerusalem: Ibis Editions, 2000), 45.

29. References to Bialik have drawn on the following sources: Shay Zarchi, "Reflections on Bialik's Conception of Halakha" in Avraham Shapira (ed.), *The Heart's Furrow: A Tribute to Muki Tzur* (Tel Aviv: Hakibbutz Hameuchad, 2006) [Hebrew]; Rani Jaegar, "Bialik's Halakha and Aggadah" (Hartman Institute) [Hebrew]; Shmuel Avneri, "Bialik and the cultural and religious emptiness; in the Land of Israel," *Haaretz* (07.07.2011) [Hebrew]; Shmuel Avneri, "Spending Shabbat With Bialik," *Haaretz* (17.07.2011), accessible at: https://www.haaretz.com/life/books/1.5367403; Ari Alon and Yona Arazi, "Secular Judaism According to Bialik," *Deot* 79 (2017) [Hebrew]; Assaf Inbari, "In the Ranks of Gershom Scholem's Zionism" in Avihu Zakai et al. (eds.), *Fields in the Wind: A Tribute to Avraham Shapira, in Friendship and Appreciation* (Jerusalem: Carmel, 2005) [Hebrew].
30. References to the Leibowitz-Neria polemic have drawn on the following sources: Yisrael Rosen, "Shabbat in an Independent Jewish State" in Yedidia Z. Stern and Yair Sheleg (eds.), *Zionist Halakha* (Jerusalem: Israel Democracy Institute, 2017) [Hebrew]; Asher Cohen, "Orthodox Halakhic Commitment and the Challenge of Jewish Sovereignty: The Leibowitz-Neria Polemic in the Early 1950s," ibid. [Hebrew]; Asher Cohen, *The Tallit and the Flag: Religious Zionism and the Vision of the Torah State in the Early Years of the State* (Jerusalem: Ben Zvi Institute, 1998) [Hebrew]; Moshe Zvi Neria, *The Contours of the Debate*, 1951 (Jerusalem: Or Olam) [Hebrew]; David Aronovsky and Gideon Sapir, "The Position of the Halakhic *Poskim* on the Matter of the Activity of the Security Forces and Vital Services on Shabbat," *Dine Israel* 31 (2016): 197-247 [Hebrew]; Menachem Friedman, "The State of Israel as a Theological Dilemma" in Baruch Kimmerling (ed.), *The Israeli State and Society: Boundaries and Frontiers* (New York: SUNY Press, 1987), 165-215; Aviezer Ravitzky, "Is a Halakhic State Possible? The Paradox of Jewish Theocracy," *Israel Affairs* 11:1 (2005), 137-164. It is worth mentioning that Leibowitz later changed some of his positions regarding the relationship between religion and state, and regarding the desired character of the State of Israel.
31. Yeshayahu Leibowitz and Aviezer Ravitzky, *Dialogue on Faith and Philosophy* (Tel Aviv: Ministry of Defense, 2006) [Hebrew]
32. Avi Gil and Einat Wilf, "2030: Alternative Futures for the Jewish People" (2010), 18, accessible at: http://jppi.org.il/uploads/2030%20ENG.pdf
33. For a substantial expansion on the nature of the Jewish people's identity crisis, see Rosner, *The Jews: Seven Frequently Asked Questions* [Hebrew].

34. 88% rank their Judaism 7, 8, 9, or 10.
35. Respondents who answered "important" or "very important." The proportion of those who answered "a little important" was 8%; the proportion of those who answered "not important at all" was 5%. The same goes for the statistic on Jewish children in the same paragraph.
36. President Reuven Rivlin, Address to the 15th Annual Herzliya Conference "Israeli Hope: Towards a New Israeli Order" on 7 June 2015, accessible at: https://www.idc.ac.il/en/research/ips/Documents/4-Tribes/PresidentSPEECH2015.pdf
37. For criticism of the Four Tribes speech, see for example: Moshe Ifergan, "The Post-Zionist Shift of President Rivlin," *Mida* (31.12.2015) [Hebrew]; Avrum Tomer, "No Tribes, and No Forest," *Hashiloach* 3 (02.2017); Ron Tira, "In his Tribes speech, President Rivlin turned Hebrewness into a relic of a forgotten civilization," *Maariv* (27.10.2016) [Hebrew].
38. Charles Liebman, "The Culture Wars in Israel: A New Mapping" in Anita Shapira (ed.), *State in the Making: Israeli Society in the First Decades* (Jerusalem: Zalman Shazar Center, 2001) [Hebrew]
39. See "Israel's Religiously Divided Society" (Pew Research Center, 2016)
40. Shlomo Hasson (trans. Eetta Prince-Gibson), *State and Religion in Israel: Possible Scenarios* (College Park, MD: The Joseph and Alma Gildenhorn Institute for Israel Studies, 2015), 40
41. Figures from the Jewish People Policy Institute Pluralism Survey 2016.
42. Noam Buksbaum, "There are two states here: of universities and hi-tech—and everything else," *TheMarker* (07.08.2016) [Hebrew]
43. Israelis in the political center and leftwards believe so. The rest of the figures are from "A Portrait of Israeli Jews" (Israel Democracy Institute, 2009). For a broader overview, see: Dana Blander, "Old and New Cleavages in Israeli Society—a Perspective from Public Opinion Polls," *Parliament (Journal of Israel Democracy Institute)* 81 (2017) [Hebrew]. For figures and analysis on these matters, see all of the Jewish People Policy Institute's pluralism surveys; Amnon Rubinstein, *Tribes of the State of Israel: Together and Separately; Liberalism and Multiculturalism in Israel* (Or Yehudah: Dvir, 2017) [Hebrew]; Yochanan Peres and Eliezer Ben-Rafael, *Cleavages in Israeli Society* (Tel Aviv: Am Oved, 2006) [Hebrew]; findings of the Institute for Policy Studies survey on divisions in Israeli society, 2015.
44. Chana Eden et al., *Being Citizens in Israel: a Jewish and Democratic State* (Ministry of Education, 2001) [Hebrew]
45. Interestingly, traditionalist Jews are divided on this question and equal shares answer either way (each 39%).

46. Alexander Yakobson, "Is Israeli Society Disintegrating? Doomsday Prophecies and Facts on the Ground," in Fania Oz-Salzberger and Yedidia Z. Stern (eds.), *The Israeli Nation-State: Political, Constitutional, and Cultural Challenges* (Boston: Academic Studies Press, 2014), 292-293
47. Hasson's work features a similar chart, with an axis he calls "national-Zionist affinity" and another he calls "religious affinity." Hasson's map does not include a statistical analysis of Israeli society along these axes.
48. See Micha Josef Berdyczewski, "Changing Values: Thoughts" accessible through the Ben Yehuda Project [Hebrew]. For more on Berdyczewski and his approach to religion and tradition, see Avner Holtzman (ed.), *Micha Josef Berdyczewski: Studies and Documents* (Bialik Institute, Jerusalem: 2002) [Hebrew].
49. It is interesting to compare these Jews to the American Jews called "Jews not by religion" in a Pew Research Center study. See "A Portrait of Jewish Americans: Findings from a Pew Research Center Survey of U.S. Jews," Pew Research Center (2013), accessible at: http://www.pewresearch.org/wp-content/uploads/sites/7/2013/10/jewish-american-full-report-for-web.pdf.
See also Shlomo Fischer, "Who are the 'Jews by Religion' in the Pew Report?," JPPI (2013), accessible at: http://jppi.org.il/new/en/article/english-who-are-the-jews-by-religion-in-the-pew-report/.
50. Protocols of the Provisional Government 1, Session 1, 4; see also Ruth Gavison, "Constitutional Anchoring of Israel's Vision: Recommendations Submitted to the Minister of Justice" (2014) [Hebrew].

**Notes for chapter 3**

51. Yaron Harel, "The Chief Rabbinate and Twentieth Century Fox Present: No Movies on Saturday: An Episode in the Struggle for Public Sabbath Observance in Jerusalem, 1930-1945," *Cathedra* 157 (2015): 113-138 [Hebrew].
52. Ibid.
53. Guy Ben-Porat, *Between State and Synagogue: The Secularization of Contemporary Israel* (Cambridge: Cambridge University Press, 2013). The paragraphs that deal with the status quo also draw on the following sources: Shmuel Rosner, "The Status Quo is Not Even Relevant: Five Observations about the Supermarkets Law," *Maariv* (02.01.2018) [Hebrew]; Merav Crystal, "'Crazy Shopping Day': a Map of the Businesses Open on Shabbat in Israel," *YNet* (31.12.2017) [Hebrew].
54. *Seinfeld* episode no. 94 "The Mom and Pop Store" (Original air date: 17 Nov 1994). Script accessible at: http://www.seinfeldscripts.com/TheMomAndPopStore.html

# Endnotes

55. Ari Paltiel et al., *Long-Range Population Projections for Israel: 2009-2059* (Jerusalem: Central Bureau of Statistics, 2012) [Hebrew], accessible at https://www.cbs.gov.il/he/publications/DocLib/tec/tec27/tec27.pdf
56. Executive summary of Alex Weinreb and Nachum Blass, "Trends in Religiosity Among the Jewish Population in Israel" (16.05.2018), accessible at http://taubcenter.org.il/are-israeli-jews-becoming-more-secular-2/. For the full report, see: Alex Weinreb and Nachum Blass, *Trends in Religiosity Among the Jewish Population in Israel* (Jerusalem: Taub Center for Social Policy Studies in Israel, 2018), accessible at: http://taubcenter.org.il/wp-content/files_mf/trendsinreligiosity.pdf.
Michael Zalba, "The Demography of Religiosity," *Chotam* (undated) [Hebrew]
57. Rebhun and Malach, "Demographic Trends in Israel." A *Haaretz*-Dialog poll found that 34% of Israelis say that they observe tradition less than their parents, in contrast to 17% who say that they are more observant than their parents. See Chemi Shalev, "Haaretz Poll for Rosh Hashanah, a Picture of Israel's Muddled Jewish Soul," *Haaretz* (09.09.2018), accessible at: https://www.haaretz.com/israel-news/.premium-for-rosh-hashanah-a-picture-of-israel-s-muddled-jewish-soul-1.6462847.
58. Yagil Levy, *The Divine Commander: The Theocratization of the Israeli Military* (Tel Aviv: Am Oved, 2015) [Hebrew]
59. Shuki Friedman, "Wage Jihad, IDF," *Haaretz* (14.12.2016) [Hebrew]
60. For the story of Kibbutz Beit Alfa, see the 2015 documentary film *The Kosher Kibbutz* produced by Hagit Yaron and Eyal Tzarfati; Yael Freund Avraham, "The Death of the Atheist Kibbutz," *Makor Rishon* (06.12.2015) [Hebrew]; "Upheaval: Dining Hall of Kibbutz Ein Harod in the North Made Kosher," *Yom Leyom* (2016) [Hebrew]; Noa Shpiegel, "From Cowshed to Synagogue: Kibbutzim Compromise on Secular Identity in Bid to Survive," *Haaretz* (03.05.2016) [Hebrew].
61. Uri Misgav, "The Religionization War: Have We Reached the Turning Point?" *Haaretz* (02.08.2018) [Hebrew].
62. These figures relate to respondents who answered 7, 8, 9, or 10 when asked to assess the prevalence of religious coercion from 1-10, and likewise with secular coercion.
63. Tamar Hermann et al., "The National-Religious Sector in Israel 2014" (Jerusalem: Israel Democracy Institute, 2014), 125 [Hebrew]. The abridged English edition of the report contains the main findings, accessible at: https://en.idi.org.il/media/4663/madad-z-english_web.pdf.

64. See also Asher Ariann et al., "A Portrait of Israeli Jews: Beliefs, Observance, and Values of Israeli Jews, 2009" (Jerusalem: Israel Democracy Institute, 2009), accessible at: https://en.idi.org.il/media/5439/guttmanavichaireport2012_engfinal.pdf. See also JPPI Pluralism Survey 2018.

**Notes for chapter 4**

65. Babylonian Talmud, *Yoma* 19b, translated by William Davidson, available from the Sefaria Library at Sefaria.org.
66. See Hizky Shoham, *Let's Celebrate! Festivals and Civic Culture in Israel* (Jerusalem: Israel Democracy Institute, 2014) [Hebrew].
67. "Ask the Rabbi: Bicycle Riding on Yom Kippur," *Kippa* (01.09.2010) [Hebrew]. The halakhic questions about cycling are complex, and there have been important rabbis (such as the Ben Ish Chai, one of the greatest Sephardic rabbis of recent generations) who allowed cycling on Shabbat and festivals under certain conditions. Rabbi Shmuel Holstein, "Bicycle Riding on Yom Kippur," *Yeshiva* (06.10.2008) [Hebrew].
68. Statistics from the Jewish People Policy Institute. Questions about fasting on Yom Kippur have appeared in many other surveys. According to data from Guttman-AVI CHAI (2009), some 64% of Israelis always fast for the whole day on Yom Kippur, 4% always fast for part of the day, a further 4% frequently fast for the whole day, 7% do so from time to time, 6% occasionally, and 15% never. See "A Portrait of Israeli Jews" (Israel Democracy Institute, 2009). The Israeli Central Bureau of Statistics (2009) found that roughly half of secular and traditionalist Israelis fast on Yom Kippur (49.4%).
69. Asked "What is Yom Kippur for you?" 55% replied "a day of atonement and forgiveness," 11% "a good opportunity for body cleansing," 9% "a forced day of rest," and another 9% "an ideal day to ride a bicycle or watch movies." The remainder of the respondents (17%) did not answer. YNet-Gesher poll conducted by Panels in 2011, see "58% of Israel's Jews fast on Yom Kippur," *YNet* (07.10.2011), accessible at: https://www.ynetnews.com/articles/0,7340,L-4132382,00.html. A poll for Or Yarok, an NGO, by Geocartography in 2013 found that 36% of secular and traditionalist Israelis said they would ride a bicycle "next Yom Kippur."
70. Daniel Mishori and Daniel Robinson, "The Israeli Yom Kippur: An Opportunity for Introspection about the Environment and Public Space," *Ecology and Environment* 4 (2011): 314-315 [Hebrew].
71. Shoham, *Let's Celebrate! Festivals and Civic Culture in Israel*, 167 [Hebrew].

72. I heard this new take from Dr. Calderon at a conference in which we both appeared (Shmuel Rosner).
73. "Tel Aviv Yom Kippur bicycle rental irks Katz," *Globes* (02.09.2012), accessible at: https://en.globes.co.il/en/article-1000781612
74. "Tel-O-Fun offers free Tel Aviv bicycles on Yom Kippur," *Globes* (01.10.2014), accessible at: https://en.globes.co.il/en/article-tel-o-fun-offers-free-tel-aviv-bicycles-on-yom-kippur-1000975676
75. Chaim Eckstein, "Yom Kippur bike rental – secular fanaticism," *YNet* (09.06.2012), accessible at: https://www.ynetnews.com/articles/0,7340,L-4277660,00.html
76. We asked two versions of the same question and received an almost identical answer: some 64% of all Jews say they read "the whole Haggadah" (in one version) or "the whole Haggadah including the sections after the meal" (in the second version).
77. Shmuel Rosner and Camil Fuchs, "Who Reads the Haggadah Until the End?" *JPPI* (March 2018) [Hebrew].
78. The odd one out among the seven identity groups defined by the JPPI is the "totally secular" group—some 30% of all Jews in Israel—the large majority of whom (71%) suffice with reading "part of the Haggadah."
79. See Zvi Shua, *History of the Kibbutz Haggadah* (Beit Hashita: Shitim, 2011) [Hebrew]. See also Joseph Tabory, *The Passover Ritual Throughout the Generations: Chapters from the History of Seder Night* (Tel Aviv: Hakibbutz Hameuchad, 1996) [Hebrew].
80. Shmuel Faust, "The Freedom to Know," *Makor Rishon* (04.2012) [Hebrew].
81. Uri Heitner, "Collaborative-Innovative," *Shavim* (06.01.2008) [Hebrew].
82. Berl Katznelson, "Revolution and Tradition" in Hertzberg, *The Zionist Idea*, 392. This quote appears in the introduction to the 1955 Kibbutz Yagur Haggadah.
83. For more on the Haggadahs of American Jewry, see: Rosner, *Shtetl, Bagel, Baseball* [Hebrew], especially the chapter "Inventing a New Judaism."
84. *Beyt Tikkun 2007 Passover Haggadah Supplement*, accessible at: http://www.beyttikkun.org/article.php/2007HaggadahSupplement/print
85. See Rebhun, which draws on: Moshe Sicron, *Demography: The Israeli Population – Characteristics and Trends* (Jerusalem: Carmel, 2004) [Hebrew]. The figures are from "A Portrait of Israeli Jews" (Israel Democracy Institute, 2009).
86. Michael Avraham, "On the 'Decree' of Kitniyot: Conservatism and Hilul Hashem (Column 2)," published on https://mikyab.net (2016) [Hebrew].

87. David Bar-Haim, "Whence Kitniyot from the Torah?" published on Machon Shilo website (www.hip.machonshilo.org) (2009) [Hebrew].
88. According to the JPPI survey. According to Pew's 2015 study of Israeli Jewry, 12% of Ashkenazi Jews are Haredi, in comparison to 8% of Mizrahi Jews.
89. Figures from the 2016 JPPI Pluralism Survey, representing both those who answered "quite important" and "very important."
90. Rachel Sharabi, *The Mimouna Holiday: From Periphery to the Center* (Tel Aviv: Hakibbutz Hameuchad, 2009) [Hebrew].
91. Neria Knafo, "Ashkenazi Men: Don't Take Over My Mimouna and Culture," *Kippa* (2017) [Hebrew].
92. See the Israeli Central Bureau of Statistics: http://www.cbs.gov.il/shnaton63/st02_24x.pdf
93. "With end of Passover, Israelis celebrate Mimouna," *The Times of Israel* (17.04.2017), accessible at: https://www.timesofisrael.com/with-end-of-passover-israelis-celebrate-mimouna/

## Notes for chapter 5

94. Uri Orbach, *Religious as Normal* (Rishon Lezion: Yediot Books, 2018) [Hebrew].
95. "Israel's Religiously Divided Society" (Pew Research Center, 2016), 23
96. "A Portrait of Israeli Jews" (Israel Democracy Institute, 2009), 70.
97. 26% say "nationality" is the main component in their eyes, 20% "culture," 11% "ancestry."
98. "A Portrait of Israeli Jews" (Israel Democracy Institute, 2009), 71
99. For a short description see: Rafi Mann, "How Were Yom Haatzmaut and Yom Hazikaron Invented?" *Footnotes to History* blog (23.04.2012) [Hebrew].
100. See Maoz Azaryahu, *State Cults: Celebrating Independence and Commemorating the Fallen in Israel 1948-1956* (Sde Boker: Ben-Gurion University, 1995) [Hebrew]; Ilana Shamir, *So They Shall Not Be As If They Had Not Been: Establishing Commemorative Patterns—The Unit for the Commemoration of Fallen Soldiers* (Tel Aviv: Ministry of Defense, 2003) [Hebrew].
101. Anita Shapira, "Berl Katznelson's Conception of Culture," *Kesher* 35 (2007) [Hebrew].
102. Amos Harel, "Israeli Government Panel Decides to Keep God Out of IDF Memorial Prayer," *Haaretz* (03.08.2011), accessible at: https://www.haaretz.com/1.5039402

# Endnotes

103. The Haredim are the exception when it comes to standing for the siren: a large majority stand for the siren if they are out in public, but only a minority stand at home.
104. "1,150,000 flags will be flown in Israel on Independence Day" *Srugim* (20.04.2015) [Hebrew].
105. 66% of somewhat-traditional-secular Jews, 53% of the totally secular.
106. Israel State Archives, file ISA-PMO-Symbols-000b0qm [Hebrew].
107. Belkind's letter to Zeev Dubnov, cited in Alter Druyanov, *From Early Days*. A replica of the original flag is on display in the Rishon LeZion Museum.
108. Quoted in Rabbi Shmuel Katz, "Establishing a Holiday: The Chief Rabbinate and Yom HaAtzma'ut" in Rabbi Moshe Taragin et al. (eds.), *The Koren Mahzor for Yom Haatzma›ut and Yom Yerushalayim* (Jerusalem: Koren Publishers, 2015), 190. For more on the subject, see: Yoel Rafel, *The Prayer for the Welfare of the State of Israel* (Tel Aviv: Kinneret-Zemora-Bitan, 2018) [Hebrew].
109. Esther 9:22-23, JPS Version
110. For records of Knesset debates, see: Protocol 105 of the Knesset Constitution, Law, and Justice Committee, Tuesday 24 Tammuz 5757 (29 July 1997; Protocols/Interior Committee/4256, 16 Tevet 5762, 31 December 2001). For reports on open and closed restaurants, see: "The Restaurants That Will Open and Those That Will Close," *Time Out Tel Aviv* (July 2017) [Hebrew]; "Attention Tel Avivians (and Inspectors): These Are the Places Open Tonight, Tisha B'Av," *Haaretz* (31.07.2017).
111. Berl Katznelson, "Destruction and Uprooting," Davar (26.07.1934), English translation taken from Yosef Gorny, *Converging Alternatives: The Bund and the Zionist Labor Movement, 1897-1985* (New York: SUNY Press, 2012), 192
112. Moshe Shner, "Between Leadership of Holiness and Leadership of the Day-to-Day," *Eretz Acheret* 11 (July-August 2002) [Hebrew].

## Notes for chapter 6

113. Moshe Nissim, "Conversion in Israel: Report and Recommendations" (2018) [Hebrew].
114. For more see the chapter "Who is a Jew?" in Rosner, *Judaism: Seven Frequently Asked Questions* [Hebrew].
115. "Israel's Religiously Divided Society" (Pew Research Center, 2016), 110
116. "A Portrait of Israeli Jews" (Israel Democracy Institute, 2009), 39

117. 90% say that it is "important" or "very important" that they and their families observe Seder night.
118. Protocol of the 69th session of the 11th Knesset, 19 Adar 5745 (12 March 1985); Protocol of the 234th session of the 11th Knesset, 28 Tammuz 5746 (4 August 1986).
119. Daphne Barak-Erez, *Outlawed Pigs: Law, Religion and Culture in Israel* (Madison: University of Wisconsin Press, 2007)
120. Ibid., 107-108
121. Ibid., 113
122. Ibid., 114
123. The figures concerning Kashrut are mostly from the JPPI Pluralism survey 2019 and also from a Midgam Project poll for Mako, May 2016.
124. See for example the Hiddush Religion and State Index 2010. 53% oppose all religious legislation, and another 17% oppose any further religious legislation beyond what already exists.
125. See the Israeli Supreme Court ruling in a case known as "Bar Ilan Street," or Horev v. Minister of Transportation (13.04.1997). Unofficial English translation taken from "Versa: Opinions of the Israeli Supreme Court—a project of Cardozo Law," accessible at: http://versa.cardozo.yu.edu/opinions/horev-v-minister-transportation
126. Poll conducted for the "Be Free Israel" and "Secular Forum" movements by the Hamidgam Project company, led by Dr. Ariel Ayalon and supervised by Prof. Camil Fuchs, 2017.
127. See Arthur J. Wolak, "Ezra's Radical Solution to Judean Assimilation," *Jewish Bible Quarterly*, 40:2 (April 2012): 93-105; see also Chapter 7 ("The Rabbinic Conversion Ceremony) in Shaye J. D. Cohen, "The Beginnings of Jewishness: Boundaries, Varieties, Uncertainties (California: University of California Press, 1999), 198-238.
128. "A Portrait of Jewish Americans" (Pew Research Center, 2013) shows that 48% of millennial Jews were born to mixed marriages.
129. "A Portrait of Israeli Jews" (Israel Democracy Institute, 2009), 69
130. Poll conducted for Bina, cited in Kobi Nachshoni, "Poll: Majority of Israelis stringently define Jews," *YNet* (18.09.2014), accessible at: https://www.ynetnews.com/articles/0,7340,L-4572269,00.html
131. Tamar Hermann, et al., "The Israeli Democracy Index 2014" (Israel Democracy Institute, 2014), 38
132. Protocol 156 of the Aliyah and Absorption Committee, Tuesday 15 Sivan 5758 (9 June 1998).
133. JPPI's Pluralism Project survey, 2018.

134. Figure from the Hamidgam Project poll for Mako, May 2016. JPPI's figure for this question is 25%.

**Notes for chapter 7**

135. Haggai Harif, *Muscular Zionism* (Jerusalem: Yad Ben-Zvi, 2011) [Hebrew].
136. Ahad Ha'am, "Shabbat and Zionism," accessible through the Ben Yehuda Project [Hebrew].
137. This chapter makes use of data and examples from the unpublished JPPI report "Seven Decades since the Status Quo Letter" by Ohad Shpak. Ben-Gurion's agreement to delay debate became a policy for coexistence. Shpak's report maps out the main lines of contention on matters of religion and state in Israel and includes a comprehensive chapter on the dispute over Shabbat.
138. Rabin's speech and further documents from the time of the "brilliant ploy," Israel State Archives file A-4245/5 [Hebrew].
139. According to the extended Hebrew report of "A Portrait of Israeli Jews" (Israel Democracy Institute, 2009), 17.2% observe Shabbat "fully" and 15.4% "to a great extent."
140. Shmuel Rosner, "The Debate Over the Character of Shabbat Has Become Righteous and Inconsistent," *Maariv* (08.09.2016) [Hebrew].
141. JPPI Pluralism Index 2017, accessible at: http://jppi.org.il/new/en/article/english-2017-pluralism-index-survey-results/#.XJZDDxMzYxd. See also the JPPI Pluralism Index 2018.
142. In their "Foundation for a New Covenant among Jews in Matters of Religion and State in Israel," Rabbi Yaacov Medan and Prof. Ruth Gavison propose a compromise formula for various issues, including the character of Shabbat in Israel. See Yoav Artsieli, "The Gavison-Medan Covenant: Main Points and Principles" (Jerusalem: Israel Democracy Institute, 2004), accessible at: https://en.idi.org.il/media/5308/gavison-medancompact-mainprinciples.pdf
143. In the survey a very small percentage of respondents identified as "religious" and said they shopped, went on hikes, or traveled.
144. Among Haredim 98%, Dati-Torani 99%, National-Religious Jews 92%, Liberal-Religious Jews 48%.
145. Cited in Itamar Rabinovich and Jehuda Reinharz (ed.), *Israel in the Middle East: Documents and Readings on Society, Politics, and Foreign Policy, Pre-1948 to the Present* (2nd ed.) (Waltham, Mass.; Brandeis University Press, 2008), 59

146. Hours of Work and Rest Law—1951, accessible on the website of the International Labor Organization: https://www.ilo.org/dyn/natlex/docs/ELECTRONIC/36146/81476/F1584867301/ISR36146.pdf. See also the Supreme Court ruling in Horev v. Minister of Transportation (13.04.1997); Aviad Cohen, "The Day of Rest in a Jewish and Democratic State," *Daat* (2002) [Hebrew].
147. Ruth Kabbesa-Abramzon, "An Answer for Anyone Afraid of the Shabbat Unplugged Initiative," *Haaretz* (31.05.2018) [Hebrew].
148. Ram Vromen, "The Empty Cart Is Full of Screens," *Haaretz* (29.05.2018) [Hebrew].
149. The figures here are based on the JPPI survey. Other surveys have produced slightly different results: 56% in Pew, 66% in Guttman-AVI CHAI.
150. The law states that local bylaws concerning the opening and closing of businesses on days of rest will be subject to approval from the interior minister, and the interior minister shall only grant approval if he believes that the businesses must be open to provide vital services.
151. For the background of some of these covenants, see: https://gavison-medan.org.il/english/faq/
152. See Uri Dromi, *Brethren Dwelling Together: Orthodoxy and Non-Orthodoxy in Israel – Positions, Propositions, and Accords* (Jerusalem: Israel Democracy Institute, 2005) [Hebrew]; see also Tova Ilan and Batya Kahana-Dror, *Covenants in Israel: Attempts to Regularize Relations between Secular and Religious: Presented to the President of Israel, Mr. Moshe Katsav* (Jerusalem: Moetzet Yachad, 2005) [Hebrew].
153. Yoav Artsieli, "The Gavison-Medan Covenant," 55
154. Ruth Gavison, "The Shabbat Chapter in the Covenant" accessible on the Gavison-Medan Covenant website [Hebrew].
155. Amnon Shapira and Yohanan Ben Yaacov, "The Issue of Shabbat in Israel: Not to Force—to Regularize," *Makor Rishon* (26.10.2018) [Hebrew].
156. Shuki Friedman, "The Erosion of the Status Quo in the Religion-State Relationship," *Parliament (Journal of the Israel Democracy Institute)*, 81 (2018) [Hebrew].
157. See Naomi Gutkind-Golan, "The Heikhal Cinema Issue: A Symptom of Religious-Non-Religious Relations in the 1980s" in Charles Liebman (ed.), *Religious and Secular: Conflict and Accommodation Between Jews in Israel* (Jerusalem: Keter, 1990).
158. Ariel Finkelstein, *The Sabbath in Israel: The Full Picture* (Jerusalem: The Institute for Zionist Strategies, 2016) [Hebrew].

159. The figure for the religious population is lower than 100% mainly because some religious men answered "no" in the survey—probably because they do not light candles, but their wives do.

**Notes for chapter 8**

160. According to Pew (2015), 56% of secularists believe in God. The breakout numbers are from JPPI (2018).
161. The figures for "totally" and "somewhat-traditional" secular Israelis are from the JPPI study. According to the Mako study (2016), 27% of secular Israelis say they do not believe in God.
162. The secular Jews are not unique in the matter of faith. See for example: "Being Christian in Western Europe," Pew Research Center (2018), accessible at: https://www.pewforum.org/2018/05/29/being-christian-in-western-europe/. In this study one can see how Christians who do not live a religious lifestyle believe in God.

    In this context, see also Sigal Samuel, "Atheists Are Sometimes More Religious Than Christians," *The Atlantic* (31.05.2018), accessible at: https://www.theatlantic.com/international/archive/2018/05/american-atheists-religious-european-christians/560936/.
163. "Israel's Religiously Divided Society" (Pew Research Center, 2016)
164. Only 1% of the totally secular and 3% of the somewhat-traditional secularists answered "to a very great extent" on this question.
165. See also Guy Ben-Porat, *In Practice: The Secularization of Contemporary Israel* (Haifa: Pardes, 2016) [Hebrew].
166. See: JPPI Pluralism Index 2016; "For the Revolution, Against the Revolutionary," *Globes* (13.09.2000) [Hebrew]; "Barak: Buses on Shabbat within Two Weeks," *Walla* (09.09.2000) [Hebrew]; "Barak Presents: The Secular Reformation," *YNet* (20.08.2000) [Hebrew].
167. Rates of reading from the Torah at bar mitzvahs: 78% totally secular, 98% somewhat-traditional secular. For bat mitzvahs, the respective figures are 14% and 15%.
168. By "like everyone," we mean at a similar rate to everyone. Around half of adult Jews in Israel dress up on Purim (51%), and around half go to Purim parties (56%).
169. "A Portrait of Israeli Jews" (Israel Democracy Institute, 2009), 13
170. Shlomo Fischer, "JPPI Annual Assessment 2016," JPPI, accessible at: http://jppi.org.il/new/wp-content/uploads/2016/JPPI_2016_Annual_Assessment.pdf
171. Three observations:

Other studies have also attempted to distinguish between different groups on the non-religious spectrum. The Israeli Central Bureau of Statistics distinguishes between two groups of traditionalists—not-so-religious traditionalists and religious traditionalists. The Guttman-AVI CHAI study identifies a (small) group of anti-religious secularists. In our opinion, the division in the JPPI study is more useful and precise for understanding Israeli society, among other reasons because the secular group is the biggest group in Israel.

It is clear that any other distribution would slightly change the size of the groups. The division by the Central Bureau of Statistics takes people out of the secular group and moves them to the not-so-religious traditionalist group. See "The Social Survey 2009-2010" (Israeli Central Bureau of Statistics).

The division in the JPPI study was performed in advance, by means of various options presented to the survey participants. This obviously has implications for the results.

172. The figures in this paragraph are from a Reform Movement survey and the JPPI 2016 Pluralism Survey.
173. These figures relate to those who ranked themselves 8-10 (out of 10) on the question of how Jewish they feel. If we count only those who ranked themselves 9 or 10, this translates as 37% among the totally secular and 62% among the somewhat-traditional secular group.
174. This figure includes those who fast all day (7%) and for part of the day (6%) among somewhat-traditional secular Israelis.
175. Rates for those who study Judaism or perform Jewish rituals (Hebrew Bible, Mishnah, Talmud, Jewish philosophy and ethics, halakhic books, Jewish history): 9% for totally secular Jews, 24% for somewhat-traditional secular Jews.
176. JPPI Pluralism Survey 2016
177. The figures pertain to those who answered "to a great extent" or "to a very great extent." 47% of totally secular Israelis said "not at all," in contrast to 21% of the somewhat-traditional.
178. Without elaborating, it is clear that this phenomenon is characteristic of a worldview (more common among the secular population) that places the individual at the center, and therefore places less emphasis on rituals and symbols that are meant to exalt the collective and obscure personal independence.
179. Examples: traditionalist Jews, 21%, Haredim, 7%.
180. A similar gap was also found in the 2018 Pluralism Index survey, in relation to the question: "Try to assess how much religious coercion there is in Israel." (The poll offered a scale of 1-10.)

181. Ne'emanei Torah Va'Avodah poll, August 2016.
182. Avishalom Westreich and Pinhas Shifman, "A Civil Legal Framework for Marriage and Divorce in Israel" (Jerusalem: The Metzilah Center for Zionist, Jewish, Liberal and Humanist Thought, 2013), 49, accessible at: www.metzilah.org.il/1153
183. See "America's Changing Religious Landscape," Pew Research Center (2015), accessible at: https://www.pewforum.org/2015/05/12/americas-changing-religious-landscape/;

   James Emery White, *The Rise of the Nones: Understanding and Reaching the Religiously Unaffiliated* (Grand Rapids, MI: Baker Books, 2014); Phil Zuckerman, "The Rise of the Nones: Why More Americans are Becoming Secular, and What that Means for America" in Anthony Pinn (ed.), *Theism and Public Policy: Humanist Perspectives and Responses* (New York: Palgrave Macmillan, 2014), 37-52
184. Shmuel Rosner, "New Poll of Parents: Is There Religionization in the Israeli Education System?" *Maariv* (26.09.2017) [Hebrew]. The Panim poll figures are from this article.
185. Yuval Noah Harari, "The Secular Truth," *Yediot Aharonot* (31.08.2017) [Hebrew].
186. Micah Goodman, "An Encounter of the Perplexed on Both Sides," *Makor Rishon* (26.10.2015) [Hebrew]. A few terms have been slightly changed from the original text in the newspaper, in order for the quotation to be clear for readers of this book. Full disclosure: Shmuel Rosner is the editor of the books written by Harari and Goodman and was exposed in so doing to the ideas mentioned herein. Nevertheless, our interpretation of these two authors' positions does not necessarily reflect their positions as they would phrase them, and it is our responsibility alone.
187. Among the general public, 91% have a Hebrew Bible at home. Totally secular—78%. Somewhat-traditional—94%.

## Notes for chapter 9

188. Many articles and books have been written about theological responses to the Holocaust, and especially the response of Haredi society to the Holocaust. This chapter makes use of the following sources: Eliezer Berkovits, *Faith After the Holocaust* (New York: KTAV Publishing House, 1973); Yitz Greenberg, "Theology After the Holocaust" in Dan Michman (ed.), *The Holocaust in Jewish History: Historiography, Consciousness, Interpretations* (Jerusalem: Yad Vashem, 2005) [Hebrew]; Dan Michman, "The Impact of the Holocaust on Religious Jewry," in

Yisrael Gutman (ed.), *Major Changes Within the Jewish People in the Wake of the Holocaust* (Jerusalem: Yad Vashem, 1996); Michal Shaul, "The Regeneration of Ultra-Orthodox (Haredi) Society after the Holocaust: Starting with the Old," *Iyunim Bitkumat Israel (Studies in Zionism, the Yishuv, and the State of Israel)* 20 (2010) [Hebrew].

189. Menachem Friedman, *The Haredi Ultra-Orthodox Society: Sources, Trends, and Processes* (Jerusalem: The Jerusalem Institute for Israel Studies, 1991) [Hebrew].

190. Blaming Zionists for the Holocaust is a recurrent motif in many studies on the response of Haredi society to the Holocaust. See, for example, studies by Menachem Friedman and Dina Porat on this issue: Dina Porat, "'Amalek's Accomplices': Blaming Zionism for the Holocaust: Anti-Zionist Ultra-Orthodoxy in Israel in the 1980s," *Journal of Contemporary History*, vol. 27, no. 4 (1992): 695–729; the chapter "Upheavals in Confronting the Holocaust" in Kimmy Caplan, *The Internal Popular Discourse in Israeli Haredi Society* (Jerusalem: Zalman Shazar Center, 2007) [Hebrew]; Haim Nirel, *The Haredim and the Holocaust: Ultra-Orthodox Accusations of Zionist Responsibility for the Holocaust* (Jerusalem: Carmel, 1997) [Hebrew].

191. Michal Shaul, *Beauty for Ashes: Holocaust Memory and the Rehabilitation of Ashkenazi Haredi Society in Israel 1945–1961* (Jerusalem: Yad Vashem and Yad Yitzhak Ben-Zvi, 2014) [Hebrew].

192. "[Hezekiah] inserted a sword at the entrance of the study hall and said: Anyone who does not engage in Torah study shall be stabbed with this sword. As a result, they searched from Dan in the north to Beersheba in the south, and did not find an ignoramus. They searched from Gevat to Antipatris and did not find a male child, or a female child, or a man, or a woman who was not expert even in the complex halakhot of ritual purity and impurity." Babylonian Talmud, *Sanhedrin* 94b, translated by William Davidson, available from the Sefaria Library at Sefaria.org.

193. Israeli Central Bureau of Statistics population forecast 2015-2065. The Haredi population of Israel is expected to rise from 12% to 16% by 2030.

194. Reuven Gal, *Ultra-Orthodox ('Haredi') Jews in Israel's Society: A 2014 Status Report* (Haifa: Samuel Neaman Institute, 2015) [Hebrew]. Gilad Malach argues that it is difficult and problematic to try to classify people as Haredi, and that there is a broad spectrum of ultra-Orthodoxy. See also Yair Ettinger, "Four Surveys Yield Different Totals for Haredi Population," *Haaretz* (21.04.2011), accessible at: https://www.haaretz.com/1.5002201.

195. Around one-third of Haredim in the study (37%) defined themselves as "Mizrahi." For further discussion, see: Shlomo Deshen, "The Religiosity of the Mizrahim: Public, Rabbis, and Belief," *Alpayim* 9 (1994): 21-22 [Hebrew]. Nissim Leon, "Soft Ultra-Orthodoxy: Religious Renewal in Oriental Jewry in Israel" (Jerusalem: Yad Yitzhak Ben-Zvi, 2010) [Hebrew]. Yaakov Lupo, "Shas: Historical Depth" in Aviezer Ravitzky, *Shas: Cultural and Ideological Perspectives* (Tel Aviv: Am Oved, 2006), 123-151 [Hebrew]. Yaron Tsur, *A Torn Community: The Jews of Morocco and Nationalism 1943-1954* (Tel Aviv: Am Oved, 2001), 44-47 [Hebrew].
196. It is important to emphasize: the JPPI survey offered seven definitions. Obviously, in a distribution that offers fewer definitions—e.g., without "Dati-Torani" (also known as national-Haredi)—the share of Haredim would probably rise.
197. Lee Kahaner, Gilad Malach, and Maya Hoshen, "The Yearbook of Ultra-Orthodox Society in Israel 2017" (Jerusalem: Israel Democracy Institute, Jerusalem Institute for Policy Research, 2017) [Hebrew].
198. Tamar Rotem, "The Haredim Are Discovering Yad Vashem," *Haaretz* (22.02.2005) [Hebrew].
199. Caplan, *The Internal Popular Discourse in Israeli Haredi Society* [Hebrew].
200. Racheli Ibenboim, "Fearful of the Holocaust: Holocaust Remembrance from a Haredi Perspective," *Tzarich Iyun* (23.04.2017) [Hebrew], accessible at: https://iyun.org.il
201. In the JPPI Pluralism Surveys, Haredim and yeshiva students rank bottom in the perceptions of their contribution to Israel by secular Israelis, somewhat-traditional secular Israelis, traditionalists, and Liberal-Religious Jews. Their average score on a scale of 1-4 (minimal to maximal contribution) is 2.27. The Israeli average is 2.96. Soldiers get the highest score, of 3.82.
202. Shmuel Rosner and Dov Maimon, "The Haredi Challenge," JPPI (21.02.2013), accessible at: http://jppi.org.il/new/en/article/english-the-haredi-challenge/#.XJ-v0-szYxc. See also Shmuel Rosner and John Ruskay, "Jerusalem and the Jewish People: Unity and Division," JPPI, 2017), especially the chapter "The Haredi Issue: Culture and Economy," accessible at: http://jppi.org.il/new/wp-content/uploads/2017/Jerusalem-Dialogue-Report-English.pdf
203. 62% believe this "to a very great extent," much more than among Dati-Torani Jews, the next group on the ranking, 44% of whom believe this to a very great extent. A further 29% of Haredim believe this "to a great extent." Not a single Haredi respondent answered "not at all" to this

question (compared to 7% of Dati-Torani Jews, 9% of Orthodox Jews, and 22% of traditionalists).
204. Chemi Shalev, "Israelis Support Equal Rights for Reform and Conservative Jews—but Want U.S. Jews to Keep Their Mouths Shut," *Haaretz* (04.07.2017), accessible at: https://www.haaretz.com/israel-news/.premium.MAGAZINE-israelis-support-non-orthodox-jews-but-want-u-s-jews-to-shut-up-1.6242552. According to the poll published in this article, only 5% of Haredim would very much want to move to the United States, compared to 32% of the general population.
205. Living in Israel: 43% answered "to a great extent" or "to a very great extent."
206. "After the Zionist Revolution: Patterns of Jewish Collective Identity among Israeli Jews" in Fischer, "JPPI Annual Assessment 2016," 129
207. Yosef Shilhav, *A Town in a City: The Geography of Separation and Integration* (Jerusalem: Jerusalem Institute for Israel Studies, 1991) [Hebrew].
208. Yishai Blank, "Islands of Pluralism: Segregation and Integration between Secular and Religious Jews," *Haifa University Law Review*, 6 (2011): 85-137 [Hebrew].
209. Israel High Court of Justice 4906/98, Am Hofshi Association vs. Ministry of Construction and Housing. This ruling drew on a ruling concerning housing for Bedouins, HCJ 528/88, Avitan vs. Israel Lands Authority.
210. "Israel's Religiously Divided Society" (Pew Research Center, 2016), 28. Secular Israelis also have mainly secular friends (90%). Traditionalist and religious Jews are more likely to have friends from other groups.
211. 2018 JPPI Pluralism Survey. Other figures on mixed residential areas in the following paragraphs are from the 2017 JPPI Pluralism Survey.
212. Yishai Blank and Issi Rosen-Zvi, "The Municipalities Bill: Present Without Past, Reform with No Future," *Hukim 1: Journal of Legislation*, 49 (2009) [Hebrew].
213. Ruth Gavison and Uri Schwartz, "Segregated Housing as an Element in Discrimination: The American Experience," *Iyunei Mishpat (Tel Aviv University Law Review)* 25 (2001) [Hebrew].
214. For detailed analysis, see the 2018 JPPI Pluralism Survey.
215. "Israel's Religiously Divided Society" (Pew Research Center, 2016)

**Notes for chapter 10**

216. On a scale of 1-10, this rate reflects those who answered 8, 9, or 10 (82%).

217. Benjamin Ish-Shalom, "External and Internal Challenges on the Agenda of Religious Zionism," *Akdamot* 6 (1999) [Hebrew].
218. See Avraham Leslau and Mordechai Bar-Lev, *The Religious World of State Religious Education Graduates* (Ramat Gan: Bar-Ilan University, 1993) [Hebrew]. See also Avraham Leslau and Yisrael Rich, *Research Report: Religious State Education, Survey of 12th Graders* (Ramat Gan: Bar-Ilan University, 2001). See also "Israel's Religiously Divided Society" (Pew Research Center, 2016), 69.
219. From the general Jewish population, 19% are National-Religious and 9% of those drop out (46%). For a different quantitative summary that points to the same trend, see: Michael Zalba, "Demography of Religiosity: Secularization in the Orthodox and Traditionalist Publics," *Chotam* (undated) [Hebrew].
220. Hermann et al., "The National-Religious Sector in Israel 2014," 53 [Hebrew].
221. In surveys by the Israeli Central Bureau of Statistics, "Orthodox" and "traditionalist Orthodox" amount to 24% together. Hermann et al., "The National-Religious Sector in Israel 2014" puts the National-Religious group on 22%. This was also the share that emerged from the JPPI study (2018) by adding "Liberal-Religious," "National-Religious," and "Dati-Torani."
222. It is difficult to precisely estimate the size of a small group within a small group, but by weighting all the data aggregated from the JPPI surveys and other polls, we can induce that roughly one-tenth of those who identify as "Liberal-Religious" regard themselves as belonging to the Reform or Conservative movements.
223. Hermann puts the proportion of those who live in the settlements at 7%.
224. JPPI Pluralism survey 2019.
225. 36% in the Israeli Judaism survey, 25% in the JPPI 2019 Pluralism Survey.
226. Kimmy Caplan, "The Scholarly Study of Jewish Religious Society in Israel: Achievements, Missed Opportunities, and Challenges," *Megamot* 51:2 (2017): 207-250 [Hebrew].
227. See Shmuel Rosner, "Rebels in Uniform: Why More Young Orthodox Women are Serving in the IDF," *Moment Magazine* (10.05.2018), accessible at: https://www.momentmag.com/rebels-in-uniform/
228. See Shmuel Rosner, "How Israel's Modern-Orthodox Jews Came Out of the Closet," *New York Times* (06.08.2016), accessible at: https://www.nytimes.com/2016/08/05/opinion/how-israels-modern-orthodox-jews-came-out-of-the-closet.html

229. See Amnon Shapira, "Religious Zionism between Ultra-Orthodoxy and Modernity," *Akdamot* 26 (2011): 117-139
230. Malka Puterkovsky, *Following Her Halakhic Way* (Tel Aviv: Yediot Aharonot, 2014) [Hebrew].
231. Yair Ettinger, "When Rachelle Fraenkel Recited the Kaddish, the Chief Rabbi Said 'Amen'," *Haaretz* (02.07.2014), accessible at: https://www.haaretz.com/.premium-the-chief-rabbi-said-amen-1.5254214. Ettinger further elaborates on this subject in his book on Religious Zionism, which was edited by one of the authors of this book.
232. Asher Cohen, "The Knitted Kippah and What's Behind It," *Akdamot* 15 (2004) [Hebrew].
233. See Racheli Malek Boda, "Shabbat Shalom, Awake? Meet the New Orthodox," *Makor Rishon* (25.07.2013) [Hebrew]. A series of news reports by Akiva Novick for Israel's Channel 10 launched this phenomenon into the public consciousness. For criticism of the culture of "the spectrum," which blurs the boundaries of religiosity, see: Yehuda Brandes, "The Price of the Spectrum," *Makor Rishon* (04.08.2018) [Hebrew].
234. Yair Sheleg, "The Split in Religious Zionism—Past, Present, Future," *Deot* 46 (2010) [Hebrew].
235. 64% of Liberal-Religious Jews, 58% of the National-Religious, and 50% of Dati-Torani Jews say the definition of "Israeli Jew" describes them. Among Haredim, only 16% say it does; among the totally secular—48%.
236. David Tversky, "We Can Still Repair," *Davar Rishon* (10.06.2016) [Hebrew].
237. Naama Tsabar Ben Yehoshua and Yona Sorek, "Tikkun Leil Shavuot: Renewal of Secular Judaism," *YNet* (11.05.15) [Hebrew].
238. Dov Elboim, "The Real First Offerings of Our Generation," *YNet* (17.05.2018) [Hebrew].
239. Yoav Sorek, "The Emergence of the Israeli Tradition," *Hashiloach* 10 (2018) [Hebrew].
240. Tsur Ehrlich, "The First Post-Orthodox Jew: With Yoav Sorek on the Renewal of Judaism and the Removal of the Kippah," *Makor Rishon* (22.01.2010) [Hebrew].
241. Sorek, "The Emergence of the Israeli Tradition" [Hebrew].

## Notes for chapter 11

242. Benny Toker, "No Reform Jews in Israel, Synagogues are Empty," *Arutz Sheva* (02.07.2018) [Hebrew].

243. Survey for the Reform Movement conducted by Dialogue, supervised by Camil Fuchs, 2018. Pew 2016, Hiddush 2016.
244. See Shmuel Rosner and Avi Gil, "Israel as a Jewish and Democratic State: Perspectives from World Jewry," JPPI (2014), accessible at: http://jppi.org.il/uploads/jewish_and_democratic-eng.pdf
245. JPPI's Pluralism Index 2019.
246. Survey for the Reform Movement conducted by Dialogue, supervised by Camil Fuchs, 2018.
247. To understand the extent of the erosion of the Rabbinate's monopoly on weddings, add to this figure the very large number of weddings performed abroad—up to around one-fifth of all marriages between Israelis—whose nature is not always known. Also add the drop in the rate of Rabbinate-officiated marriages because of the sharp rise of unmarried cohabiting couples. For the data, see: Feferman, "Rising Streams"; Shahar Ilan, "Voting with their Rings," *Hiddush* (21.08.2014) [Hebrew]; Israeli Central Bureau of Statistics data on marriage, 2016.
248. For data on this issue see the JPPI Pluralism Survey 2016, also Hiddush polls: for example, the Hiddush Tu B'Av poll—"67% of Jewish Israelis support freedom of choice in marriage," *Hiddush* (07.08.2017), accessible at: http://hiddush.org/article-23232-0-67_of_Jewish_Israelis_support_freedom_of_choice_in_marriage.aspx. In the 2016 Pew study, the rate was even lower, at around 40%.
249. The data here are from the second iteration of the JPPI survey (for a methodological explanation of the two rounds, see the appendix). In the first round, the proportion of Reform and Conservative Jews was slightly lower (9%). The Reform Movement poll found 11% of secular Israelis are Reform or Conservative, as are 17% of traditionalist Jews. Among *dati* Jews, none are Reform or Conservative—11% from the total sample.
250. These facts emerged from a follow-up survey by the JPPI (Pluralism Survey 2019). They do not appear in the Hebrew edition of the book that was published prior to this survey. See: Shmuel Rosner, "The Challenge of Counting Israeli Reform Jews," *Moment Magazine* (May 2019).
251. The association between Reform and Conservative that this chapter espouses can be misleading. For example, when asked to what extent they feel Jewish, or are confident their children will be Jewish, or believe their grandchildren will be Jewish—Conservative Jews are significantly more likely to answer in the affirmative than Reform Jews.

252. Chaim Burgansky, "Zionist Halakhah in the Rulings by Rabbi Herzog" in Yedidia Stern and Yair Sheleg (eds.) *Zionist Halakha* (Jerusalem: Israel Democracy Institute, 2018) [Hebrew].
253. Data from the Reform Movement poll and the 2016, 2017, and 2018 JPPI Pluralism Surveys.
254. See for example: Liam Hoare, "Reform and Conservative Judaism Have Failed in Israel. And It's Their Own Fault," *The Tower* (March 2015), accessible at: http://www.thetower.org/article/reform-and-conservative-judaism-have-failed-in-israel-and-its-their-own-fault/
255. The question was on a scale of 1-10. The figures here pertain only to those who answered 10.
256. JPPI Pluralism Survey 2018.

**Notes for chapter 11**

257. i24NEWS interview with Tzipi Hotovely (22.11.2017), accessible at: https://www.youtube.com/watch?v=MZ-ELTSytuc
258. Stuart Winer, "Netanyahu bashes deputy FM for saying US Jews have it easy," *The Times of Israel* (23.11.2017), accessible at: https://www.timesofisrael.com/netanyahu-bashes-deputy-fm-for-criticizing-us-jews/
259. "The Peace Index—October 2017," *Israel Democracy Institute*, accessible at: http://www.peaceindex.org/files/Peace_Index_Data_November_2017-Eng.pdf
260. Chemi Shalev, "Netanyahu Owns Hotovely's Arrogant, Hypocritical anti-Semitic Attack on U.S. Jews," *Haaretz* (23.11.2017), accessible at: https://www.haaretz.com/israel-news/.premium-netanyahu-owns-hotovelys-hypocritical-anti-semitic-attack-on-u-s-jews-1.5626735
261. Shmuel Rosner, "The Lazy Jew—Keeping Jewishness Alive," *RealClearPolitics* (27.12.2018), accessible at: https://www.realclearpolitics.com/articles/2018/12/27/the_lazy_jew_-_keeping_jewishness_alive_139025.html
262. JPPI Pluralism Survey 2019. 30% completely agree, 28% agree, 17% somewhat agree, 23% disagree.
263. Elan Ezrahi, "Israelis, American Jewry, and American Judaism: Analysis of Israeli Attitudes, Mapping of Interventions, and Reflections," 2018.
264. Shmuel Rosner and John Ruskay, "70 Years of Israel-Diaspora Relations: The Next Generation," JPPI (2018), 18, accessible at: http://jppi.org.il/new/wp-content/uploads/2018/07/Dialogue-at-70-English.pdf
265. Michael Chabon, "Those People, Over There," *Tablet Magazine* (23.05.2018), accessible at: https://www.tabletmag.com/jewish-arts-and-culture/262965/michael-chabon-commencement

266. Data from: Sylvia Barack Fishman and Steven M. Cohen, "Family, Engagement, and Jewish Continuity among American Jews Sylvia Barack Fishman and Steven M. Cohen," JPPI, accessible at: http://jppi.org.il/new/wp-content/uploads/2017/06/Raising-Jewish-Children-Research-and-Indicators-for-Intervention.pdf
267. Steven Cohen et al., "Together and Apart: Israeli Jews' Views On Their Relationship To American Jews And Religious Pluralism, Findings from UJA-Federation's Survey of Israeli Jews 2017," accessible at: https://www.ujafedny.org/api/assets/789241/
268. In our study we sought to rank confidence levels from 1 (not at all certain) to 10 (completely certain). The figure of 86% represents those who answered 8, 9, or 10. If we add those who answered 7, that rate rises to 91%. The same goes for the calculation regarding grandchildren; if we add those who answered 7, that rate rises to 87%.
269. Data in the following paragraphs are from Pew 2013; Ira Sheskin, "2013 Comparisons of Jewish Communities: A Compendium of Tables and Bar Charts"; and Rosner, *Shtetl, Bagel, Baseball* [Hebrew].
270. See Rosner, *Shtetl, Bagel, Baseball*. See also Shmuel Rosner, "Sukkot, the holiday of appropriate balance," *Jewish Journal* (09.10.2017), accessible at: https://jewishjournal.com/rosnersdomain/225528/sukkot-holiday-appropriate-balance/.
271. The question of what constitutes Jewish values is discussed in depth in Rosner, *Seven Frequently Asked Questions*. The relevant chapter raises substantive objections to the assumption that there even exist discernible, agreed Jewish values beyond trivial matters (the day of rest, etc.). For the choice by American Jews to rely on values more than rituals, see: Steven R. Weisman, *The Chosen Wars: How Judaism Became an American Religion* (New York: Simon and Schuster, 2018).
272. Shmuel Rosner, "Do Israeli Students Need to Visit Auschwitz?" *New York Times* (14.02.2018), accessible at: https://www.nytimes.com/2018/02/14/opinion/israel-poland-holocaust-auschwitz.html
273. Dan Feferman and Dov Maimon, "An Integrated Jewish World Response to Israel's Migrant Challenge," JPPI (03.08.2018), accessible at: http://jppi.org.il/new/en/article/english-an-integrated-jewish-world-response-to-israels-migrant-challenge/
274. Anti-Defamation League, et al., "Letter to Prime Minister Netanyahu Concerning the Safety and Future of African Asylum Seekers" (05.04.2018), accessible at: https://www.adl.org/news/letters/letter-to-prime-minister-netanyahu-concerning-the-safety-and-future-of-african-asylum

275. Babylonian Talmud, *Yoma* 57, translated by William Davidson, available from the Sefaria Library at Sefaria.org.

## Notes for the afterword

276. Many studies, including our own, point to this phenomenon. Among Israeli Haredim, almost everyone donates to the poor at least once a month (97%). Secular Israelis do so much less (25%). Among religious Jews in Israel, three in four donate to non-governmental organizations or social charities (75%); somewhat-traditional secular Israelis do so much less (51%). According to the Israeli Central Bureau of Statistics, around one-third of Israelis donated a sum of 100 NIS, another roughly one-third donated up to 500 NIS, around one-tenth donated up to 1,000 NIS, and around one-fifth donated more than 1,000 NIS. The upper band of donations is more common in the Haredi (45%) and religious (41%) populations. The situation is similar in studies on charitable giving by American Jews.
277. Ranked 7, 8, 9, and 10 out of 10.
278. Around one-tenth of respondents (9%) expressed a desire for the state to be a "state of all its citizens," not a Jewish state.

## Note for appendix 1

279. Smith, T. and Dennis, M. 2008. "*Mode Effects on In-Person and Internet Surveys: A comparison of the General Social Survey and Knowledge Network Surveys*» *JSM, Section on Survey Research Methodology.*

# *Acknowledgments*

We would like to thank all fellows of the Jewish People Policy Institute. Many of them read chapters in the book, commented, offered, contributed insights, saved from mistakes. Many of their articles served as a theoretical basis for the book.

The institute's president, Avinoam Bar-Yosef, enabled this project and supported it from its inception. Noah Slapkov helped with the statistical analysis and was a sounding board for many of our ideas. Adar Schiber assisted with the research and handled the tedious work of compiling endnotes and bibliography. Ita Alkalai made sure we kept our sanity, even in the difficult moments.

Thank you to Barry Geltman, Ambassador Avi Gil, Dan Feferman, Dr. Shlomo Fischer, Dr. Inbal Hackman, Brig. Gen. (res.) Mike Herzog, Dr. Dov Maimon, Dr. Gitit Levy Paz, Prof. Steven Popper, Prof. Uzi Rebhon, John Ruskay, Rami Tal, Prof. Shalom Wald, Tanya Perlin, and Sharon Shilo. Thank you to Menachem Lazar, who conducted the surveys of JPPI's pluralism project.

We thank the professional team of Kinneret-Zmora-Dvir Publishing for the work on the Hebrew edition of this book. We thank Stuart Schnee and his team for his work on the English version of this book. We also thank Yaacov Katz, Matti Friedman, Aron Raskas, David Suissa, Adi Schwartz.

Shmuel Rosner wishes to thank some of the thinkers and writers with whom he worked as an editor while working on this book.

Almost inevitably, their thinking influenced me. Thanks to Asael Abelman, Yair Ettinger, Regev Ben David, Ruth Gavison, Micha Goodman, Yuval Noah Harari, David Zoldan, Yoel Rappel.

Special thanks Daniel Goldman, for his friendship, his support of this project, and his good advice.

# The Authors

**Shmuel Rosner** is a senior fellow at the Jerusalem based The Jewish People Policy Institute (JPPI). He writes columns for The *New York Times*, The *Jewish Journal*, and *Maariv*, and is the non-fiction editor for Kinneret-Zmora-Dvir Publishing House.

**Camil Fuchs** is a professor emeritus of mathematics and statistics at Tel Aviv University. He is an advisor at the *Dialog* polling institute, conducts surveys for Israel's *Channel 13 News*, as well as for *Haaretz Daily* and many other organizations.